BROTHER IN ARMS:

AN ENGLISHMAN IN

VIETNAM

Gay Holden

Reading, Berkshire, England

For Jake and Oliver,
so that they will know and remember their
Great Uncle Tony

_____

CONTENTS

Chapter One

CHAPTER ONE

January 1999

A s B-52 bombers go, this one was a wreck. Shot down by the North Vietnamese during Operation Rolling Thunder, the United States' carpet bombing campaign, the crashed plane serves as a reminder to all who visit the War Museum in Hanoi that America lost the Vietnam War. Proudly displayed inside the museum are captured trophies, such as the flying helmet belonging to one young unfortunate US Air Force pilot, killed in an air attack over Hanoi in 1966. His name, printed in red plastic Dymo tape, was still stuck to the front of his helmet. DUCAT. I made a note of it and moved on. I would look his name up on the Vietnam Veterans' Memorial Wall on the Internet when I returned home to England in a few days' time.

Why was I, a middle-class, middle-aged woman from middle England making notes in a Hanoi museum on New Year's Day, 1999? The fact was that two months previously my daughter Katy had written from India, where she was travelling, to say that she and her boyfriend would reach Vietnam by Christmas, and could I possibly fly out and meet up with them. I could have caught up with them in India, Thailand, Laos or New Zealand, but Katy knew how important Vietnam was to me. I needed to find out more about my brother Lt. Tony Harbord who, as far as the records show, was the only Eng-

1

lish officer to lose his life in the service of the United States Army in Vietnam. He had died, just two days short of his year's tour of duty, in January 1969. He has his place on the Vietnam Memorial Wall in Washington DC. And so, of course, does young Major Ducat who, the Internet revealed, was shot down on the very first day of his tour of duty in December 1966.

*

September 1992

"Do you want a lift up, Ma'am?" asked the tall young blond American courteously. He had appeared as if from nowhere, out of the silent crowds of people slowly milling around in the steadily falling rain. Overcome with emotion and only able to nod her head, the slight, elderly woman was gathered up in his arms and raised like a feather high enough for her to touch the inscription on the top row of the mirror-like black granite panel. Panel 33W of the Vietnam Veterans' Memorial Wall in Washington DC. I watched as, biting her lip from the pain in her heart, she ran her arthritic fingers slowly along the name, only half an inch high, engraved in the smooth jet-black matrix: Anthony G Harbord, her only son – my brother. Returning my mother to terra firma, like a Nureyev gently lowering his Fonteyn, the anonymous American melted into the crowds and we stood, bareheaded in the rain, overwhelmed at the enormity of the tragedy that was Vietnam.

It was late summer 1992 and we had made the pilgrimage to Washington from England before my eighty-year-old mother Vivien became too infirm to travel.

Since the memorial's dedication on November 13 1982, several people known to us had visited it to pay vicarious respects on our behalf and one American friend, Abigail, had thoughtfully written to us describing the experience:

"As you get closer, you see that the people are walking down a curving ramp along a black marble wall that is cut down below ground level. When you come to the ramp, you can see that there are names cut into the marble, first a trickle, then, as you go

2

deeper, they increase to a flood along high panels that loom over you. The names are those of each person who died fighting for the USA, and are listed chronologically by date of death. I found Tony's name. He was about half way along, on a top line. I could just reach up and touch the letters, and send him a little prayer."

Another friend had sent us a pencil rubbing of Tony's engraved name, achieved by balancing his daughter on his shoulders for her to reach the inscription. Others, as yet unknown to us, had visited the memorial to remember Tony as a fellow soldier. One, former US Army Captain Tom Coffey, who had been Tony's closest friend at Officer Candidate School in Fort Benning, Georgia back in 1966, wrote down his thoughts on the 1982 inauguration ceremony. He described the search that day for his dead friends:

"As I found my way through the names on the wall to the location of my first friend's name, I was unprepared for what was about to happen. I found his name and wept. Finally he had his rightful place in our heritage and our history. Before turning away I had to reach out and touch his name as if to say 'I love you' one last time. This memorial can bring the strongest of men to his knees in tears."

That friend was Tony, and those words of Tom Coffey's only became known to me in 1999 when, thirty years after Tony's death, I began my own search to find the man my brother became. So, unaware of the existence of Tom and the many other people I was later to locate who helped me build a picture of the last four years of Tony's life in America and Vietnam, my mother and I were paying our own, very personal respects.

Abigail's description had prepared us to some extent for the experience, but what we had not anticipated was the overwhelming sense of sadness and communion amongst the visitors. The silence is rarely broken by anything other than footsteps, murmured voices and stifled sobs. Occasionally a voice cries out "There he is!" in a mixture of triumph and anguish as someone identifies a loved one on the Wall, just as I did when I found Tony's inscription. Apart from being a focus for quiet contemplation, grief and gratitude, the Wall also generates a tangible feeling amongst visitors of incomprehension at the sheer scale of the tragedy, such as is present at the vast cemeteries in Northern Europe where the graves of the dead of two World Wars stretch across the landscape. Both carry the same powerful impact whilst visually expressing the horror of war in very different ways.

In 1981 the memorial's design had been unanimously chosen, from 1,421 entries, by a team of nationally recognised – yet anonymous - artists and designers in a competition open to all US citizens aged 18 or over. Controversially, because of her origins, the first prize had gone to a 21-year-old south-east Asian girl student, Maya Ying Lin, of Athens Ohio, and although the vivid black gash of the design caused great dissent, uproar and controversy, time would tell that the engraving of all the names on the monument was Lin's greatest inspiration. It is the names that make the Wall speak, crying out to humanity not to make the same mistakes; it is the names that enable us to grasp the enormity of the disaster. To the east and west, for 250ft in each direction, the walls of the V-shaped memorial stretch, bearing their poignant burden of over 58,000 names which are set out chronologically by the date of death, beginning and ending at the vertex, where the panels are at their highest – 10 feet tall. They gradually diminish in height out towards the easternmost and westernmost tips of the memorial, tapering eventually to nothing as one climbs the slope back up to ground level to the familiar – yet oddly out-of-place – sights and sounds of the fast-food and souvenir stalls and people enjoying the surrounding parkland. Looking back, the Vietnam Veterans' Memorial Wall seems embedded in the earth like some huge crashed stealth bomber, its black wings testimony to the ultimate disaster of mankind, war.

Countless Vietnam veterans, and others, still harbour strong emotions of outrage. Outrage at the then Administration for pouring the cream of its youth into a theatre of war so far away over so many years; outrage at the draft-dodgers and anti-war demonstrators who never pledged their lives to their country; outrage that it took a group of veterans themselves, instigated by former infantry corporal Jan Scruggs, to raise the necessary $7m from private donations to build the memorial, the US Government having refused to fund the project. Above all they still feel outrage at the vilification and neglect meted out to so many of them by Government and fellow Americans after their return home. Defeat of one nation by another is hard enough to accept by its people, but denigration by their fellow countrymen of those who fought was intolerable. It has been estimated that more veterans than the total number of US fatalities in the war subsequently found life unbearable and have, over the ensuing years, sought the only way out of their misery and pain in that most wretched of acts, suicide. There had been no troop-ship cooling off period for the men returning home; they were air-lifted swiftly to their US destinations from one kind of hell often straight into another. The US Forces air communications system was so efficient that a soldier could be fighting for his life in the jungle one day, yet walking the streets of his home town the next, where all too often the sight of his uniform prompted hostile comments and behaviour. Never before had fighting men been repatriated so swiftly, nor had the magnitude of their disorientation been foreseen.

But it was not just the living who were swiftly despatched home. The formidable scale of Vietnam casualties at the height of the war in the mid 1960s had oiled the gruesome wheels of logistics and thousands of bodies were returned within days, even hours, to their homelands. On America's West Coast, as the huge freight planes prepared for their flights back to Vietnam, they took on board their sombre return cargo of hundreds of empty coffins, one of which would eventually be used to transport my brother's remains back to his final resting place in the village churchyard in Datchet, England, where we grew up. Promptly and efficiently, Tony's body was duly flown home from Vietnam via the American east coast Air Force Base at Dover, Delaware, and was delivered to the premises of a funeral director near Datchet a mere six days after his death on 27 January 1969.

We as a family were uncomprehending, numb. It didn't make sense. Tony had been due home any day on leave. His bed was made up, the clothes he had had made for him on R&R in Penang had been sent direct to England and, at his request, were hanging in his cupboard, pressed. But he was lying lifeless in a box two miles away in Slough clothed in his dress uniform, awaiting the final return home to his village. We had been told by the US authorities of his head injuries and had made the decision that we would prefer not to see his body, rather to remember him as he had been. Had we but known of the skilful work carried out by the embalmers in Delaware, who had rendered his handsome face apparently flawless, we would undoubtedly have plucked up the courage to say our goodbyes in person. However, the closest we ever got to him again was to stand by his coffin in church at the funeral on February 6.

We were still in a state of shock. How could the big brother I'd always looked up to, feared, admired and loved have faced that ultimate experience, death? It did not seem possible or rational. But there was his light oak coffin inside which his body lay, his blue-grey eyes forever closed, perfect white teeth never again to flash from his crooked smile.

What was the sequence of events which led to this young Englishman's name being engraved on a war memorial thousands of miles away from his home? How can we identify and evaluate the influences that ultimately seem to have shaped our own and others' futures? On one level, my brother's story naturally began with his birth in 1941 at a crucial point in one war and ended with his death twenty-seven years later during the height of another. On a different level, perhaps his story could be seen to have begun in an earlier theatre of war, the Great War of 1914-18. It was there that our valiant grandfather Brigadier General Frederick Hoghton died in 1916, in the terrible siege of Kut-al-Amara in Mesopotamia, modern day Iraq. Yes, this could be the key to understanding Tony's restlessness

6

Chapter One

and his driving need to prove himself in that most virile of scenarios, a life in the military. As he was to write home from a gruelling U.S. Army course to our mother in 1967: *"You know, it's funny that I should have started off in such casual professions as filming and music, and ended up in the military like your Dad"*. But I am fast-forwarding too soon. The one hundred and twelve letters of Tony's that survive, written over the four years of his search for the American Dream between 1965-69, will speak for themselves in due course.

From our earliest years Tony and I, three years younger, were aware of our mother's pride in her father, a British officer in the Indian Army. Vivien had vivid – if few - memories of her tall, twinkling-eyed, moustachioed father, even though she was only three years old when he died. Turbaned menservants and elegant *ayahs* looked after the four little sisters, three of whom were old enough to recall attending parties at Vice Regal Lodge in Simla. The British in India were in their element, leading the kind of life which – for many of them at least - would never have been afforded them back home. But the Great War of 1914-18 ended the Indian idyll for countless thousands of families, not least my grandmother's. Both her brothers were killed – Oswald, an Army chaplain, blown to bits in Cambrai, northern France, in 1915, and Hyla, *aide-de-camp* to the Viceroy and an expert horseman who commanded the Jodhpur Lancers, killed in Aleppo, Palestine, just before the Armistice in 1918. Sandwiched in between these two tragedies my grandmother learned the bitter news of her beloved husband's agonising death. She and her four little girls – the baby, only 5 months old, never did see her father – had had to face the hazardous journey back to England, when their convoy was struck fore and aft by German U-boats.

The stories of Frederick Hoghton's bravery and the respect he received from his fellow officers and men are not something dreamed up by our mother in some sentimental and retrospective act of wishful thinking, a trap into which many orphaned children are prone to fall. On the contrary, my grandfather's character and cour-

7

age are well documented, as are his last days when he was dying from the enteritis and dysentery which ravaged the defending forces in the blistering heat of Kut.

The siege had come about because of one man's pique and lust for glory. Major General Charles de Vere Townshend, affronted at his superiors' orders that he was to manage the logistics of army transportation up and down the River Tigris when he would rather have been distinguishing himself on the battlefields of northern France, resolved to gather his forces around him and go for the big prize, Baghdad. There being no roads and no railroads south of Baghdad, the army had to use the waterways. Nevertheless, they had success after success in capturing towns along the way, including Al-Kut as it is now known. Then came the advance to Ctesiphon, the ancient winter capital of the Parthian empire whose famous ruins are dominated by a gigantic vaulted hall, built by the Sasanian kings in the first few centuries AD. The site of a sack by the Romans and in AD637 by the Arabs, Ctesiphon's astonishing royal palace was to witness yet another bloody battle, for the Turks, allies of the Central Powers, were waiting for the British. It was a disaster for the British Indian Army; the Turks gained a resounding victory for they were able to call on thirty thousand reinforcements whereas Townshend had neither sufficient supplies nor reinforcements to sustain and augment his troops. This lack of resources is evident in a letter written by my grandfather to an unknown General from the besieged town of Kut dated February 14, 1916, several weeks after the retreat from Ctesiphon:

"What we lacked was just that one desideratum, that the U.S. General Grant [American Civil War] *lacked in his attack on the bloody angle in the Wilderness, viz a good stout 3ʳᵈ Line left intact to clinch the victory – and to keep enemy on the run. The huge extent of the position as compared with the numbers left to the attacking force precluded our doing more than to adopt a defensive role. Had we but left one solid Brigade to take on the enemy second line and to repel counter attacks, I believe we should have walked through. But*

8

Chapter One

how long we should have stayed at Baghdad is quite another question.

"My own experiences I could enlarge upon to a great deal, but I am so afraid of treading on contentious ground that I have to be careful. My Brigade was the containing force that day and took on the position in front on a frontage of 1500 yards. I was ordered to make a decisive attack when Delamain's flank attack had developed. This I did and pushed through capturing the central large redoubt and 2 others. But my line was a bit thin as you may conceive, and had it not been for the grit of my troops and the magnificent leading of their British and Indian officers, things might have been very different! I arrived with a small reserve, all I had left (50 rifles 22nd Punjabis), at the central main redoubt to find the whole line from enemy left to the said redoubt in our possession and as Delamain's troops were co-operating to the North I directed my Brigade (or such scattered remnants as I could collect) to sweep down the works to the southward and round up the remaining garrisons (enemy). I had just begun to do so when I had an urgent call from Delamain, on my right, for immediate assistance to repel a strong counter attack. I was only able to collect 250 men made up of detachments of 6 different units. Of these some 60 were British. We only had an average of 50 rounds per rifle and there were no reserves to be found. With this small body I at once moved out to Delamain's assistance. The Britishers led the advance and behaved heroically. The remainder, except for one brilliant exception, did not do much. However, we got up to within 300 yards of the enemy who now had taken up a strong position on some sandhills 1200 yards N.W. of their original left. We held on until dark and then as heavy enemy reinforcements began to arrive, had to fall back."

Townshend was forced to retreat to Kut where the siege began in December 1915 and lasted four months, one of the longest in British military history. Having had his dreams of glory shattered at Ctesiphon and as a consequence being robbed of the glittering prize of Baghdad (and possible eternal fame as 'Townshend of Baghdad')

9

he now set his sights on distinction by way of a glorious siege and famous relief at Kut. Honours galore had been bestowed upon Ba-den-Powell after the courageous siege and relief of Mafeking in the Boer War just 16 years previously. Moreover, Townshend believed that he would be given command of the relief force and that he would resume his advance on Baghdad. However attempts to relieve Kut failed with terrible loss of life. Townshend had lied about the amount of food still remaining; in order to force the issue of a relief he reported that the situation was far more critical than indeed it ac-tually was. As a consequence of his 'crying wolf', the relief force felt compelled to get through, despite Kut being surrounded by a powerful Turkish presence. Twenty-three thousand men died in fu-tile attempts to relieve their comrades. Eventually, however, the supplies within Kut did run out and starvation and disease claimed many more lives. My grandfather is mentioned several times in the diary of the Reverend Harold Spooner, MBE, MC, the Army Padre who often visited General Hoghton's dugout. His entry dated 27 March 1916 records one of these last occasions:

"I had a long talk with him [Hoghton]. We discussed what we had both been through since we had met on the boat coming from Basra to Amara – the forced march to Azuzyah when the General was so weak from dysentery he could scarcely sit on his horse – Cte-siphon – the Retreat – the Siege – shells, bombs, &c. &c."[1]

Food supplies in the fort had by this time reached crisis point, and horses were being slaughtered to feed the men. My grand-father abstained from eating horseflesh, probably because his constitution was severely weakened by the siege and his digestive system could not have tolerated it. A diet which included wild green grasses contributed to the swift progression of his dysentery. An-other source reports:

[1] SPOONER, Rev. H, Manuscript Diary, Library of the Imperial War Museum

10

"He died on the 12ᵗʰ [April] and was buried the same day. All who could do so attended his funeral to bid farewell to a good man and to mourn his loss. Silent and sorrowful we stood around and listened to the well-known service recited in the padre's solemn tones. They ceased – a brief pause, and then the bugles took up the refrain, and clear and mournful rang out those wonderful notes of the 'Last Post'. Were they prophetic, we wondered, of the fate of Kut?"²

A third account echoes these feelings of deep sadness and presentiment. *"The death of Brigadier General Hoghton caused great sorrow amongst his men who were devoted to him. He had done wonders in maintaining the moral courage of the troops billeted in the Fort. Even the enemy refrained from bombarding when the sad, haunting wail of the bugle sounded the Last Post, filling the air with its shrill notes, till it plaintively faded away over the strangely stilled desert. 'There was a great glow shimmering over the land', says Major Anderson, 'which shrouded the horizon, and a strange mirage formed by great clouds appeared above the swamps, where flies in their myriads rose and blotted out the landscape, after the beloved General was laid to rest. How more fortunate was his lot than that in store for others, few present realised."³*

Those who were still alive at Kut's fall in April 1916 were marched off to an appalling fate as prisoners of war, of whom 60 per cent died. It has been estimated that some 40,000 men died as a result of Townshend's personal ambition. He himself became a honoured 'guest' of the Turks and lived a life of luxury until the war's end. He neither cared nor asked about the fate of those he left behind. He never held a senior military post again. This disaster

---

² BARBER, Major C. H. *Besieged in Kut – And After* (Blackwood 1917) p219
³ NEAVE, Dorina. *Remembering Kut – Lest We Forget* (Arthur Barker 1937) p72

became a national scandal for Britain and led to the immediate resignation of India's secretary of state, Austin Chamberlain.

These contemporary accounts of a brave, approachable general who was held in high esteem by those he commanded as well as by his fellow officers, clearly found their mark in the boy who was to follow extraordinarily closely the fine example set him by his grandfather. But why did Tony choose to become a professional soldier in another country's army, and why America? The baton of influence which shaped his future is now handed down a generation to our mother who, as a young woman of twenty-two, accepted a job in America in 1935 looking after the three children of a beautiful and aristocratic American divorcée, Margaret Adams Bok. Known to us since our infancy as Peggy, the provider of wonderful food parcels and clothes in early post-war Britain, Peggy would eventually play a key role in both Tony's and my life and was to be the source of great strength and comfort to us when trying to come to terms with his death.

Young Vivien Hoghton had left her widowed mother and three sisters at their home in Weston-super-Mare, Somerset, to seek her own American Dream, crossing the Atlantic to New York in March 1935 by ship and firing off long, descriptive letters home, just as her son was to do exactly thirty years later. Peggy Bok quickly became more of a friend to Vivien than an employer and the whole family, with several other friends in tow, moved about America that summer, from Santa Fé in New Mexico to the Grand Canyon where they slept under the stars, back to Pennsylvania and on to New York City. As children in rationed and bomb-devastated England, Tony and I used to get out our mother's old photograph albums and marvel at the faded pictures of her adventures in a fabled country so far away from ours; the East Coast city streets with their soaring buildings were clogged with Bonnie and Clyde-type motor cars with running boards; in Arizona there were pictures of real Indians, our mother horse-riding and – best of all - views of Monument Valley, a scene so familiar to us from the cowboy films we saw at the cinema.

Upon her return home to England in the spring of 1936, Vivien realised that the only thing she really wanted to do – had only ever wanted to do - was to dance. At the age of twenty-three the odds were stacked against her – ballet dancers must of necessity start training seriously at a very young age and Vivien had only attended dancing school as a child and then a few adult classes courtesy of Peggy in New York - but she displayed a grim determination to succeed in this notoriously gruelling and extremely competitive profession. Her innate tenacity, a quality she was to pass to her children, had been fuelled by a memorable meeting with the fabled ballerina Anna Pavlova who, towards the end of her career, had been forced to perform in some lowly venues including the Pier Pavilion Theatre in Vivien's west country home town of Weston-super-Mare. That evening the great Russian ballerina had danced her most famous role, the *Dying Swan*, and on emerging from the stage door had taken eight-year-old Vivien's hand in hers and walked down the pier with her. Vivien was smitten. Thus began her love affair with ballet which was to last all her life. Even in her eighties she was still going to class, her grace and ability quite remarkable for one so advanced in years.

With very little formal training but a great deal of natural aptitude she doggedly pursued her dream of dancing professionally. She had the temerity to audition for Col. De Basil's Ballets de Monte Carlo for their 1936-37 London season under the direction of the great Michel Fokine. She was successful and, in the years leading up to the Second World War, went on to join the cast of dancers supporting the duo Jack Hulbert and Cicely Courtneidge in three of their major West End musicals and a film. Not bad for a relatively untrained beginner. It was during this time that she met and fell in love with Bill Harbord, a debonair young theatre producer. Vivien was sitting in a café in London's theatreland when he first set eyes on her, very Garbo-esque and dressed *à la mode* with a saucy little hat and long cigarette holder. During a prolonged courtship, when Vivien tried repeatedly to tie down the ever-independent Bill, they finally joined the stampede of couples rushing to marry at the beginning of September 1939, when Britain declared war on Germany.

The fashioning of Tony's future seems to have depended upon three key qualities, courage, adventurousness and tenacity. The first characteristic was evident in the gallant example of our grandfather, the second in the exhilarating stories of our mother's American adventure and the third in her stubborn determination to succeed in spite of overwhelming odds. These three constituent parts gave Tony a feeling of family pride, a sense of adventure and inordinate persistence, but welding them all together was his love for - and trust in – our mother.

Like many a wife and mother in the middle decades of the 20th century, the raising of children was left up to her. Of course the war had accounted for the prolonged absence of countless young fathers, but child-rearing was nevertheless seen as women's work and as a consequence our father, Bill, never formed the close relationship which such a large proportion of today's fathers have with their children. We loved him, of course we did, but we tiptoed round him. We worshipped her. I adored her until she died; Tony adored her until he died. His letters home, though addressed to both parents, were - consciously or unconsciously - directed primarily to her. He was able, time and time again, to unburden his often heavy heart with surprising frankness, knowing that she would always try to understand and to help whenever and however she could. Such intimacy and trust was forged in the crucible of our childhood, creating a very precious relationship indeed.

Tony was born at the Shrubbery Road Maternity Home in High Wycombe on the afternoon of 1 August 1941, just a few miles from the family's home in Iver, a small Buckinghamshire village. It came at a point in the war when Britain stood very much alone and the future of its children was highly uncertain. The disastrously heavy and prolonged German bombardment of Britain in the Blitz of September 1940-March 1941 had left many towns and cities in ruins and millions of children from these target areas had been evacuated to the relative safety of the countryside such as Iver. A further 15-20,000 children were shipped to destinations as far distant as Canada and Australia and most would never see their families, nor their homeland, again. In June of 1941 Germany had invaded Russia and by the end of the year Japan's bombing of the US naval base at Pearl Harbor, Oahu, would bring America into the war. This, then, was the England into which Tony was born, but despite the understandable misgivings and deep apprehension felt by Bill and Vivien as to the kind of world into which their baby son had emerged, his arrival brought great happiness. A record of Tony's first months was enthusiastically and meticulously kept by Vivien in her copy of the "Little One's Log", a baby record book with abundant advice for the new mother, written by one Eva Erleigh, Marchioness of Reading. An early entry records, *"Bill carried Tony into the drawing-room and I saw on his face the look I have been waiting for – the realisation that he was holding his own son."*

As a baby, Tony's hair was golden, and a lock of it is still safely pressed between the pages of the Little One's Log, which recorded his progress for the first year of his life. His Christening at six weeks was documented and amongst the presents he received were War Savings Certificates. Sensible, if somewhat uninspiring. Rather ambitiously, the Little One's Log provided space for the proud parents to enter details of the child's first seven years of life. Pages and pages filled with dotted lines expectantly awaited the mother's pen to provide information on every conceivable aspect of development from "Progress in the Arts – first dancing/gymnastics/riding/drawing/music lessons" to "Religious Record – first prayer/attendance at Divine Service/Confirmation". That was the way things were then. Everything done by the book. It even exhorted mothers to *"train baby from birth to sleep with his mouth shut, for by encouraging nose breathing the correct formation of the mouth will be much helped."* The legendary British obsession with regular bowel function was evident in another chapter: *"Regularity is one of the most important factors in the successful management of a baby, and he should be trained from the first to have regular bowel movements every day – these should take place two or three times daily at the same time each day."*

Due to the happy and relaxed personality of our mother, Tony thrived, and the gospel according to the Marchioness of Reading was probably all but forgotten. Because of Bill's age (he was thirty-one when war broke out), his contribution to the war effort was for a long time at home in the ARP (Air-Raid Precautions), rather than as a conscript in the military and as a result he was able to witness the first three years of his son's life. However, by September 1944, with Vivien due to give birth to me, her only other child, at the end of the month, Bill received orders from the RAF and the news was bad. Barely able to frame the question, she asked him "Where are they sending you?" He replied, sadly, in mime, making a sign of waves with his hand, "Overseas".

Although the war in Europe was entering its last few months, Britain was now being attacked by the new pilotless V-weapons, the flying bombs and rocket projectiles launched from sites across the English Channel. Hearing the so-called 'doodlebugs' motoring overhead held no terror, however, as long as they kept on going; the moment the engine cut out was the signal that the bomb was immediately going into free-fall and would explode in the few seconds it took to reach the ground. There was no opportunity to run for the air-raid shelters; time enough only to dive beneath a table or under the stairs. More deadly was the V2 rocket missile, which made its dreadful debut right at the end of the war. Designed by Werner von Braun, who went on to become a leading contributor to the American space programme, the V2 was much faster than previous models, coming as it did out of the blue with no advance warning. These early guided missiles caused real fear amongst Londoners and others living in south-east England as they could appear unexpectedly at any time, any place. As a result of the V-weapon attacks, some 23,000 buildings were destroyed, one million were damaged and 5,000 lives were lost.

Chapter One

Meanwhile the war in the Far East was still raging and Bill was sent out on a troop ship to India to join an RAF munitions unit as an armourer, loading bombs on to planes bound for destinations further east. Not knowing when, or if, she would see him again, Vivien was overcome with emotion. She had a little son just three years old and a baby due any day. Bombs were still falling over Britain and no-one had any clear idea how much longer this five-year-old war would last, even though the Allied invasion of France - 'D-Day' - had taken place early that June followed by the liberation of Paris on August 25. To add to the general concern, the Allied Forces had just suffered a terrible strategic disaster at Arnhem in Belgium during Operation 'Market Garden' under the command of Field Marshall Sir Bernard Montgomery and Lieutenant-General Brian Horrocks. The biggest airborne invasion in history had tried – and failed - to hasten the end of the war by capturing the vital bridge which would have laid the way open for the Allies to march on Berlin. Thousands of aircraft had taken part in the operation; two airborne columns, each a staggering 94 miles long and three miles wide, crossed the Channel to their targets. But what had been predicted as the decisive blow in Western Europe against Germany turned into a bloody fiasco resulting in the deaths of more than 1400 men. Montgomery had predicted that the war would be over by Christmas, but it became horribly clear that such optimism was seriously misplaced. The war was anything but over.

Tony had been born into a violent and uncertain world at war. Three years on his baby sister was about to arrive at another cliffhanging period of the conflict. Desperately saddened and apprehensive after Bill's departure, Vivien wrote a poem about Bill's unspoken goodbye to his son:

GOODBYE
Rosy walls, a little bed,
A sleeping child with tousled head.

Smiling lips and dimpled hands,
Who can doubt Christ by him stands?

Goodbyes to say and tears to shed,
But I'll not wake my sleepy head.
Tiptoe out and down the stair;
God be with you, Tony dear.

Looking back on our childhood, as I have done so many times when trying to understand what shaped Tony's future, I am more and more struck by the integral role our mother played in our lives. She was such a friend, such fun, sometimes so outrageous and always genuinely interested in all our activities, unlike our father's much more detached approach to parenthood. He saw his role as breadwinner, with weekends as 48 hours of well-earned mannish self-indulgence – some gardening in the vegetable patch, some cricket or golf and some dozing. Vivien on the other hand had not only her own full-time job teaching a class of more than thirty five-year-old infants in the local village primary school, she also had a household to run, with shopping, cooking, cleaning and home decorating to be done. She still found time to make me dresses on an old Singer treadle sewing machine, staying up late into the night to get them finished. Despite this heavy load, it was she who arranged our excursions, family treats, Christmases, birthdays and holidays. We children did help quite considerably around the house, though – we were responsible for our pet guinea pigs and mice, we tidied our bedrooms, Tony walked and groomed the dog, I looked after some of the flowerbeds and on Sundays three of us would go to church, leaving Dad happily behind with the newspaper. But when our tasks and obligations were done, we were off in a flash to play outside.

It has often been said that childhood was innocent, inexpensive, fun and simple in the middle decades of the 20th century. It was, I was there. True, my retrospective view may be somewhat softened by the years, but as far as we children were concerned at the

Chapter One

time, what little we had – in today's terms - was sufficient. The adult world, in contrast, was as beset with problems and tragedy as it is today, but we were blissfully unaware because the television age with its facility for instant communication had not yet arrived. What newsreel footage we did see was at the cinema once every few weeks and it was generally rather jolly. Or perhaps that is my perception of it. However, our mother did make sure that we were aware of others less fortunate than ourselves. We were not allowed 'down' from the table until our plates were empty (in recognition of the starving millions in India), we prayed for the poor children of the world, and for one or two pence (in aid of the Sunshine Babies' Home) we sold pictures of orphaned babies which we tore out of little booklets like raffle tickets.

For most children in early post-war Britain, life really was what you made it. There were no theme parks to visit, no foreign holidays to take or expensive toys to expect as presents. We enjoyed simple pleasures which our mother planned and arranged, such as picnics on our (second-hand) bikes to the Thames at Windsor where we would fish for little muddy-tasting gudgeon and roach. Tony had far more patience than I, and would sit for ages on the riverbank concentrating on the brightly coloured float at the end of his line and willing it to show that first exciting bob below the water indicating that a fish had taken the bait. Little did that small boy realise that one day he would be fishing for marlin in the blue waters off Florida for a living. As for holidays, we – and our many cousins, aunts and uncles - spent two weeks every summer at Granny's house in Bexhill on the south coast to which we travelled by steam train, an exciting enough experience in itself except for one thing. I always dreaded the lurching walk down to the lavatory because of the terrifying swivelling, creaking metal plates where the carriages joined together and the brown leather concertina'd sides that shuddered with the train's efforts. We never seemed to be in the same carriage as the lavatories, and Mum would have to go ahead and coax me over the monstrously groaning link with an encouraging smile as I blanched at

19

the sight of the rail track slipping past beneath my feet. Dad didn't come to Bexhill. It was not his idea of fun, and by 1955 we had acquired our dog, Mikey, which gave Dad what he thought was a good excuse to stay at home. So, wearing our new summer sandals whose crepe soles - for a day or so at least - looked just like lightly fried bread, Tony and I hurried to keep up with our mother who, miraculously it seemed, knew not only how to get to London, but underneath it too. How she knew which of the panting steam trains was ours remained a mystery to me for many years. She knew everything.

Vivien supervised our homework; she was an inspired teacher of both infant and junior children and knew how to make learning fun. She oversaw our scratchy efforts with pen and ink as we traced over perfect italic script templates in an effort to improve our handwriting. She coached us and disciplined us. She taught us manners, to write prompt thank-you letters, how to swim, to say our prayers, the facts of life, cookery and gardening. It was she who sometimes gently woke us, with an excited smile, on a winter's night when the snow had started falling long after everyone in our quiet little road had gone to bed. To the sleepy sounds of Dad muttering "You're mad" from their bed, she would take us outside in our dressing gowns, slippers and gloves to catch snowflakes and to make the first footsteps in the squeaky snow. On other occasions she woke us so that we could watch meteorites silently pursuing their transitory courses across the night sky. We knew the names of the constellations (Tony's star sign was Leo, which was a far more visually interesting celestial outline than my very dull Libra) and we could identify countless wild flowers by both their common and Latin names. Wizened little stems of flowers such as Lady's Slipper, Ragged Robin and Shepherd's Purse fall out of my *Observer's Book of British Wild Flowers* as I turn the pages some fifty years later.

CHAPTER TWO

L ike countless other demobbed men, Dad returned home
after the war not only to try to pick up the pieces of
family life but also to meet me, the new addition to the family born in
his absence and now a toddler of almost eighteen months. Tony may
have had some vestigial memory of his father, kept alive by Vivien,
but for me this man was an interloper and by all accounts I did not
appreciate being picked up and swung around by a joyful stranger
holding his little daughter for the first time. Or the second, or the
third. And that was another sadness of war, for all too often war-
weary men returned to their families after prolonged and sometimes
tortured months and years away having nurtured dreams of the happiness of reconciliation with their children, only to find that at best it
took weeks or a few months to kindle or re-kindle the relationship,
and at worst that the bond between father and child would never be
happily established. Luckily for Dad and me, though, he very soon
settled fairly seamlessly into family life once more. However, finding
suitable work was difficult for him, trained as he was in theatrical
production. Furthermore, he was unable to work for eighteen months
due to a serious eye problem, so times were often very hard and resulted in us eventually having to move downmarket.

The terrible winter of 1947 held Britain in an icy grip for
months, during which time we as a family moved into one downstairs
room and ate and slept on beds and cots pulled up close to the open
fire. One day in particular remained forever in our parents' minds; a
water pipe in the loft had burst, the last chicken had died of the cold,

and Dad had had to resort to chopping up the kitchen table and chairs in order to keep the fire going. After settling us all down in front of the fire that evening muffled in coats and gloves, Dad put the wireless on, to be greeted by the sentimental strains of someone crooning "When You Come To The End of a Perfect Day". They cried. And then they laughed.

Laughter played a huge part in our childhood. Tony and I were good companions, despite the three-year age difference. We played a lot together, often laughing so helplessly that we got bad attacks of hiccups which, when still present at the dinner table, resulted in our mother requesting that we get down from the table and to return only when we could control ourselves. Amused glances between her and Dad told us that we were not in trouble, just a bit of a nuisance. Tony took full advantage of having a kid sister to boss around, but I obeyed his commands because I admired him and wanted always to be in 'his gang', even though he often got me into trouble. One such occasion was when he appropriated my first very precious white T-shirt, explaining that if he cut the cap sleeves into fringes and boiled the garment with an onion in a saucepan of water to dye it a streaky brown, I would look much more the part for our next game of cowboys and Indians. Our mother was not pleased. I can't say I was all that enthusiastic either. Then there was the time he dared me to recite a rude poem at the top of the stairs, at the top of my voice; I have to confess that I did know it was rude, but in my innocence I did not know which of the words were offensive or why, or indeed quite how bad they were. A hiding from my mother did not at the time improve my knowledge of swear words, but it did convince me that to repeat the dare would be tactically unwise.

In 1950, when Tony and I were aged eight and five respectively, we moved to a little semi-detached house in a quiet cul-de-sac in Datchet, a small village near Windsor. Our parents were to live in that house for the rest of their long lives. Central heating, double glazing and electric blankets were almost unheard of in those days, and our only sources of warmth in winter came from a small coal fire

22

downstairs, a paraffin stove on the landing and a hot-water bottle in every bed. Ice would form on the inside of the windows overnight and we would wake with dread at having to leave our snug nests, to the point where Tony and I would often skip washing and get dressed in bed. I got quite adept at leaving my clothes at night already assembled, with vest and blouse inside my jumper, and knickers inside my leggings, thereby minimising the number of fumbling manoeuvres necessary beneath the heavy blankets.

Every back garden in the road contained a newly defunct air-raid shelter. Ours was a monstrous reinforced concrete shed which was home not only to my beloved dressing-up box (a large wicker hamper from Dad's theatrical days, full of wonderful evening dresses including one by Molyneux), but to some horrendously large spiders too. Also stored there was Dad's wind-up gramophone and treasured collection of classics on 78rpm records. Each symphony, concerto and opera was recorded on to several discs, and in our early years Tony and I were willingly fed a diet of this wonderful music. We would take it in turns to change the steel needle when necessary, selected from a little metal tin of spares. The record would be carefully removed from its brown paper sleeve and placed on the turntable, the gramophone wound up and the catch released. Then the heavy arm was lowered on to the record where an initial hiss was soon replaced by the sounds of music. Dad had a trained voice, and often he would sing along with the likes of Caruso and Björling. That always made us feel especially happy and all these years later it has only just occurred to me why that should be; I think that Dad had always found it hard to express himself – certainly he hardly ever mentioned Tony after his death – yet through song he could really open his heart. A great shame, for him and for us.

I went to the Church of England primary school in the village, while Tony cycled two miles to Long Close, a boys' preparatory school just outside Slough. He was not altogether happy there, hating in particular the boxing lessons which all the boys had to take. School dinners were almost as unpopular, featuring all too often copious amounts of cabbage from the headmaster's wife's kitchen garden. So Tony and his friend Michael conceived a plan to put an end to the monotonous presence of greens on their plates. One weekend they collected as many caterpillars as they could find and on the Monday morning took them to school in their satchels. At playtime they broke bounds and crept into the kitchen garden with their jam jars full of caterpillars, scooping them out and placing them on the serried ranks of cabbages in the certain hope that before long the leaves would disappear into the caterpillars and therefore not into the boys. They were found out, duly punished and the cabbages continued to thrive.

Irritatingly for Tony, I loved school and found the learning process easy; he, on the other hand, found it more of a challenge and did less well. Away from school, however, Tony was in the ascendant and I was his willing slave. I was Robin to his Batman and the Indian to his Cowboy. He would send me into murky frothing ponds to collect frog-spawn, get me to bait his fishing rod with squirming gentles, tie me to a tree as a captive Indian and leave me for dead. But I loved him. We collected stamps by the hundred and giggled over the dark-skinned bare-breasted ladies on the ones from Niger. For a couple of days each week our noses were buried in our comics and over the childhood years our games were influenced by the characters from *Dandy, Beano, Hotspur, Lion* and *Eagle*. However, he never agreed to play games using the daring sixth-form Secret Society girls from my comic *The Girl's Crystal*, because he said that girls were "feeble". Surely he didn't he mean me?

In our road a few families had a car but we weren't one of them. Three doors down lived my friend Mary Crook whose father was a tiny little man who wore a bowler hat and proudly drove around in a bulbous black Rover, the 1950's equivalent of today's small man/red Porsche syndrome I suppose. Despite the sporadic nature of the passing traffic, Tony would occasionally equip both of us with a pad and pencil and we would sit at the end of the road waiting patiently for the opportunity to take down car numbers. I never did see the point of this, but went along with him because he knew best. Not only did our family not own a car, we had no television either, and on an unseasonably cold, wet day in June 1953 we crowded into our neighbours' house along with about forty others and sat in rows on benches to watch the Coronation of Queen Elizabeth on a tiny television set which needed some time to warm up. But we did have a wireless. Tony and I, washed and in our dressing-gowns, would settle down in the evenings and listen, totally enthralled, to *P.C. 49, Journey into Space*, and our favourite programme, *Dick Barton – Special Agent*. In winter we would drink our mugs of cocoa as we listened, and in summer suck away at an orange with a sugar cube buried in its middle.

Every day, rain or shine, we children who lived in the Close were out in the road playing. Sometimes we would all play hopscotch together, chalking out impossibly large grids which needed a run-up of several yards and huge leaps into the air to reach the right square. In the surrounding fields we made 'camps' in the undergrowth or up trees, with Tony directing operations. The best field was the one called the 'German Man's Field' or 'Jerry's and then 'Jez' for short. About two hundred oil drums, in various stages of rusty decay, had been dumped there and made a wonderfully dangerous surface on which to play tag. In the same field, in springtime, was a vast area of cow parsley whose frothing lace umbels towered above us. We made peashooters out of the stalks and tracked each other in the undergrowth, popping up every so often to aim and fire.

At other times the girls played separately in a small field we called the Girls' Palace, where no boys were allowed. We made our own camp there and would sweep the earthen floor, pick wild flowers and put them in jam jars and sit hidden under the leafy canopy eating sticks of rhubarb dipped in sugar, giggling. There we would play games of fivestones, Jacks and cat's cradle. Meanwhile the boys raced up and down the road on go-carts made with planks of wood and pram wheels (Tony had convinced me I should volunteer my doll's pram wheels for the purpose), steering inaccurately with rope attached to the front axle. Every so often would come the un-mistakable sounds of a collision, a yell and – even worse – boyish sobbing. All of us had permanently grazed knees, the tight scabs sometimes making cycling difficult, but they would have to be really restrictive to stop us belting around on our bikes, into the spokes of which we would stick playing cards so that the machines sounded like motor bikes – or so we liked to think. Sometimes we would all hobble several hundred yards to the top of the road on roller-skates, making our painful way around potholes in the uneven concrete to the only piece of smooth tarmac for miles. Why we didn't walk, and carry our skates, I cannot imagine. Perhaps the discomfort was all part of the experience, and anyway, Tony said we had to skate to the end of the road and back, so we did. The wonderful smell of that tarmac on a hot summer's day was matched only by our delight at being able to swoop effortlessly around its small area of dead flat, sound-absorbent blackness, before the long, uncomfortable stumble home.

Not so happy was the time when we found builders' pegs hammered into the ground in 'our' fields – the Jez, even the Girls' Palace. It was horrible, horrible; we felt someone had come in and desecrated our land and spoilt our lives. The sacred mulberry tree in the Jez, out of which Tony had once fallen and broken his arm whilst trying to swing on a rope like Tarzan, would now be in somebody's back garden. We pulled out as many pegs as we could, in the belief that by so doing we could stop the inexorable spread of house build-ing in our road, in our village, and that the builders would give up and move on. We failed, of course. But we did have some great times playing in and around the foundations, and when the houses began to go up, Tony found some gadget that enabled him to unlock the doors. In we would all go, and dash up and down the wooden stairs playing 'he'. I would gather the corkscrew-like wood shav-ings, take them home and pin them to my hair, pretending they were my ringlets. I now realise that even the catastrophe of building de-velopment did not, in the end, dampen our spirits. Nor did it curtail our ability to dream up new games for new situations. Whenever I smell new plaster I recall the fun we children had in those half-built houses.

It really is quite extraordinary how even a moderate sense of smell can transport us back to past moments in time, especially childhood, on catching the faintest whiff of a particular scent. Sometimes the speed of such 'regressions' can be quite dizzying as the years peel back in a split-second and place one, like a beamed-down character in Star Trek, in another almost forgotten world. Along with new plaster and hot tarmac, my childhood is recalled instantly by more fragrant smells such as Sweet Williams and phlox, which grew in abundance in Granny's garden. Not all smells from our childhood were pleasant, however. Once a fortnight the malodorous 'lavender cart' which emptied each house's septic tank would make its dreaded journey down the road, the tanker's big vacuum pipes seeming to bounce with glee as the villagers' waste products were sucked greedily into its interior.

Happy childhood memories contain an inordinate amount of sunshine. Was the weather ever too bad to go outside? Sometimes it must have been, because we had a much-thumbed standby on the bookshelf entitled *The Children's Make-and-Do Book*. Resorting to this book usually meant that conditions out of doors really were bad, or that we were ill, or perhaps we'd done something particularly naughty. We came to both love and hate that book. The reason we loved it was because it told you how to make all sorts of things, from the simple - but hideous - flower pots which involved heating and reshaping old 78rpm records (those of Dad's which were already cracked or badly scratched), to such sophisticated delights as a zoetrope, whose 'moving' pictures you viewed through slits in a revolving cylinder. The origami teapot, though, always defeated us. The reason we hated the book was that the very act of opening its pages was confirmation that we had to stay indoors when we would utter the rare words "We're *bored*".

Datchet was a small, pretty village with three pubs, a church, timbered buildings and a few shops. It is mentioned in the Domesday Book of 1086 but settlement there goes back at least five thousand years to the Neolithic, due in part to its convenient riverside location. In the 1950s Datchet had its own dairy and bakery and a grocer's where pregnant or elderly customers could sit on conveniently placed chairs while they were being served. In February 1953 sweet rationing ended and the village sweet shop became my favourite place in all the world and accounted for my all-too-frequent visits to the village dentist whose foot-operated drill and 'laughing gas' dealt with my fillings and extractions. Tony, who had less of a sweet tooth, only ever visited the dentist for the occasional check-up and went through life with nothing more than a scale and polish.

A few miles away from our house was London Airport, where occasional, propeller-driven planes landed. Enclosed by a wire perimeter fence, the airfield comprised a few tents and temporary buildings and a windsock or two; by the time my quest for my brother began in 1999, London Airport had become London Heathrow, the busiest international airport in the world where 57,000 people are employed. As children, we never flew anywhere, of course. 'Abroad' was somewhere Dad had been during the war, or somewhere Mum had visited before she married. In any case, we had a grandmother who lived by the sea, and that's where we went on holiday every year to join our many cousins and aunts and uncles.

Bexhill was heaven. Tony was the eldest boy, and organised the cousins (we children numbered 10 at our maximum). We would go shrimping in the rock pools before breakfast if the tide was low and then come pattering back with bare feet on the pink pavements with our little metal buckets full of sandy water in which pathetically small grey shrimps darted around. Kate, Granny's aged retainer, who still wore a long maid's uniform and frilly cap, would mutter darkly and complain that she had more than enough to do without boiling up shrimps for breakfast. But Tony was persistent, and we would sit out in the garden for ages pulling off the heads and

28

cracking open the skins of the tiny bodies, now pink from cooking, savouring every morsel. Then, weather permitting, it was back down to the beach for all of us and we children would have to pull on our bathing costumes once again, now horribly damp, clammy and sandy from the morning's expedition. Tony also supervised the trolley bus tickets. The bus stopped almost outside Granny's house, and long before it came into view we could hear the singing in the overhead wires, signalling its approach. With such a large party boarding the bus on our outings into Bexhill or to Eastbourne or Hastings, the continuous ticket that issued from the conductor's machine could measure several feet. It was only fair that each cousin – babies excepted - had a turn at keeping the ticket. When it was my turn I used to fold it into a concertina and tear it into the shape of a person with hands out to the side. Unfolding it to reveal maybe twenty little joined up people was always a magical moment.

We must have been an odd sight - ten children, most of us in hand-me-down clothes, looking like a bunch of refugees. But then few people had much money in those early post-war days, or if they did, we didn't know them (apart from little Mr Crook in his huge Rover). To add to the comic nature of our collective appearance, Tony often wore on his head our grandfather's white sola topi from the First World War, complete with brass spike and chinstrap. He wasn't allowed to wear the precious plume of feathers, but he cut a dashing figure nevertheless. At other times he wore a cut-down version of grandfather's dress uniform, cap and all, and marched around importantly trying to create some semblance of an orderly line amongst the cousins. I now realise that our mother must have had to pack all this paraphernalia and take it down to Bexhill. No wonder she used to struggle so across London with the luggage.

A favourite trip each summer holiday was to the huge, enigmatic figure called the Long Man of Wilmington, which was cut into the chalk slopes of the South Downs. Uncle Bernard the vicar and Uncle 'Squib' (the one with the short temper) had cars and somehow we would all pile in to these tiny sit-up-and-beg vehicles and hang out of the windows, making faces at pedestrians and motorists as we made our way slowly along the country lanes to our destination. I was already impressed that my cousins had fathers who owned cars, but even more so when Uncle Squib fooled me into believing that he knew personally every brown-uniformed man in jodhpurs who, standing beside a large motorcycle, would salute him when we puttered past. I knew nothing about motoring organisations and cared less.

Once we had paid our annual homage to the Long Man by scrambling up his long body and running down the staffs he held in each hand, we split up and followed our own pursuits before reassembling for the picnic tea. Tony would disappear to fly a kite or spot butterflies while Mum and I danced till we dropped amongst the harebells, daisies and blue flax growing bravely on the chalky soil. Exhausted and dizzy, we would lie on our backs laughing, the sun on our faces and the larks sending out their ecstatic trill from some invisible point high in the sky as the world spun round and round.

Towards the end of our holiday we would notice more dew on Granny's lawn in the morning, more spiders' webs in her garden to catch the unwary child and the combine harvester would begin reaping the corn from the field at the back of her house, the farm labourers piling the sheaves together in stooks to dry. These were the dreaded signs that what had seemed an endless summer was drawing to a close and that we would soon be back at school, where the offerings for the nature table would include hips, haws and conkers, a world away from the sticky buds and bluebells of spring. Plans would soon be under way again for November's Bonfire Night, when Tony would supervise the meagre display of fireworks, obeying the quaint firework code clearly printed on each item: *"Light the blue touch-paper and retire immediately"*. It was time to pay another visit to the shoe shop, this time for our winter lace-ups.

Our childhood days were thus punctuated: some school, much playing and Bexhill. But slowly and imperceptibly things changed. They became much school, less playing and no Bexhill. I had won a place at Sadler's Wells Ballet School (later the Royal Ballet School) at the age of ten and although initially thrilled at my achieving the rare place at this prestigious school, Mum realised that there was no way that she and Dad could possibly afford it, until Peggy from California stepped in with financial assistance. She enabled me to follow my dream, just as she was to enable Tony to follow his, many years later. Academically he still struggled, but in 1957 Dad promised he would buy our first TV set if Tony managed to improve his performance in class by ten places. This carrot-dangling resulted in Tony's jumping from 22nd to 6th place in one term and, true to his word, Dad arranged for the television set to be delivered the very next day. The new arrival in the home widened Tony's knowledge of – and love for – all things American. Up until then our information had come from the cinema and Peggy's regular parcels of National Geographic magazines in whose pages I would lose myself looking at the extraordinary tribal people, exotic birds and beautiful American ladies wandering around the national parks in full skirts, high heels and white gloves. Tony, meanwhile, marvelled at the skyscrapers, the streamlined cars and photographs of places such as Monument Valley and the Grand Canyon. But now we had a television and could tune in to something American most evenings and it was not long before Tony, by then aged sixteen, shocked us all by coming home from school sporting probably the first crew-cut in the village. Soon after that, and bought with the earnings from his Saturday job at the village greengrocer's, came what we called his 'Bilko' outfit of beige shirt and slacks, just like the army uniform worn by Phil Silvers and his men on Tony's favourite TV Show. We still listened to the radio, but it had certainly taken second place to the television. One programme that was never missed was the luna-tic *Goon Show* with Peter Sellers, Harry Secombe and Spike Milligan. Tony knew virtually every line of every script, having re-corded each show on to his reel-to-reel tape recorder and he would play them over and over again up in his bedroom from whence guffaws and giggles regularly emanated. Ridiculous little 'Goon-like' comments were to pepper his letters home.

With the advent of skiffle Tony's love affair with music began and he organised us into his own family band. My diary records that *"Tony has made a bass drum for our jam sessions"*, when he played his drum, Mum strummed the ukulele and I was inveigled into thrumming on the bass - a tea chest to which had been affixed a broom-handle and long taut piece of string. Dad was not invited to sing, much to his relief, I'm sure. Whereas skiffle made a brief appearance in Tony's life, drumming was there to stay. With every penny he could muster from odd jobs and pocket money, he managed to assemble a full drum kit in his bedroom where he proceeded to teach himself and to practise. We were, of course, living in a small semi-detached house where every-day sounds such as doors shutting and curtains being drawn were conveyed through the walls to the neighbours next door. Now they had drums and cymbals to contend with. Complaints soon began to roll in as the cymbals crashed and the paradiddles became more intense and prolonged. Inside the house itself it was sometimes unbearable and once Tony had the cheek to complain about the noise issuing from a little portable typewriter upon which I was learning to type in my bedroom, saying that it disturbed his concentration. I felt like knocking his block off. Fed a daily diet of drumming, Duke Ellington, Miles Davis, the MJQ and Thelonius Monk, a solution to the noise had to be found, so Tony agreed to soundproof his bedroom. Up the narrow stairs came boards of thick compressed hessian and plywood, which he hammered on to battens affixed around the room. Unfortunately the soundproofing was largely ineffective because he had been unable to treat the ceiling and floor, and the end result was that he was eventually banished to the local cricket pavilion to practise, where he drummed away in peace surrounded by fields, trees and startled wildlife.

The rhythms were with him – and us - day and night; while sitting watching television he would use his thigh as a drum and restlessly tap out complicated patterns until we cried for mercy. More acceptable were the records he played, however, and he succeeded in teaching Mum and I to appreciate the sounds of the big jazz bands and many solo artistes, though we always had trouble seeing the finer points of Monk's music. Mum did try her best, even going to one of his concerts at the Festival Hall in London with Tony, but she remained unmoved. Although by our teens we had begun to develop separate interests, I still wanted Tony's approval and friendship and knew I would maintain it if I were seen to join him in his love of jazz. Although still preferring Tchaikovsky's original, I bought an LP of Duke Ellington playing his own version of the *Nutcracker Suite*, put it on the turntable in my bedroom and waited for the reaction. I remember so clearly Tony's crooked smile as he popped his head round my door. He said "Hmm. Getting quite grown up aren't we?" I was thrilled.

Tony left school just before his seventeenth birthday, in July 1958. He had not distinguished himself, despite examination retakes, and found work at Beaconsfield Film Studios as a sound assistant. Initially the work was mostly for advertisements, but then he moved on to more interesting projects such as the dubbing of Cliff Richard's first film *Expresso Bongo*. His work often took him up to London where he could wander around the musicians' haunts in 'Tin Pan Alley' – Charing Cross Road – and window-shop for drums, buy music and generally wise up on who was playing where. Ronnie Scott's famous club became a favourite venue and many years later he and I went there just weeks before his departure for America in the spring of 1965.

He and some friends formed a small band and played at local dances and pubs, often coming to our house to practise, so not only did we have drums, we had sax and clarinet too. It was before the days of the small keyboards, otherwise the pianist would have been upstairs as well. Presumably the neighbours had given up complaining, taking some comfort in the fact that Tony would, one day, leave home. Many's the time that a strangely sweet smell emanated from his room, and a peep round the door would reveal three young men smoking what looked like badly-rolled cigarettes, giggling help-lessly, the windows wide open even in winter. I knew that the clarinettist was a bit of a weirdo, walked around like a zombie and grew some sort of plant in his bedroom he wasn't supposed to, but I was so innocent that it wasn't until several years later that I put two and two together, but by then there were other things to worry about.

With the fruits of his labours at the studios Tony bought a motorbike on hire purchase and gave Mum the first of many sleepless nights worrying about his safety on the roads. Progressing half a rung up the production ladder to become a clapper loader on feature films at Pinewood Studios, it was Tony's job to chalk up the scenes on to the board and to snap it in front of the camera before each take. The next step was camera assistant and he worked on a Walt Disney film, which naturally contained several animals. He was told to climb a ladder with a cat and repeatedly drop the animal for several takes so that the cat would appear to be flying, but here his film ca-reer hit a snag. Tony was an animal lover. We had Mikey his beloved dog, a cat, guinea pigs and mice and we'd nursed numerous birds with broken wings and legs (without much success it has to be said) and there was no way that Tony was going to perform this act with the cat. He argued the point, lost, and quit the set.

In October 1959, when he was eighteen, Tony enlisted in the Royal Marine Volunteer Reserves, the marine equivalent of the Territorial Army. He had been just a few months too young to have been eligible for call-up as a conscript under the compulsory Na-tional Service policy, but clearly fancied the challenge such an experience presented. It meant that he could continue his day job, with the odd day-release for unit operations. He was neither tall nor broad – his enlistment details note a height of 5' 8½ ", chest 28", hair dark, skin fair, eyes blue-grey. His lack of height and breadth had been a constant disappointment to him during his teenage years, but our parents were both short in stature and it was unlikely that Tony would ever be a tall man. Once, in desperation aged sixteen, he sent off for a Charles Atlas chest expander which he used diligently. From behind his bedroom door we could hear the grunts and gasps as he grappled with the device, fiercely determined as he was to improve his physique. But with a chest of 28 inches at the age of eighteen it soon became clear to Tony that his dreams of rippling pectorals, bulging biceps and six-pack abdominals would not be achieved by way of Mr Atlas' appliance. He was not to be deterred, however, and took up Judo which was an excellent way of combining both physical and mental exercise and was to stand him in good stead when he joined the US Army. His keenness to achieve and maintain a well-toned physique remained very important to him for the rest of his short but eventful life. He may not have had the body he wanted, but on entering the RMVR he did get something else he had coveted, the entitlement to wear a uniform in his own right instead of the cut-down ones of our grandfather. He loved the Marines and went away on his motorbike for weekend exercises with a sparkling kit, which he would not let any of us help him clean, whiten or polish.

For Tony, the ensuing few years continued to be a mixture of movies, Marines and music, until the latter became dominant. Gigs were becoming more frequent and better paid, and the chance to tour the American Air Force bases in Germany for a couple of months was too good an opportunity to miss, so he took leave from the Marines, gave up his job which was freelancing anyway, and left for mainland Europe. The tour was not a success. 'Harbord's luck' as he often called his bad breaks in life, had struck. The tour man-ager cheated the musicians out of money and at one point Tony ended up in hospital with a broken arm, the result of his swerving to the wrong side of the road in his van to avoid an oncoming motorist. Worried as we were, we trusted he wouldn't make the same mistake again, either with a rogue manager or on the road. But it was good experience, and was his first prolonged period away from home. On his return it was clear to him that music was to be his immediate fu-ture.

Though self-taught, Tony was clearly a talented drummer and set about looking for more permanent work. One late summer's day in 1963, aged 22, he went up to London to Archer Street, Soho. It was a Monday, the day when out-of-work musicians hung out for news of work and auditions. Word was out that Don Smith, then Britain's highest paid resident bandleader, was looking for a new drummer. It was a rare vacancy, particularly as Don usually only needed to make a phone call or two to get musicians to come running. Both the previous drummers had left to join the renowned Johnny Dankworth band, one of whom worked also with Ronnie Scott, and they were clearly going to be a hard act to follow. Tony, with all his inexperience yet charged with hope and the determination to do his best, auditioned for Smith for the coveted position at the Oxford Gallery in Newcastle-upon-Tyne along with other far more seasoned professionals. Tony got the job. Oh, happiness! Harbord's luck had changed at last. For £1.10s he bought himself out of the remaining time he had to serve with the Marines, packed his bags for the north-east and said goodbye to Mikey. Once there, he began to write home regularly, and these early letters form the basis of the story which now unfolds of Tony the man. It is structured around the surviving one hundred and twelve letters he wrote during the last four years of his life, from places as far distant as Florida, California, Guam, the jungles of Vietnam and finally Saigon.

CHAPTER THREE

E ven though the process upset her deeply, my mother
read and re-read Tony's letters over the years following
his death in 1969. They represented a tangible link with her beloved
son, and she scoured them for many different reasons: to feel close to
him, to try to understand what had made him take the path which
ultimately led to his death, and indeed to try to find out how her gentle son had become a hardened killer in a foreign theatre of war.
Hardest of all for her to bear were the occasional, reasoned, admoni-
tions contained in his letters and directed to her, prompted no doubt
by acerbic comments in hers to him criticising his pro-war attitude.
Although this two-way intermittent heated exchange was done out of
love, each for the other, she felt utter despair and guilt on re-reading
his words and recalling her own. I remember her asking me in anguish, following one of her punishing letter-reading sessions fourteen
years after his death, "Do you think he loved me?" Unwillingly, for
I too found it a tragic process, I agreed to read a bundle of them.
Returning it by post with a covering letter, I did my best to assuage
her fears and to comfort her:

"The sheer volume of letters is indication enough of Tony's
love for – and ties with – you, with all of us. Even when his – and
America's – motives and politics were criticised by you, he still came
back with his point of view, trying to make you understand, where
others would have said 'that's it, I'm not writing again'.

"He was able, through his letters, to pour out his heart to you, telling you things few men would confide to their parents. That in itself shows love and trust."

Upon her death in 1996 I took over guardianship of the letters, medals and other documents, although I did not at the time know quite what to do with them. The letters were stacked together haphazardly, out of order, some with no envelopes by which to date them and, feeling unable to cope, I put them back into the drawer of the desk I had inherited from my mother and which had been their home for nearly thirty years. I had other letters to deal with first.

Whilst carrying out the sad and unenviable task of clearing out my mother's house (Dad having died eight years previously in 1988), I had found, tied up in red ribbon, a bundle of intensely intimate love letters he had written to her both before and during the war. How well he had expressed himself then! How deeply he had loved her! I felt like an intruder, put the letters back into their envelopes and then spotted, too late, a note from my mother to me, tucked into the bundle: "Do not read. Please burn after my death". She had left me many notes – they were all around the house and varied from the instructional and funny to the loving and encouraging. They made the miserable job of clearing up easier, and had the poignant effect of making me feel I was not alone in the quiet little grieving house, which had once echoed with our childhood laughter. But this note I had missed, and somewhat belatedly and guiltily I obeyed her command, and went out into the garden where I lit a small bonfire upon which I placed the letters. As the flimsy sheets of paper with their burning messages of love caught the flames, they ascended haphazardly, smouldering, before breaking into fragments of ash, suddenly dispersed by a strong gust of wind. It felt as if I was burning my parents and I watched as their passion, their essence, blew away. I felt totally bereft.

It was to be another two years before I could bring myself to read Tony's letters thoroughly and methodically for the first time. I had suffered some major upheavals in my life, but decided one day in

1998 that the time had come at least to try to put the letters into chronological order. Not easy, when some had been placed into the wrong envelopes, others had no envelope at all and those letters with an indication of the date often simply *said "Monday the 1ˢᵗ"* or *"I think it's my birthday"* or some other fairly unhelpful pointer. Having achieved a pile of certainties and a much larger pile of 'don't knows' I realised that there was nothing for it but to read all one hundred and twelve of them and I spent days sifting, scanning, filing, learning, absorbing, laughing, crying. Here was a young man I thought I knew. I was wrong. For the four years since Tony's departure for America I had clearly been too busy with my life, work, holidays, falling in love and getting married to have given more than half an ear to my mother as she relayed the contents of Tony's latest letter home. I could now understand why she had read them over and over again after his death, trying as she had to pick up threads, look for thought processes, indications as to how things had ended the way they did and, saddest of all, to worry that in some way she might have been to blame. Was this young hero, decorated with a Bronze Star with 'V' for Valor really my big brother? And this citation for bravery: "...with complete disregard for his own personal safety, 1ˢᵗ Lieutenant Harbord braved a murderous hail of fire". Why hadn't I known about this, or, if I had, how come I had forgotten, or had dismissed it from my mind? I had a lot of catching up to do and reparations to make. For his sake I vowed there and then to find out as much as I could about the last years of his life, particularly the period in Vietnam, and to write it all down, though how I was to go about it heaven only knew.

The best place to start was with the four letters that were saved from Tony's fifteen months with the band in Newcastle. Quite why there were so few is not clear, for he wrote regularly. Indeed as a family we were very good correspondents, the telephone being an expensive and often complicated way to communicate in those days when operators across the country would talk to each other as they sat at their manual switchboards, surrounded by wires and plugs, trying to connect the parties. For some inexplicable reason, domestic telephone points were always placed in the hallway which, in those pre-central heating days, made prolonged long-distance phone calls a freezing misery in winter as you stood, shivering, clinging to a heavy, cold Bakelite receiver, every so often hearing the operator chip in to ask if you wanted to pay for more time. It was certainly a good way of keeping call charges down, but we preferred the written word anyway.

Soon after his arrival in the north-east in October 1963 aged twenty-two, Tony had written to say that following a week in digs, he had found his own accommodation in the seaside town of Culler-coats, comprising two attic rooms in a house overlooking the grey and unfriendly North Sea, and he reported on those first bachelor days from his meagre pad:

"The crumpet in the Oxford Gallery is quite fantastic. The trouble is that there are so many girls you can't make up your mind which you would like to meet most. Very disconcerting! Needless to say I haven't got organised along those lines yet. I'll have to soon, because I've got all my shirts to iron ha! ha! I do them in a launder-ette, as one a night is too much for the laundry at 1/6^d a time. I have got to buy myself an iron and one of those folding clothes-horse things."

His keenness to stay fit continued, despite the unsociable hours the band was forced to keep. He kept up his Judo and in their spare time he and the band's bass player would go to the gym to do weight training, play tennis (weather permitting in those days before indoor courts) and often finish with a Turkish bath.

Tony had written that we were welcome to go up and stay with him, as he could rent a spare bedroom for only ten shillings ex-tra a week. Mum and I did visit, on separate occasions (clearly Dad was not keen and although it must have been something of a disap-pointment for Tony, it would not have come as a surprise). The flat was cold and rather grim, but it was fascinating to go to the Oxford Gallery and watch him at work for the first time. There he sat in a smart suit on the bandstand behind his drum kit, aware of a family presence up in the gallery and trying hard to look cool but having the greatest trouble suppressing his familiar, slightly lop-sided grin. I was impressed – the last time I had seen him drumming was up in his bedroom in his underpants, Mikey sleeplessly but obediently keeping his master company. After the gig I was introduced to so many of the band members that I couldn't possibly have remembered their names, but here I was, thirty-six years later, combing Tony's letters for clues to the identities of those long-forgotten musicians. And I found what I was looking for - Brian Whittle and Roger Garrood on sax and Kay Rouselle the vocalist. My mind was whirring. I had started my research.

A plea to the *Searchline* section in the Newcastle Evening Chronicle for information on these people resulted in my letter being printed the following day. Within minutes of the paper hitting the streets my telephone was red-hot. One call was from Kay herself. We didn't know where to start. We didn't know how to finish. Over the following months, including a visit to Newcastle to see her, I got to know this warm, funny, sensitive woman who – still singing – had known and loved Tony and had corresponded with him during his tour in Vietnam.

What had she and her colleagues in the band thought of this green young man stepping into the hot seat vacated by one of Britain's best drummers? "He was a handsome 'divil' with his crew-cut" says Kay, laughing. But what of his talent? "Don would never have engaged anyone who was not a gifted musician, nor did he ever settle for second best, he didn't need to. The band didn't use the standard arrangements which you could pick up at sheet music stores; Don had all our numbers arranged specially. The new music would arrive on a Tuesday, we had a rehearsal the next morning and were playing them that evening." Quite a challenge for the new drummer who was very much feeling his way.

Roger, one of the sax players, was Tony's roommate during 1964-65 when they lived in Dunston, Co. Durham. Now a University Lecturer in Jazz Saxophone at the Western Australia Academy of Performing Arts in Perth, he remembers the days when they shared "time, job, house and personal stuff". Indeed, Tony's personal life had just come alive with his first love affair. Unfortunately for him, his girlfriend Ronnie was married, but that did not stop him falling for her hook, line and sinker. Indeed, Ronnie made a great play for the handsome new drummer on the bandstand. What Tony did not know – and realised too late - was that she was using him to win back her errant husband. For the time being he was smitten and saw her as often as he could. They would both take time off to visit the beautiful Lake District and once he brought her down to stay with us in Datchet. But Mum was worried. She sensed that Ronnie was not nearly as in love with Tony as he was with her. Her instincts were proved right when Ronnie's plan soon bore fruit. Her jealous husband wanted her, and back she went, without so much as a backward glance. I found Ronnie, thirty-six years later. She agreed to talk about those times, but her voice over the phone was cool, monosyllabic, unhelpful. She had heard long ago that Tony had died but said that with the passage of time she really could not remember much about him. No crumbs of comfort there. Even so, I decided not to tell her what Tony had written about her in a letter from the jungles of Vietnam.

His distress and pain at the end of the affair hit him hard and as time went on Roger noticed him becoming unsettled, restless, with a desire to explore new avenues even though the one he was following was perfectly good, and indeed highly promising. He tells of Tony's search for "chivalry and fairness" and recalls his close relationship with our mother. But a conversation Roger has carried with him to this day strikes a chill note. Tony told him that he envisaged meeting his end leading his men into battle - an extraordinary thing for a young musician to say whose country was not even at war. The next saved letter is perhaps the real beginning of his story. Almost a year after he arrived in Newcastle he was clearly some way down the road to implementing a plan for his future, possibly influenced in

some part by his introduction to sailing by another of his saxophone-
playing friends, Brian. He wrote:
  *"I have a new plan of campaign. It's going to take a bit of
doing, but I want to have a go. I have decided to go to America at
last! I intend in three months' time to sell my car, drums etc. and go
to California. I can work my passage and try and get a job when I
get there. I am doing some weight lifting at the moment to get fit, as
I would like to work as crew on private yachts etc. There are a lot of
these in California with rich people taking trips to the South Sea Is-
lands etc. I wonder if Peggy will stand as sponsor for me. I am
determined to really have a go at last, but it will be so easy to put it
off and never go, so I hope you will help me to keep at it and this time
do it."*
  In December 1964, Tony wrote from Newcastle: *"I have
written to Peggy but if America is ruled out I will go anywhere. I'll
put an ad. in the Sunday Times: IDIOT REQUIRES SUITABLE
POST ABROAD, PREFERABLY NOT WITHIN 2,000 MILES OF
DATCHET.*
  *"I've even written to the Congo Embassy to see if they want
any more mercenaries, but I know you will all do your nuts at that
so...* [and here a *Goon Show*-type ditty] *1,2, 1,2,3,4 Ying Tong Ying
Tong Tiddle-I-Po, Stick it up your ---- and a Huh-Huh-Ho. So when
life is boring, and you haven't got a chance, JUMP INTO A
DUSTBIN, AND DANCE."*
  Congo Embassy? Mercenaries? What on earth was going
on in his head?   The troubled central African country had obtained
independence from Belgium in 1960 and become self-governed under the inexperienced leadership of Patrice Lumumba.   Army and
police mutinied and UN peacekeeping forces were called in, but their
intervention failed to prevent the murder of Lumumba just three
months after he took control.   Upon the UN's withdrawal in 1964
widespread rebellion broke out and political stability was in part
achieved as late as 1967.   Just which faction Tony thought he might
support after the UN's departure is a mystery, as is the reason why he

should wish to give up his life as a musician and fight someone else's war, to say nothing of his vision of dying in the process. Perhaps he had been moved by reports and pictures of atrocities and felt a basic instinct to try in some small way to right a terrible wrong. Roger's recalled 'chivalry and fairness' perhaps.

Peggy readily agreed to sponsor Tony in order for him to obtain a US immigrant visa allowing him to work. He was quietly overjoyed that his registered address would thus be hers, in exclusive Beverly Hills, California. Peggy also promised to help in any other way she could. Over the next four years she certainly fulfilled that promise.

Tony came home to Datchet for Christmas 1964, having left the band. His plans were beginning to take shape and his spirits were rising like yeast, as evidenced by entries in my diary:

January 7th, 1965: *"Tony had a cable from Peggy in California!"*

January 16th: *"Tony's made more brown bread. He never stops."*

January 20th: *"Met Tony and Brian J after work & went to see Sonny Rollins at Ronnie Scott's. Absolutely fabulous. Dick Morrissey was fantastic, he played 'Down Home' for me."*

January 22nd: *"Tony's put an ad. in the local paper about selling his car."*

January 29th: *"Tony has secured his visa for America. He had to raise his right hand and take an oath. Tickled him pink!! I went to Winston Churchill's lying-in-state in Westminster Hall".*

February 4th: *"Put an ad. In Melody Maker for Tony's drums and sax".*

February 6th: *"Someone rang up about Tony's car and he'd just left so I went tearing off to Windsor Park to find him".*

February 12th: *"Skiing holiday! Had to say final goodbye to Tony. Awful."*

Chapter Three

And on my return from holiday:
February 26th: *"Tony's still here! Delayed visa or some-*
thing. He met me at the airport with Mum".
March 3rd: *"Felt rotten. Stayed at home. Dad has a pain in*
his side. Tony got ready for his departure tomorrow. When
will we all be together again?"
March 4th: *"Stayed at home again. Tony left in fantastic*
blizzard for America. Dear Tony. With a rucksack on his
back. Fell asleep for 3½ hours & let fire out. Mum came
back from school in bitter cold and had to chop wood in
snow. Washed hair."

How heartless that makes me sound. It was a dreadful day
for her. I remember she and I waving Tony goodbye at the front door
that bitterly cold Thursday morning as, heavily laden, he crunched
down the road in the driving snow to the train for London where another would take him to his ship docked at Southampton. Mum made
a big sign of the cross in the same way that a priest gives the Bless-
ing. Dad had already left for work, and fortunately it turned out that
his pain was nothing sinister; it was probably an inward-turning
manifestation of his own sadness, unable as he was to express himself. For Tony, however, the big adventure had begun, the dream
was becoming reality and he was crossing the Atlantic by ship just as
our mother had, exactly thirty years earlier.

The first letter from his new life was written on board ship
where he had clearly lost no time in seeking out American companions to get him into the real feel of things:

"I have met quite a few people including a very amusing
Texan who tells marvellous stories in a real Huckleberry Hound ac-
cent. We've been drinking together every night and had a lot of
laughs. The funniest thing is every night we have to put our watches
back an hour and a half! This makes the evening kinda long! The
food is very good, the service good, my coloured bedroom steward
called 'Brownie' is awfully delightful, the band is pretty awful, and
the crumpet pretty fair."

45

A picture of Tony and Ralph the Texan on a bunk, glasses in hand, red-faced and giggling, arrived soon after with the first box of slides and demonstrated the effects of the extra drinking time rather more clearly than his letter had. Also in the first batch of slides was one of Tony on deck looking at his New World as his ship docked – a world which was at war with communism thousands of miles away in south-east Asia.

Like many another nation where unrest was to surface in the 20th century, Vietnam's problems could be seen to date back a hundred or so years to the days of western imperialism and it is necessary to go back this far in order to understand how America became so tragically involved. Vietnam had become a French colony because of the richness of its resources and for its strategic position on the trade route into China. For seventy years Vietnam was ruled by France, during which time – in 1890 - one Ho Chi Minh was born. Ho's dream of freeing Vietnam from colonial rule led him to France where he became a founding member of the French Communist Party. The Great Depression of the 1930s caused France to downsize the resources being committed to its colony and thereby created a situation ripe for unrest and insurrection. Moreover, France's own occupation by Germany in World War II demonstrated to Vietnam's citizens the vulnerability of their own colonial masters. Vichy France permitted the stationing of Japanese troops in the colony and by 1941 Vietnam's economy and military bases were under Japanese control which lasted until the dropping of the atom bomb on Hiroshima in August 1945. Within three weeks the nationalist coalition had won independence and Ho Chi Minh declared the establishment of the Democratic Republic of Vietnam. However, France was not going to give up so easily, and in 1946 an eight-year war with France began. It ended with the terrible 59-day battle in the valley of Dien Bien Phu in May 1954, which culminated in French surrender and the splitting of Vietnam at the Seventeenth Parallel under the terms of the Geneva Accord that July. A demilitarised buffer zone (DMZ) was established on either side and the following year saw a great movement of people from north to south and vice-versa, as they headed to the predominantly communist north or non-communist south. However, many active guerrilla cells remained in the south which would eventually amalgamate and resurface as the National Liberation Front, better known as the Viet Cong.

The north counted on the support of China and the USSR, whilst the administration of the President of South Vietnam, Ngo Dinh Diem, had the backing of America under President Dwight D Eisenhower. The US government feared the likely 'Domino Effect' of south-east Asian countries falling one by one to communism and began pouring money and advisory manpower into military aid programmes. Since 1950, American dollars had been supporting the French war effort in Indochina and by the end of 1963 America was involved to the tune of $500,000 a year. As far as manpower 'in-country' was concerned, by the summer of 1962 there were already 12,000 American advisors in South Vietnam. This policy continued and developed under President John F Kennedy, although he was against large-scale intervention. Diem was fighting a losing battle against the Viet Cong and three weeks before the assassination of Kennedy was himself deposed in a coup and shot.

In America, President Lyndon B. Johnson was handed the hot potato. The Viet Cong were winning popular support in the rural areas in the south as the administration in Saigon tottered under corruption, nepotism and repeated coups. The north meanwhile was sending thousands of infantrymen down the infamous Ho Chi Minh Trail whose three main arteries and feeder roads totalled an amazing15,000km, beginning north of the DMZ and running south to the Mekong Delta. The administration in Saigon, such as it was, was under threat from both the Viet Cong and now the North Vietnamese Army (NVA) which was pouring down the Trail. President Johnson began enlarging the US commitment in Vietnam and the situation was kept continually under review. In effect, this development committed America to fighting a war in Vietnam, but what she needed now was a legitimate way of entering the conflict.

On August 2 1964, North Vietnamese torpedo boats in the Gulf of Tonkin attacked the destroyer *USS Maddox*. The *Maddox* had been taking part in a covert coastal surveillance operation, but the US government at the time did not declare this. Two days later a second North Vietnamese PT boat attack was reported to have fired on the *USS Maddox* and her escort the *USS C. Turner Joy*, although whether this second incident ever actually occurred has never been satisfactorily substantiated. Having been assured that the attack did occur, however, President Johnson ordered retaliatory air strikes against North Vietnam and a few days later Congress passed the Southeast Asia Resolution empowering him to take "all necessary measures to repel any armed attack against the forces of the United States and to prevent further aggression." Currently seeking re-election, Johnson's stand against communism was fortuitous and widely approved. He won the Democratic nomination on August 26 and on November 3 polled the greatest percentage of the total popular vote (61%) ever attained by a presidential candidate.

Johnson was in the fourth month of his second term in office as Tony's ship docked in New York after five days at sea. With thoughts only of commencing his long-planned adventure, Tony made his way to the YMCA on West 34th Street where he soon had a taste of life in the Big Apple. His wallet was stolen.

March 13th: *"Thanks for the letters and the money belt. Guess what happened the same day it arrived? Somebody stole my wallet. I think it was lifted when I was in the elevator. I got it back, as the thief threw it out of the window, after taking $31 out. The security men attached to the YMCA are very good, and they really tried to find the thief as soon as I reported it. I'm not sure if they 'shook the guy down' that I reported as having been hanging round the shower room, but they said they were going to, and I know they do these things. Rather different from the YMCA in Newcastle where you tell the office and they let you know if your wallet 'turns up'.*

"The highlight of New York is definitely the view from the Empire State Building at night. I went the first night and although I

was tired I haven't seen anything to compare with it yet. I am at this moment waiting for Ralph as we are going to Coney Island. He's so funny because he always has a saying for everything. When we were on the street, I said 'Brrrr, isn't it cold?' and he replied 'Yep, colder than a well-diggers ass in Montana!'

" I have seen so few girls it's ridiculous. I've even been to Peppermint Lounge where they invented the Twist and there weren't that many there. I did better on the boat.

"I am leaving New York tomorrow for Philly, Baltimore and Washington. When I get south of Washington I'm going to start looking for a job. Ta Ta for now."

YMCA Washington DC: *"Hi there all you wunnerful people! The buildings here are absolutely fantastic. You will see some of them on my next roll when I send it. I know how Gay loves buildings, buildings and still more buildings. The Capitol has to be seen to be believed. The architecture is wonderful."*

Indeed it is. Unable to have the time to walk around Washington when my mother and I visited the Vietnam Wall in 1992, I savoured the opportunity when I revisited the city for Veterans' Day in November 1999. On an unseasonably warm early winter's day I walked for many blocks up and down the wide boulevards, map in hand. I could almost imagine myself as a citizen in Pericles' Athens of the fifth century BC, strolling amongst the amazing white stone buildings with their lofty columns, porticoes and flights of steps. Washington seemed so familiar, but then Tony and I had seen it 'at the pictures' since we were quite young, had sat glued to the television for President Kennedy's funeral in 1963 and watched Martin Luther King's "I have a dream" speech delivered during the march on Washington soon afterwards.

"Today I had a conducted tour round the FBI headquarters. This is the most exciting thing I have ever seen. They show you all the departments, finger-printing, this-ology, that-ology, and we even went down into the basement and watched a special agent firing a .38 revolver and then a .45 Thompson sub-machine gun. The guide

was a real nice young fellow who is at present working in one of the clerical departments but is studying law in the hope of becoming an agent. I had a very interesting talk with him after the tour."

Did he see the anti-Vietnam War protesters camped at the gates of the White House? Did he know that Operation Rolling Thunder, the sustained carpet-bombing campaign against North Vietnam, had just been initiated by the Johnson administration? That some 75,000 American troops were currently in South Vietnam? If he did, he made no mention. He left the next day to hitchhike south, stopping along the way to look for work.

"I hit the road at 12 o'clock Tuesday morning. I didn't get a lift for about half an hour, but then I got four for very short distances and was only a way past Fairfax, Virginia, by 3 o'clock and walked with my pack for 2½ hours before being picked up by two guys in a beat-up 1951 Buick they had bought for $30.

"Having arrived in Greenville, S. Carolina, in the pouring rain at 8.30 the next morning, I staggered to a crummy hotel (the Hotel Windsor, $2.50 per night) and flaked out until 3 o'clock. The manager always seems to be in pyjamas, and has a great big Confederate flag on the wall in his bedroom.

"Then this morning I tried looking for a job, but nothing so far. I put an ad. in the paper tonight: YOUNG ENGLISHMAN REQUIRES WORK IMMEDIATELY, DRIVING, ANYTHING. If nothing turns up I'll head south."

And head south he did. Clearly work was not going to be that easy to find. Down through Georgia he travelled – the state whose army parade grounds, jump towers, swamps and deadly snakes were to become very familiar to him, but not yet. Shedding clothes as the temperature climbed, he reached the Sunshine State of Florida four weeks after arriving in New York and again immediately set about looking for a job, only this time his search was more focussed, centred now upon the charter fishing scene.

6th April, Fort Lauderdale: *"I luckily got a ride to Tarpa Springs, Florida and stayed a couple of days in a cheap rooming*

house there. I tried to get on a boat. No luck again. The manager-
ess was very kind and took me round to a shrimp boat captain she
knew. I missed a job on a grouper boat by a day and a job driving a
shrimp truck by about 3 days. The nearest I got was the captain of a
drift fishing boat (with people on board fishing) who told me to come
back in about 6 weeks as some of his crew were being drafted to
Vietnam. They have a fleet of charter fishing boats, two man crew
jobs, and they take people out for fifty dollars a day – absolutely
great, just like in Flipper! But I am the world's unluckiest when it
comes to either jobs or women."
    Harbord's luck again, or that is how it must have seemed to
him. He had certainly been unlucky in love so far, with at least one
unhappy affair behind him, which may have been an added spur to
his leaving England. He had been used to watching his two best
friends collect girls with ease, but handsome as he undoubtedly was,
Tony's slight diffidence and shyness worked against him when it
came to charming the female sex, even, apparently, in America,
where an English accent was widely considered an added attraction.
    It seemed that wherever he went looking for work it was the
wrong time of year, as the season was just ending. Undaunted, he
left his name with all the dock-masters and at all the yacht basins he
could find, hoped for the best and went off to explore Fort Lauderdale. He was smitten. He found it *"just like something out of a Cliff*
Richard musical, with hip, good-looking sunburnt youngsters danc-
ing on the beach and driving enormous cars in just trunks and
bikinis. Of course I have drawn all the usual blanks, female-wise,
and last night I tried three times in a club. I think I must have lep-
rosy or something.
    "I really love this way of life, so casual and fun loving. The
woman at my rooming house is awfully nice and it's not all 'tip-toe
and peering and aspidistras' at all. Nobody seems to be like that at
all here". This was of course a reference to the legendary English
boarding-house landlady behind whose net-curtained windows lay

rooms stuffed with dusty pot plants, unplayed pianos, artificial flowers and gloomy dark wooden furniture.

"If I could just get what I had before at home, a job, a car, and a few friends, life would definitely be very, very pleasant here, no shit! My opinions haven't changed, in fact it is almost better than I expected, and I haven't even got west yet. Really, the picture we get in England of a violent, greedy, boastful, sickly sentimental nation is most terribly overdone.

"I got a letter from Peggy today... and she says I must write a book one day so you better keep my letters, or I will forget everything!" We kept them, Tony.

His next letter early in April 1965, was addressed to 'The Datchet Hill Billies' and continued his job-searching narrative.

"I put an ad. in the paper and had four replies altogether. The first one was a call at 8 Friday morning from a lawn maintenance man who collected me at 8.30 and I sweated my balls off all day in the hot sun snipping and raking and mowing private lawns at a fantastic rate. The man told me 'you gotta work fast, everything's that way in America'. The next call was from a man who runs a janitor service, and I could be driving around cleaning up people's offices. I reserved judgement on that one.

"Luckily I met a fellow in a bar who was a captain on a private power boat and he offered me a week's work helping him 'decorate' it. The pay is $1.50 per hour and I started Monday sandpapering all the varnished woodwork in the wheelhouse. Bill is a nice fellow and he's going to talk to the captain of a boat that goes north. If I got that job I would get a khaki navy-type uniform with a CAP! Just like a proper captain!"

April 26 1965: *"Yes it's me folks! (Pause for Applause)"*

Tony's spirits were clearly in the ascendant. His new employer, Bill, regarded Tony's work highly and considered the $1.50 per hour wage such a paltry amount that he made it up out of his own pocket to something more reasonable. Tony had by now moved out of his lodgings and on to the boat, Santena III:

"The weather is really wonderful down here, I knew I wouldn't hate the heat, and I sleep naked with a fan blowing on me. I have decided not to go west until the Fall, as it will be too hot in Texas in the summer. Tell everybody to write to me; mail means a lot when you're on your jack, as you know."
May 1965 and along came the break.
"HULLO FOLKS HULLO FOLKS HULLO FOLKS HULLO FOLKS!
"Well, at last I'm a fisherman. I have got a job on one of the charter boats at last, Kingfisher V. The other day my new fishing mate John and I took out a rich American wearing long shorts and a golf cap and caught him a sailfish. He gave me a $10 tip! Altogether that day I made nearly $40! Two half days that's $16, $11 total in tips, $10 commission on the cost of mounting the fish from the taxidermist, and some fish money (selling the edible fish).
"One day Jack (John's weather beaten old captain) decided to go out for a morning's fun-fishing as his boat did not have a charter. Luck seemed bad until we hooked onto a hammerhead shark. I was in the chair to begin with and later I finally brought it in. John pulled it up to the boat by hand and Jack shot it through the head with a long pole and a shotgun cartridge in the end. I'm now at last a real fishing mate on a big game fishing boat with chrome chairs and padded seats!"
Tony's cup began to run over, for not only did he have a job which he enjoyed so much that working seven days a week was no chore, he had made several good friends who clearly enjoyed his company as much he did theirs. In just a few weeks he was well into his American Dream and his letters described his thrill at encountering drive-in banks, eateries and in particular the joys of drive-in movies where there was no *"pushing past, farting or smoking.*
"I wish y'all could make it over here, I'm sure you would enjoy it, even square old Dad would get a laugh out of baseball games!"

In June 1965 an exuberant letter arrived containing our parents' birthday presents. His intoxication with life appeared to have had a little help.

"Dear Jim Crint and Mrs Gladys Pukes,
The blouse is for dad and the golf hat for mum ha! ha! Gay
says I'm always pissed. It's a lie I tell you. Do you know the differ-
ence between a drunk and an alcoholic? Well, us drunks don't have
to go to all them meetings! Hee! Hee!

"Last weekend I had a wonderful time. The sun blazed down
on my mate Fred and I as we sailed along Miami Beach waving at
the crumpet. Next day we moved on down to Key Largo and an-
chored offshore in a little bay. Real Bahama Jim type stuff! We
soaped our bodies down with washing-up liquid from head to foot
and then dived into the clear, warm water and swam round the boat
to wash off.

"We had already blown up the dinghy when two guys came
out in a power boat to have a chat and look at the boat. The brought
us some barbecued ribs and chicken which we hungrily consumed,
and then took us and our dinghy to shore. We hit the local beer
joints and actually drank beer which, believe it or not, brought about
a very slight state of inebriation, yes, we were pissed. There, I've
said it. How naughty. (When my letters lack humour and jokes
about being pissed, that's the time to start worrying.) I am as fit as a
fiddle and brown as sixteen berries, just for the record."

Later that month, Tony and his mate John moved into a furnished apartment in Isle of Venice, Fort Lauderdale. It was quite luxurious and not spoiled, as it would often have been in England, *"by stacking it with all the cheapest junk they can find, just so they can say it's got furniture in it.*

"I went water skiing a week ago. It's such fun. John was
almost sick, he was laughing at me so much from the boat. I got up
first time, but apparently was skiing knock-kneed with eyes as big as
saucers, bouncing ungainly over the waves produced by a passing
boat until finally a spectacular leap through space with arms and

legs and skis all waving in opposite directions caused me to disappear beneath the surface."

The American car culture had made an instant impression on Tony who divulged his plans to buy a 1957 Plymouth for $100. *"It's not exactly immaculate, but for 30 quid it's pretty damn good value. It has automatic transmission and the engine sounds good."* In response to a question from home, which presumably asked him how long he was intending to stay in America, he wrote, *"I am a registered alien with an ID card, and the only thing I need extending is my bank balance. Haha."*

Tony wrote regularly to Peggy too, keeping her up to date with his news and plans for the future and also testing her out with ideas that, for the time being, he kept from us. Trying not to betray his confidence, Peggy wrote to Mum *"I think – but don't breathe it to a soul – I think he is going back to school! Next autumn. I think he realizes he needs more education and I believe he is going to get it. Of course, the draft may catch him, but if it does, he will try to get all the free training they can give him.*

"I gather he is in fine physical condition – the work is hard, but he likes it. I don't think you need worry about him. I believe he can look out for himself and is doing some really hard thinking about his future. He asked me what I thought of the idea of his going to college and I was enthusiastic, but he asked me to say nothing about it, because he wanted to think some more.

"And here I am telling you – but only because I know that every scrap of information about him will be eagerly awaited by you. But I want him to trust me, and not to think that I will repeat his random thoughts before he is sure of them, so you and Gay must not let him know until he tells you."

Peggy, mindful of the feelings of all of us, had told us only a half-truth. She had indeed kept from us a crucial aspect of her conversation with Tony, which would be revealed in one of his August letters to us. Meanwhile, in Florida, Tony's twenty-fourth birthday approached.

July 1965: *"I had my first lie-in this morning for about 3 weeks. I have been getting up at 6 o'clock and 5 o'clock for weeks, every day. Actually, it's lovely getting up the same time as the sun, and so warm too. Haven't been pissed for ages. Too tired to go out after work! Happy birthday to me."*

The first indication that things were going to change rapidly and radically came in a letter dated 16 August 1965.

"Thanks ever so for the prezzies which I only received a few days ago. I haven't got much time, as there is a lot to do. I am moving out of the flat and giving up my job here and setting off tomorrow for California. I think I am going to be called up, so I had better get over to see Peggy quick. I am going to drive across. Love, Tony."

"I think I am going to be called up." And Peggy's letter had said, "Of course the draft may catch him." Alarm bells rang and the tension was palpable in our little house. We knew a little about the war in Vietnam, but surely, for aliens, there was no compulsory conscription anyway? Mum walked around the house, one hand on her chest as if finding it difficult to breathe. Dad was very quiet and sat, motionless, in his chair, staring out of the window. I, with the benefit of youth, shrugged it off. I was planning my twenty-first birthday party.

What we had not fully realised in our corner of the world was that the American war in Vietnam had escalated to a point where men in their thousands were now being conscripted and sent off to fight in south-east Asia. The first regular American troops to be sent there were US Marines who landed at Da Nang in March 1965, just as Tony's ship was sailing across the Atlantic. Their original brief was to defend the airbase there, but it soon widened to embrace offensive action in the field. That month the Americans began Operation Rolling Thunder, a sustained carpet-bombing campaign that was to last for three and a half years. Its 350,000 sorties dropped twice the tonnage of bombs as had fallen on all World War II's theatres of war. By the end of 1965 200,000 GIs were in Vietnam, a figure that was to double within a year and approach half a million by the winter of 1967.

It was against this background of the escalation of the Vietnam War that Tony found himself being drafted. Under a 1951 amendment to the Military Selective Service Act of 1948, 'all male persons now or hereafter in the United States' were subject to registration if they were between the ages of eighteen and twenty-five. Tony was twenty-four and therefore in a high 'draft-eligible' age group. However, posting to Vietnam would, for him and other aliens, only occur if the individual volunteered to go. A huge sense of relief settled on our house once this last fact had been established.

Had he wished to avoid the draft, Tony could have left the United States altogether, as countless thousands of panicking American citizens did, for whom the spectre of Vietnam was a certainty. The same alarm spread amongst male college students who could only qualify for deferment from the draft if it could be shown that they were making satisfactory progress towards a degree. Many and varied were the pleas by students to college staff to enhance their marks in order to achieve that level of 'satisfactory progress'. Countless lecturers were faced with a dilemma for, in awarding honest marks for indifferent achievement they were all too well aware that they could in effect be signing a death warrant for their least able students.

But no thoughts of draft dodging entered Tony's mind. Quite the reverse, for his sense of adventure clearly took hold of him and he began his journey west in the old Plymouth to Peggy's plush California home in Beverly Hills, where he was registered.

Friday 20 August 1965: *"I am at present staying in Greenville, S. Carolina, visiting the red-haired English girl I met on the boat. Next stop will be St. Louis, where another bit of crumpet lives. After that I shall head for Peggy's, seeing as much of Colorado, N. Mexico and Arizona as possible on the way. It looks like I will almost certainly be drafted as they are taking everyone they can now, especially single, over 21.*

"In a way I am looking forward to it, as I have always had a sort of sneaking feeling towards it as you know. I shall not let them draft me with all the other Herberts, but shall volunteer for either the US Marine Corps or the Army Airborne (the toughest outfits of course) because if I have to go in, I have to go in the best or not at all.

"I am hoping to pass the tests and IQ exams for Marine Reconnaissance or 82nd Airborne Intelligence, and really make a go of it and get trained for perhaps a career in Intelligence. If I take advantage of the college opportunities offered free to servicemen, I hope to study law and this would qualify me for the very highly esteemed FBI.

"If only I could make it in this field, maybe I would find the answer to my problem of doing something worthwhile and being a member of something that is perhaps the best in the world. I probably haven't got a chance, but I'm going to have a go, and if I fail I'll go back to Lauderdale and fish."

The unwritten words of Peggy's earlier letter were now revealed, *"I mentioned my plans to Peggy about 3 months ago and she thinks they are splendid. I didn't tell you, in case you thought I was being ridiculous, or in case you might worry that I was going into something dangerous. Like I say, if I could make it I think it would be the answer, but I'm going to have a long talk with Peggy first.*

"Ying-Tong-Tiddle-I-Po
Signed, 007"

So. Tony's secret was out, and he gave himself up wholeheartedly to the delights of the drive across the continent. It was a wonderful experience for him. He looked up his friend Ralph from the boat crossing in Lubbock, Texas, and fell in love with New Mexico and Arizona. Of the Grand Canyon he said: *"I can't believe I actually lived for 14 years in Datchet when places like this exist.*

"I went to a drive-in movie in Flagstaff, Arizona, situated just off the main street with the screen in the west. So I was sitting in my car at sundown, with the sun setting behind the screen and the

Chapter Three

Santa Fé railroad trains hooting away on my left. It was something absolutely American west.

"The Grand Canyon is 80 miles from Flagstaff, and most of the land along the road is national forest. However, an Arizona Land development company has acquired some land either side of the highway and has subdivided it into plots to be sold. I managed to get one the farthest away from the road, overlooking the range with mountains in the distance. It is nearly 2 acres for $895 (£300). Ridiculous really, as I only had $40 in my pocket but I just put $5 down and will pay the rest at about $20 per month while I am in the service. Nothing ventured, nothing gained. If the area gets spoiled I will just sell it and if it doesn't, maybe one day I'll put a house on it. At least when I get out of the army I will have something of my own to stand on and shout 'It's all mine, I tell you, get off my land!' Dad can come over and help me build a log cabin, and Mum can dig the garden. Gay can dig the cesspit. Two acres is enough to have a corral and a couple of horses instead of a boring old garden.

"You're going to have to retire sometime, so why not get ready now and buy a plot of land thirty miles from the Grand Canyon? For $3-4,000 you can get a smashing 3-bedroom bungalow-type American house with central heating and the lot. I intend to nip out on leave and keep an eye on the place.

"I went out to look at my plot. It's pretty wild, and there was an enormous anthill in the middle of it. I told them all to get off my property but they didn't take a blind bit of notice. I nearly went and got the sheriff, but I told them I would be back in three years, so they better watch out.

Signed, Governor of Arizona."

Oh Tony. Such plans. You never did see your plot again, never built your cabin. None of us even knew where it was, until in 1999 I made contact with the Flagstaff Recorder's Office and a kind lady sent me a map of the development area. The company never even began work on it. No services were ever supplied, and a few families who had put money down on plots lived on for a while in trailers but eventually moved off. I wept for you when I found out.

On arrival in Beverly Hills, California, that September, Tony wrote, *"This parcel contains Gay's 21ˢᵗ birthday present which, though simple, was more than I could really afford. It was made in Anandarko, Oklahoma, the capital of the Plains Indians, by Kiowa and Cheyenne. I thought it would look original against a plain sweater. I couldn't help it being red, white and blue, the Indians seem to like that combination."* It was a pendant made of beads and shells and mounted on buckskin. I treasure it to this day. He continued, *"Tomorrow I go downtown L.A. to have a whole day of tests and a physical examination. I am hoping to do quite well, as I took the preliminary test in the recruiting office and got 45/48 which is considered brilliant – many high school grads fail to make the pass mark of 28.*

"I first go to Fort Polk, Louisiana, for 8 weeks basic training with all sorts. I then go to another 8 weeks advanced combat training, then to Fort Benning, Georgia, for 3 weeks jump school and if I pass through everything I get awarded my silver wings and I am a paratrooper.

"At sometime in the future, I intend to volunteer for the Special Forces, which is another year's training. These people have now become the finest soldiers in the world. They are extensively trained in everything, including how to survive in the jungle carrying only a knife, how to handle snakes (don't fancy that!), how to do an emergency appendix and above all how to be the toughest, most intelligent, efficient combat soldier in the world, and ultimately how to teach everything they know to others.

"The training is so hard and the qualifications so high, that I don't really expect to get through, but if I do, I think our military ancestors will be proud of me, because once I am awarded the green beret at the end of the year's training, I really will be one of the best soldiers in the world." Grandfather Hoghton was clearly very much in his mind.

"One thing that will amuse dad, in the Airborne when you jump out, you yell 'GERONIMO!' All paratroopers do it by tradition, some Indian started it in the war and it caught on. It's going to be a tough life, and I shall probably hate it, but I am looking forward to it in a way, as you know. I have always had a military 'bug' to get rid of, and if you go to it with the right attitude, I think there are lots of worse things to do. Next time I write, it will probably be from Louisiana giving you my new address (be a bit of a joke if I failed the medical through flat feet or something!)"

That was his last letter as a civilian and he was about to give his military bug a very good airing.

CHAPTER FOUR

The fingerprints of my brother Tony appear on his army enlistment record. Dated 17 September 1965, it marks a new and challenging twist to his American adventure. Ten times his signature appears, countersigned by the enlisting officer, one Floyd W. Blunk. As I look at the document and touch those finger-prints, I can sense his excitement that day, I can see him trying to suppress a grin as he held out his hands for the fingers to be inked and rolled on to the page. He was not to know how those prints would ultimately be used, for they would help identify his body three and a half years later.

So, back across the continent he travelled, this time by mili-tary plane to Fort Polk in Louisiana for eight weeks of Basic Training. His first letter as Private Harbord was dated Friday 24 September and was written late at night when everyone else was asleep:

"This is the first chance I've had to write since I entered the army. The lights are out in the barracks and I have finished polish-ing my boots and brass buckle. I am sitting on the lav. writing as the latrine is the only place where lights are allowed.

"My head has been shaved shorter than you have ever seen and the sergeants are just as mean as legend has it.

"When we arrived at Fort Polk at 4 o'clock in the morning after 8 hours' flying, we were herded around in the rain, shouted at, and seemed to do nothing else but stand in lines in the rain either for chow, or uniforms, or anything."

That was his first taste of 'hurry up and wait', that most fundamental of army lessons. *"We spent 3 or 4 days there taking tests and 'processing' as it's called and then we were moved out in teeming rain in trucks like cattle to South Fort Polk. Here we were moved into barracks, screamed at by sergeants and had all our belongings checked, books confiscated, and all civilian clothes locked in a room.*

"There are four platoons in Bravo ('B') Company, one in each barracks. Each platoon is immediately commanded by a platoon sergeant who is chosen from the ranks, usually for prior service or previous military training. When we were asked who had this, I stepped forward (because of my Royal Marine Volunteer Reserves record) and ended up a squad leader. I am very much hoping to keep the job, as this is the first step to getting recognised as a possibility for promotion.

"One of the older sergeants here likes me, I think, as he has talked to me a couple of times about England. When he first played the mean act with me he said 'Of course you know we work harder here than the British do?' and I said 'No, sergeant' and he said 'Oh you don't know that?' And I said 'No, sergeant'. Instead of giving me the third degree like some of the other tough sergeants probably would, he said 'You're damn right; you've got a fine army!' I think this is one reason why he chose me as squad leader, because I stood up to him.

"It's amazing the difference in these mean sergeants when you are sitting talking man to man, than at other times. They turn on the meanness like a light switch. I feel rather sorry for one or two rather pathetic youths who get shouted and screamed at and made a fool of. I don't think I would ever make a good sergeant! What will be worse than this though will be Airborne School, which is three weeks of hell to try to make you into a paratrooper who will never lose his nerve. If you're going to crack, they want you to crack in training before you ever see an aeroplane, so they give you hell.

"I am determined to give it all I've got. I made pretty good scores in all my tests, and just passed the officers' school by 4 points, so at some time I will have a chance to go to the Officers' Training School. I'll make those military ancestors proud of me yet!"

A typical day in basic training began with running a mile a 5 a.m. and ended late at night cleaning equipment. In a PT test Tony scored 447/500 and was proud to report that he was the only squad leader to have beaten the rest of his squad. The test involved the low crawl pit, hand grenade throw, monkey bars, run-dodge-jump and the mile run in boots, achieved by him in a time of six minutes thirty-four seconds, the standard pass mark being eight minutes thirty.

Unlike many of the other draftees, Tony was relishing the new experience and any misgivings we at home may have had were largely allayed by his cheerful letters which would be read by the three of us as we got home from work. Mum would cycle the two miles back from school and force herself to leave any letter from Tony unopened until she was sitting down with a cup of tea, I would skim through them after dashing home from *Newsweek* magazine and before rushing out again, and Dad would read them in his armchair with a well-stoked pipe when he got back from his job as theatrical agent in London.

In week five of Basic Training, Fort Polk held an Open Day for family and friends of the new recruits. Eager to become involved, Tony kept us informed of events:

"I have volunteered for the drill team (much piss-taking about my erect posture and high arm swing) and I have been 'discovered' as a drummer, so will be playing in the band for the guests. I wish you could all come over for Open Day!"

It was a great success. Tony was *"rushing around playing drums in the jazz group, faking sax in the main band and also appearing in the drill team doing some fancy rifle stuff."* The Company Commander, Lieutenant Mason, congratulated everyone personally and asked the performers to do a twenty-minute spot in the Officers' Club as result.

Chapter Four

With Open Day over, it was back to business. The last three weeks of training were particularly hard – a week's bivouac exercise with live machine gun fire, beating the hell out of each other with pugil sticks, hand-to-hand combat which involved kicking your opponent once he was down, and instruction on how to strangle a man. *"Neither I nor my opponent succeeded in this last delight, so I had to suffer, wide awake, a man trying to strangle me with all his strength, with his arm round my throat pulling up into my Adam's apple. Charming! Several guys went right out for quite a few seconds. You can imagine what it was like at first, seeing the big burly evil-looking Negro sergeant demonstrating this strangle, and seeing his subject, one of us, pass out and make little twitching movements until he woke up."*
Rifle target practice, involving man-sized targets which popped up all over the range up to 350 metres distant, was another area in which Tony particularly wanted to do well. A score of 30-44 conferred Marksman status, 45-59 Sharpshooter, and 60+ Expert. Tony made 59, having nervously wasted a few shots. So anxious to excel in everything he did, he was understandably disappointed, but it seemed that nothing was going to quell his enthusiasm and determination to succeed and improve in everything he did. Having had second thoughts about the immediate future, he wrote:
"I have decided to postpone Airborne School and go to Officer Candidate School (OCS) after my eight weeks Advanced Individual Training. This will be six months of hell, but the training is second to none, and if I make it, I will come out a LOOTENANT! Then I will continue my plans for Airborne, Ranger School, and possibly Special Forces." No lack of keenness there. No mention of Vietnam either.
By November 1965 there was just one more week of Basic to go:
"We marched twenty miles out to bivouac, and spent four days and nights in the field, shaving out of our steel helmets and getting smellier and smellier. We had some special night training

65

including the grand finale on Thursday night, the infiltration course. This little gem consists of climbing out of a trench and crawling 80m on your stomach cradling your rifle, with live machine gun fire over your head and explosions going off in demolition pits all around you. All this takes place in the dark and you can see the tracers above you as you crawl underneath barbed wire.

"The barracks was in an uproar tonight. Everyone had the giggles and kept playing jokes on each other, like waking each other up to tell them something ridiculously unimportant, or everyone would start saying 'goodnight' to everyone else all at once until it sounded like a zoo. As squad leader, I had a job getting them all quietened down but it was difficult because I had to hide my own laughter while trying to keep a straight face. Next Saturday my buddies Chip and Jim and I are going to try to get a free military hop from an Air Force Base to Arizona for our leave."

A letter from Peggy dated 2 December 1965 informed Mum of Tony's visit to her after Basic Training. *"Your boy telephoned me within minutes of arriving in California and asked if he and his two friends could come and see us. 'Lovely', I said, 'would you like to come some day this week?' 'Could we come right now?' came his answer, and of course I said yes. Vi, you would be pleased. He looks wonderful – fit and lean and good colour. But what would give you great satisfaction is the quiet self-confidence, the almost shy feeling he has – a sort of 'I've made it'.*

"The three of them talked it all out for two hours – and I feel they were all in good shape emotionally. They have been through a tough experience and they are quietly proud to have weathered it and be looking ahead to officer training.

"I felt that Tony was quieter, more controlled, less nervous than he was before. He's a man now. Frankly, I hope he goes on and on taking courses and further training – <u>anything</u> to put off going to Vietnam. But certainly they have convinced the recruits that Vietnam is a holy war. I wish I was as sure!"

There it was. The dreaded 'V' word. It came as something of a shock, not simply because we believed that going to Vietnam was something Tony as an alien would not wish – nor be obliged – to do; what was unsettling was the natural way in which Peggy had alluded to it, giving us the impression that it was very much on Tony's agenda and that the topic had been fully and frankly aired on his visit to her.

Having taken a two-week leadership course at Fort Polk, where demerits were given for petty misdemeanours such as a table lamp being set one-sixteenth of an inch too low or socks not being evenly rolled, Tony continued his training in preparation for Officer Candidate School. Christmas 1965 came, his first in America, and he had nowhere to go. He got on a bus with his buddy Tim to Houston, Texas, and ended up in a burger bar. *"While we were there, this rather sweet looking girl came in and Tim, knowing I would be left in Houston alone, got up and insisted she sit down with us."* She only stayed a few minutes, but Tony got her phone number, Tim flew off to Phoenix, and Tony had two or three lonely days wandering around the town with nothing to do. *"Judy had mentioned calling her on Saturday, Christmas Day, so I did, just to say 'Merry Christmas'. Luckily I was invited over, and as you now know, very hospitably treated in the good old American fashion. You could have knocked me down with a feather when Mr Whyman said I could call you."* That was an understatement. Twenty-five years later Mrs Whyman clearly recalled Tony's surreptitious, grateful tears at the opportunity to call home on such a special day. Taken aback at the kind offer, he later wrote home, *"I couldn't remember our number! When a London operator answered, the voice sounded so funny. Mum, you sounded exactly the same. I wish I could call you every night."* I remember that call well. We were all fast asleep after the traditional surfeits of Christmas Day. I heard the phone ring at about 1 a.m. and, startled, dashed downstairs in my pyjamas to the bitterly cold little hallway where the heavy old phone with its permanently twisted cord sat in pools of frozen condensation on the window sill. Nobody would ever call that late unless it was terrible news. I must have shrieked and woken my mother who stood at the top of the stairs in her night-dress, eyes wide, hand over her mouth, but once she realised it was Tony and that all was well, she flew down the stairs with joy and talked to her son for the first time since he had left England nine months before.

Tony was invited back to the Whymans for another meal, and then took Judy to a movie. *"That was the last I saw of her. Rather a pity, I thought the impossible had happened, a girlfriend near enough to the post to be able to get out and see at weekends to help preserve my sanity. Unfortunately, she goes back to college in Lubbock, Texas, much too far away. Balls!"*

From January through to April 1966 Tony underwent Advanced Individual Training. In his own words it was *"an absolute bitch"* and towards the end of January he faced the OCS board. *"What an ordeal. I was quizzed by a major, a captain and two lieutenants for fifty minutes. They asked me all sorts of tricky questions, like 'What would you do if England and the United States went to war?' and 'How do you feel when you salute our flag?'*

"I made one of them chuckle when I was asked 'Why do you choose infantry as your first choice?' I replied, 'Well, sir, it's a sort of love-hate relationship. When I'm out in the cold I hate it, but when I'm back in the warm I'm proud of it'.

"Don't be disappointed if I'm turned down."

Meanwhile, the course got tougher. *"Next week we have another particular ordeal to go through, the Escape and Evasion course. This is a classic legend. Apparently all the awful things we have heard are true. You are released in teams of six at night and have to go a certain route through a certain area without being caught (they have another company as the searchers). If they catch you, they take you to a prison compound where there are sergeants who interrogate you and actually beat the shit out of you. It's not as bad as it used to be, but they really do punch and kick you, and push your face into the mud with their boots. It's amazing that they get away with it, when all you have to do to get a Federal investigation into a complaint of 'ill-treatment in the army' is to write home to Mom who contacts her Senator.*

"The week after that we have a five-day bivouac which promises to be the hell of all hells. Chip's company just came back and says it's terrible. The Yanks aren't quite as soft as we thought. I can only just take it!

"P.S. Don't worry about the training. It's rugged, yes, but there are 250 of us all taking it together, so it's not as if thousands are dropping out and dying by the wayside."

But Mum did worry, and wrote to him expressing a mixture of anger and scorn at the methods of training he was undergoing. Square-bashing was one thing, but true-to-life interrogation and beatings were just not British. Despite her love of the country, she was never able to accept that 'American' could be better.

Back came Tony's wry response. *"I thought you would be indignant about the E&E course. Actually it was the best training we had. It was so exhilarating and realistic, trying to navigate silently through the woods at night, knowing full well what would happen if you got caught. We crept along, every footstep on the dead leaves sounding like a gunshot. Luckily I did not get captured, but veered off course and did not actually get all the way to the finishing point. About 23% of the company were caught and taken to a compound where some tough, ruthless sergeants were waiting. The men were interrogated and actually beaten, punched and kicked. One of my men felt bad for a couple of days with a bruised jaw and head where they banged it against a wall."*

He went on to explain the reasoning behind this brutal training. *"The American GI, though a dogged fighter when the going gets rough, fell down badly in the POW camps in Korea due to bad treatment and brainwashing methods used by the Chinese Communists. Not one American soldier escaped during the Korean conflict and several opened up under interrogation – which had been so much more subtly and evilly improved by the Communists since WWII –*

giving valuable information to the enemy. The main trouble seemed to be that a guy, used to living in a world of luxury, was suddenly taught to march and shoot and was then shipped to a horrible country where he had to fight under conditions he could not have imagined possible. When captured, instead of being determined right away to try and escape and resist the enemy, his attitude was one of bewilderment and indignation. How dare anyone put him in a pig pen and make him live like a pig? He was a perfect subject for psychological interrogation and subtle brainwashing methods.

"Because of great criticism of this failure on the part of the American GI, a program of special training was introduced to teach – primarily – escape and survival techniques and secondly, if captured, what sort of treatment to expect and how to resist and avoid giving away any information under strain.

"What we went through was just an introduction. From time to time, regular units will have large scale E&E exercises, over many miles of rough country and lasting for two or three days without food. If you get captured on those, you've really had it! One guy in our outfit was very brave, gave no information and actually punched the sergeant who was ill-treating him and escaped."

Tony was, meanwhile, rather enjoying being a 'cadre' man. *"It's kind of cool being on almost equal terms with the sergeants, having a room to sleep in instead of the bay area of the barracks and to be able to order trainees around as if I had stripes, but I couldn't stand going to all the same classes again and again with each cycle. I would much rather be training again myself.*

"You would be surprised how neat I have become! I try to keep our room perfect, always clearing out my lockers and keeping them neat, polishing my boots and arranging them neatly on a boot-rack we made, sweeping and polishing the floor and generally fussing around and tidying up like you!"

Life on the post was shaping up nicely; Tony was doing well, working extremely hard, he was moving upwards – albeit very gradually – and he was full of plans. But the desire to taste life outside was a frequent lure. *"My buddy Tim and I really wanted to get off the post for the weekend but we were both broke as usual. We were so depressed at having a pass and not being able to go anywhere when I suddenly remembered I had a $100 money order that I was saving for OCS. With a loud cry of 'Bullshit!' we ran down to the post office, cashed $40 of it and took off. We went to a nearby town, stayed in a motel, had a good meal, a few drinks and slept like babies."* Not exactly the riotous behaviour expected of soldiers let out to play.

"Yesterday we had a weapons demonstration. An officer gave the orientation while the NCOs demonstrated firing everything from pistols to a tank. The beginning was awfully funny. Only Americans would be so amusing at a serious army subject like this. While the officer was explaining the development and improvement of weapons, a sergeant dressed as a caveman, carrying an enormous club, chased a tiny little man dressed as a blonde cave woman across in front of the stands. Next, a Roman soldier solemnly walked out to the front, stopped, and threw his spear which only went about five yards and dropped with a clatter to the ground. Then a tall idiot dressed like Robin Hood with a handlebar moustache fired a bow and arrow at a target, hit it near the edge, bowed proudly, and leapt gracefully out of sight. Then came Davy Crockett firing a musket and an amusing duel between two cowboys who appeared from each end of the stands and walked dramatically towards one another."

The 'hell of all hells' – the bivouac course – to which Tony had referred in an earlier letter was scarcely mentioned again other than to tell us that they had attacked 'Viet Cong' villages and slept in foxholes, and that he had taken some photographs during the course which he would send on to us. *"I am also going to send one with an autobiography to the Slough Express, just to surprise the locals! I suddenly thought the other day that it was rather an interesting thing to put in the paper (the fightin' Harbords etc) so I am writing them a letter. Must go and clean my rifle. Love, Tony."*

The Slough Express, like most small regional papers, was always strapped for interesting news and duly printed his article and photograph in the next edition. And there was the 'V' word, in black and white and, presumably, from the horse's mouth: "Datchet Man May Fight in Vietnam with US Army". Not so, we told ourselves. He is an alien. It's just the paper being sensationalist. We read and re-read the article, trying to determine which words were Tony's and which were reportage. The result was inconclusive but we all felt distinctly uneasy.

With the worst of AIT behind them, Tony and four of his friends hit New Orleans for Mardi Gras. For Tony it was an eye-opener, a festival like nothing he had witnessed before, and the tensions of the last weeks were waiting to be released.

26 February 1966: *"FABULOUS! Unbelievable! Never have I seen so many people having such a wild time. Never have I seen such varied and extraordinary fancy dress.*

"We all walked along Bourbon Street, or rather squeezed our way, drinking bourbon as we went. There were people having parties on the balconies and everyone was laughing and shouting to each other and throwing things.

"Allen and I decided to try and join a party! Being well pissed and adventurous by this time, we rushed round to a back street and shinned up a pillar onto a balcony. We then started scrambling along balconies over roofs and along walls until we came just above the desired balcony party. Unfortunately a girl saw us and gave the alarm, whereupon two large individuals took offence and tried to chase us. We escaped easily until Allen decided to open a pair of shutters and walk into someone else's room. Some seedy looking people were lying around and apparently were a little put out. I say apparently, because I was half way across the next roof by this time.

"The next thing I knew, Al was scrambling towards me with coke bottles flying after him. We escaped again, laughing like hell, and dropped back down to the street. What fun we had, bitchin', as the Californians say."

Chapter Four

Of his return to Fort Polk, he wrote: *"After the company graduated, half of them went straight to Vietnam. The new trainees start coming in on Thursday. It's great not to be a trainee any more. We wear the red 4th Army patch on our left shoulders and blue scarves or stocks or cravats or whatever we used to call them. I'm having my uniforms tailored to fit me. I should look bitchin' in them! You have to look smarter than the trainees, so we have our shirts taken in and trousers too."*

But there was disappointing news about the OCS Board. *"All this time eight of us have gone through processing together, forms by the thousand, fingerprints, medicals, interviews by officers, and the final board. I got excellent ratings all the way and my application went in to the 4th Army along with the others. Today I found that it has been sent back as I need a background clearance. Apparently all aliens need this security check and it takes between two and four months to complete. That means I could be here with the same company, fucking around marching trainees from one place to the other for six months before I eventually get my orders. I have therefore decided to withdraw my application and apply for my enlistment commitment (Airborne) back. Once in an Airborne unit I can apply again and wait there for all this bullshit to go through, rather than here.*

"A few days ago I was offered the job of lifeguard at the post swimming pool. You can imagine how tempted I was. It was a hard decision but I decided I was in the army to be a soldier, so I intend to go Airborne. I have put off jumping out of a plane long enough. If I graduate from jump school I intend to try and get into the 101st 'Screaming Eagles' Airborne Division." Aiming for the top, again.

The 101st Airborne Division's record of action in WWII and Vietnam in particular is both exemplary and impressive. Modelled on the concept of Airborne divisions in the British Army, the 101st was formed in June 1940 at Fort Benning, Georgia, where a test platoon made its first jump that August. Upon America's entry into the conflict after the bombing of Pearl Harbor in December 1941, the new airborne division intensified its training under the command of the then Major William C Lee, 'Father of the Airborne'. Once Lee was satisfied that the 101st had proved itself in manoeuvres he oversaw its deployment to England in September of 1943 where a further ten months were given over to exhaustive training before the division embarked upon active duty.

The 'D-Day' invasion of northern France by the Allied forces, code-named Operation Overlord, took place in June 1944 and the mission of the 101st was to jump in and secure exits from the 'Utah' beachhead before the waterborne invasion forces arrived, but the airborne troops landing in occupied France encountered heavy German flak and were widely scattered. Nevertheless, they secured a causeway leading to Utah Beach before proceeding to Carentan, a strategically crucial town which they captured from the German 6th Parachute Regiment after five days of bitter fighting.

The 101st are perhaps best remembered for their involvement in the Battle of the Bulge in December 1944. Under the command of Brigadier General Anthony C. McAuliffe, their mission was to hold the Belgian town of Bastogne, thus disrupting German lines of communication which were vital to Hitler's planned attack in which he deployed thirteen German armoured and infantry divisions. It was his intention to paralyse Allied forces in the west, a plan that seemed likely to succeed when the forty-mile front occupied by the Americans in the Ardennes began to collapse. Arriving in Bastogne on the 20th, the 101st was soon surrounded by German troops to the point where, after several days of continuous assault, the German commander felt confident enough to issue a demand for surrender, eliciting McAuliffe's famous retort of "Nuts!" The 101st continue to resist German attack and were finally relieved on Boxing Day when the American 4th Armoured Division broke through. A bloody Christmas indeed. In recognition of the 101st's heroism, the entire Division was uniquely awarded the Distinguished Unit Citation. One Umberto Flores, a US Army Scout who was not only badly injured by mortar fire but nearly lost his feet to frostbite from lying in the snow for days at Bastogne, survived to father a son, Ernesto, who became the new Lt. Harbord's eyes and ears, walking point in the jungles of Vietnam twenty-four years later.

He did not know it at the time, but Tony's involvement in the 101st was still two years away. Meanwhile, he was back at Fort Polk, biding his time and waiting to hear whether or not he had been accepted for jump school. He wrote with pride, *"I now wear real corporal stripes (only because I am an OCS 'holdover' though) and am the best 'Drill Sergeant' in our company. I do all the cadence calling while we march. I sing all kinds of shit and the troops sing the repeats.*

"Example: There ain't no use in lookin' down
There ain't no discharge on the ground.
Sound off 1 – 2
Sound off 3 – 4
Bring it on down 1 – 2 – 3 – 4, 1 – 2 -------3.4!
Eight more weeks and we'll be through,
I'll be glad and so will you
Sound off....

Airborne, Airborne have you heard?
We're gonna jump from a big-ass bird.
If that chute don't open wide
We'll be spots on the countryside!
Sound off..."

"The sergeants just walk along and leave it to me to call the cadence. *I wish you could hear me. It's so much fun to sing on the march and so much more enjoyable than just 'left, right, left.'"* There was to be a great deal more Jody cadence calling at jump school, which was not going to be quite such a picnic.

It was now a year since Tony's snowbound departure from England. In that time he had tasted the delights of Florida, driven across the continent, bought a plot of land, enlisted in the army and begun to plan what seemed a serious future in the army. Pleas from our mother for him to consider some home leave were met with delaying tactics. *"It all depends on how things go and when and where I end up during the next couple of months. Also, if IDIOT FACE* [meaning me], *and I repeat IDIOT FACE, is going to plunge headfirst into holy mackerel, I suppose I ought to make the effort to be there. Make sure ITN knows when I'm coming so they can do a 'Returning Hero' TV news coverage!"*

Had I not known him better, I might have thought that publicity had gone to his head. The Slough Express newspaper cutting we had sent had tickled him pink, for sure. *"Boy what an article that was! A bit over-dramatised as usual, but at least 80% correct. What a record for the Express."* At the same time he realised that the story could have caused disapproval, especially in our small community, and asked wryly *"Am I a hero or a traitor?"* a question which reflected his understanding of the stance which many British politicians were currently taking against America's involvement in the Vietnam War. He went on, *"I wrote to the Daily Mail last week, not asking them to print anything about me, but I was angry and ashamed when I heard on Louisiana radio that* [Prime Minister] *Harold Wilson had forbidden volunteers to fight in Vietnam. Really, it's too bad Britain not sending troops to help, after all America has done for us. Having lived over here for a while, I can understand the United States' reluctance to get involved in Europe's squabbles, especially during times when she was busy with her own growth. I know we always get annoyed when they imply they won the war, but really what would we have done without their money, equipment and men? It's hard on me when I have to agree with my friends who criticise England for being ungrateful. I tell you, I wrote a stiff letter on a piece of cardboard to the Mail, saying that I will probably volunteer for Vietnam and to hell with Wilson's 'pull up the ladder, Jack, we're all right' attitude. I also urged all Englishmen who still had a little pride and guts to come over and join me. America has 835,000 serviceman around the world protecting freedom and trying to prevent the spread of Com-*

76

munist terror. Why the hell should they have to do it all? Are we so small and helpless? Bullshit. Wilson is letting England down, he's almost as bad as de Gaulle. Send some more heroes like me over, America could do with them, there are too many draft card burners over here." Fair comment, but then hardly surprising given the life he was leading with its inescapable mix of politics and the military. Pity, though, that he had withheld permission to publish such powerful thoughts. But only six words really struck home – "I will probably volunteer for Vietnam." Oh God.

By this time, April 1966, there were almost a quarter of a million GIs in Vietnam. Tony's letters not only reflected this escalation and his need to get on and actually do something practical after all his training, but they also began to address the inevitability of his participation in the war. Rather like the way an incurably sick person hangs out for a miracle cure to be discovered in the nick of time, so Mum – and of course Dad and I too – put much faith in the hope that, as an alien, Tony could not be sent to Vietnam, nor would he be foolhardy enough to volunteer. British TV news bulletins were by now covering the Vietnam War in greater depth and detail and we knew too much for our own good.

Tony's comment about volunteering for Vietnam had provoked the expected reaction from home. He was not surprised and wrote at length gently trying to explain his thought processes.

"I expected your reaction to my feelings about Vietnam. I can assure you I will never do anything without thinking carefully and rationally and intelligently, or whatever it is I usually do. You must remember I get first hand information on what Vietnam is like, as there are many NCOs and officers here and at Fort Polk, who have returned from there. Believe it or not, most of them want to go back. They say it is not as bad as it is made out to be. With the fantastic efficiency of the Medical Corps and their evacuation techniques using medically equipped helicopters, 99% of all wounded recover. This is not propaganda but facts published in Life magazine.

"I have no intention of rushing over there like an idiot, but I am rather tired of being 'the alien who can't go'. All the guys I trained with went, and all the guys I will shortly be training with in Airborne will go at the completion of jump school.

"I am a good soldier, and have a lot more pride in myself, my appearance and unit than most. Sometimes I feel it's wrong <u>not</u> to go and do my part. This is the fourth time that American youth has gone overseas to fight for somebody else, and to tell you the truth, I feel rather bad about being nice and safe here while the other boys go. I wonder what your father would have done, Mum? I rather think he would be the kind of man that couldn't stand garrison life, polishing boots while others were fighting, and doing what soldiers were meant to do.

"The way I look at it is, it's a shitty war, all wars are, and it's a pity that America got itself mixed up in it, but the facts are that it has, and somebody has to be there to do the job. My captain, CO of Cobra Company at Fort Polk, had an experience which touched him. On approaching a village while on patrol, a woman came running out and made him eat some rice, which was the only food she had. He could tell she was half-starved but realised he would offend her deeply if he did not accept this offering. She was so grateful to have the VC scared away, as they had been terrorising the neighbourhood and taking all the food by force. It is this feeling of having done something worthwhile (our old theme) which makes Captain Treadwell want to return to Vietnam.

"I'm just a normal man, just like normal men have been for the past thousand years, and want to prove my manhood and test my training. The lure of danger is as old as the hills, it's a purely natural, healthy reaction, and it's better than being a draft card burner, I'm sure you will agree.

"Don't get me wrong, I repeat, I do not intend to rush forward waving a flag and volunteer. I have a lot more thinking to do first. Anyway, don't worry about a thing. Everything will be okay."

Chapter Four

The letter was completed the next day telling us, " *I found out today that I cannot be sent abroad as an alien anywhere other than Alaska, even with a secret clearance. I filled in a preference sheet today, bypassing the Vietnam column and putting in for Fort Campbell, Kentucky. This is the unit I wanted, the Screaming Eagles (101ˢᵗ Airborne Division)."* That was what we all wanted to hear. He was safe.

Arriving at 'The Home of the Infantry' at Fort Benning, Tony commenced Airborne training and soon found he was facing yet another enormous challenge.

"I am now undergoing the toughest training I have ever received. Airborne is definitely <u>it</u>. We get up at 3.30 (just harassment). We run until we drop, singing in cadence all the time, then do PT until we ache, and all before 8 a.m., which is when the training really begins! We have just completed our first week, Ground Week, (two to go) and it really has been something. Apart from all the PT and harassment and being dropped for push-ups every time you do some little thing wrong, we have been jumping out of a 34' tower with a harness. Can you imagine how I felt when I first got into the door and was told to jump? But the sergeants push you so hard and fast, everything is snap, snap, and you are more frightened of saying 'no' than you are of jumping. You leap out into space with your heart in your mouth, fall about eight feet when the harness comes tight, jerking your body up and nearly cutting your balls off. Then the pulley slides down a horizontal wire and you float about fifty yards until you hit a mound. There you are released from the risers and you double back to an NCO for a critique of your jump.

Next week is Tower Week. The PT increases and so do the runs. We have more practice at parachute landing falls, mass exits from the 34' tower and then dropping by parachute from a 250' tower. I'll be as fit as a fiddle when I get out. Graduation is a proud day as there is always a percentage of guys that don't make it, quitters, injuries, drop-outs and recycles. I am just as scared of heights as everybody else, so it will be quite an achievement to me if I get my wings." His letter was illustrated with cartoons of little men jumping from both the 34' and the 250' towers, the former with a speech bubble saying "Oh my balls!" and the latter simply saying "Gulp". The three 250' towers dominated an area known as Eubanks Field. Today there are only two, but both are still in use for Airborne training and they are an awesome sight. I should know. Keen to find out as much as I could about the life Tony lived away from England, I travelled to Columbus, Georgia, in October 2000 where a reunion of part of the 101st Airborne Division was taking place. Air France had lost my baggage and there I was, stranded in leather trousers, boots and a fleece jacket in 80°F temperatures. I was welcomed with open arms by Vietnam veteran Joe Garcia and his wife Kathy, with whom I had until then made only email contact in the course of my research. It was the day before the reunion began, and they lost no time in taking me to the nearest mall to buy some more suitable attire. We then drove the few miles from Columbus to the post at Fort Benning. They knew that although the following day included a trip to the post plus a demonstration by students of some of the elements of Airborne training, I wanted to be there on Eubanks Field by myself. And there I was, thirty-four years on, looking at exactly the same intimidating but thrilling sight of those enormous towers, stretching up into the blue Georgia sky, as had met Tony on his first day at jump school. Joe and Kathy stood back as I walked on to the field, which was deserted. The whole post seemed to have gone quiet. No marching men, no army vehicles to break the silence. An enormous sob rose in my chest and the tears spilled down my cheeks as I tried to focus on the structures which were so familiar. Tony's cartoons had captured them perfectly. He must have sat in the bleachers behind me sketching, writing to us. I whispered to him, "I've made it. I hope you're proud of me." I could feel his presence, imagine his approving, crooked smile. It was one of the most uplifting moments of my life and the closest I came to him during the years of research and writing.

Chapter Four

I got pretty close to him the next day too. Coach loads of
101St Airborne Vietnam veterans and their guests were bussed to Fort
Benning for a whole day which, apart from the airborne demonstration, included a graduation ceremony and a memorial service, all
conducted outdoors in the beautiful early autumn sunshine. Able this
time to relax, enjoy and note what was going on around me, I took
much more interest in the journey. Rows of eateries and pawnshops
screaming out slogans such as "OUR BACON IS TOO THICK TO
SEE THROUGH" and "BEST A1 PAWN" heralded the approach to
the post. Then in through Fort Benning's entrance we went. No
fuss, no intimidating barriers, just a gentle transition from a somewhat run-down area of Columbus to the green, wooded countryside
that surrounds the post where the Chattahoochee River forms its
south-western boundary. I was struck by the neatness, the clipped
lawns, the immaculate officers' housing, and the clean cars. I was
looking forward eagerly to the Airborne demonstration and was not
disappointed, nor were the Airborne veterans for many of whom this
was their first trip back to Fort Benning since gaining their Vietnam
orders more than three decades previously. Sitting in the bleachers,
just like Tony had all those years before, we were given an expert
display of each stage of airborne training except for the aircraft jump.
Sympathetic grunts came from all around me as we watched men
jump from the 34' tower, jerked uncomfortably upwards by their
torturing harness and I could tell I was in the company of those with
first-hand experience and long memories. Tony's words "Oh my
balls!" was all I could think of as I suppressed a giggle. The descent
by parachute of the 250' tower was spectacular; a man with an open
parachute attached to a frame was raised from the ground up to the
top of the tower until he was pretty well invisible to the naked eye.
At a given command the 'chute detached itself and down floated the
man to make a perfect landing.

That day the base was busy. In almost every direction there
were squads of soldiers, male and female, marching, jogging, some
unencumbered by equipment, others heavily laden. One veteran re-

81

called how he and his buddies had applied sticking plaster to their nipples before exercising. After 'breaking starch' the uniforms were so stiff that unless they kept on their T-shirts (which in the heat of summer they preferred to put on after a run) the rubbing of stiff cotton on to those vulnerable areas could cause great discomfort.

Around us there were OCS students and Rangers as well as Airborne contingents. Jody cadences issued from a hundred and more mouths. Spotless vehicles of all shapes and sizes cruised slowly and silently along the roads and the general hustle and bustle made me feel as though I was seeing the post through Tony's eyes. The veterans assured me, however, that it was nothing compared to the mid-1960s when the Vietnam War was escalating. Then, every element of the post was full to bursting with men being trained for the real thing, the towers on Eubanks Field were frantically busy and the ancient C-119 'Flying Boxcars' made constant flights to the drop zones where, at an altitude of 1250 feet, they spilled out their contents of Airborne students. That was week three, Jump Week, and a fitting climax to the course.

Tony and his fellow students were to make five jumps, the last jump in full combat equipment.

"Here is an Airborne song we sing while running:

"I don't know but I think I might
Jump from an aircraft while in flight.
Stand up, hook up, shuffle to the door,
Jump right out and count to four.
If-my-chute-don't-open, gonna pull my reserve,
Reserve don't open gonna lose my nerve!
If I die on the old drop zone
Box me up and ship me home.
Pin my wings upon my chest
Tell my girl I done my best."

Chapter Four

Well, he didn't 'die on the old drop zone'. On the day of his first jump he wrote home exhilarated. He marked the envelope "Deliver by parachute".

"Today I had one of the most unique and exciting experiences of my life. I made my first jump from an aircraft!

"Can you imagine what it was like sitting in the plane waiting to shuffle into the door? Remember Alan Ladd in the Red Beret? How they sat in solemn silence with their stomachs turning inside out? Well it was just like that.

"I was second man out in the first plane. We all hooked up our static lines and waited for the 'go'. The officer in front of me shuffled into the open door and was given 'go' by the jumpmaster. I followed, my heart in my mouth, as the wind from the prop-blast tore at my face and clothing. Just as I felt like screaming I was tapped on the buttocks and out I went, thrown towards the rear by the tremendous force of the wind. For a moment I seemed to hang in space while I counted 'one thousand, two thousand, three thousand, four thousand' with my eyes tightly shut. The next thing was a jerk which seemed to lift me upwards and I looked up to see my parachute open wide above me. It was the most beautiful sight I have ever seen. I shouted 'Oh you beautiful canopy, you!' as I realised I really was going to live! I then started to look around at the wonderful view and the other jumpers as they floated below me, the last ones still exiting from the diminishing aircraft. All was so quiet and serene and unbelievable. The experience was like making love for the first time!

"The whole operation went well, that is except for the two broken legs, one arm, one concussion and a cut nose. There are always injuries in training, men who stiffen up before they fall, spread their feet etc. But if you act the way you have been taught, knees slightly bent, balls of the feet pointed slightly downward, eyes straight ahead, relax, hit, shift, rotate the body, the chances are excellent that you will make a good parachute landing fall. Heavens, we have practised them for two solid weeks. I landed softly in the

83

grass scaring a hare. I ran round my 'chute, collapsed it as I had been taught, folded it, put it in the kit bag and doubled over to the assembly area.

"Tomorrow we jump again (apparently the second time is more frightening for some reason), then we have to complete five jumps to graduate, the last one with extra equipment. Let's hope the wind holds down and my luck holds out as far as soft landings go. You can imagine how demoralising it is seeing almost every other GI on post walking around with a cast on his leg. The injured are evacuated with typical American efficiency. No sooner is a man injured than a pink flare is lit and a helicopter arrives in seconds to take him to hospital. There were three 'Mae Wests' today, but I don't think anyone was hurt. It happens when the skirt of the canopy gets blown under and comes out the other side, making the whole thing look like a giant brassiere. However, it still holds quite a lot of air and we also have a hand operated reserve for such emergencies. I wish you could see a stick of jumpers coming out of a C-119 over the drop zone – it's really something.

"All other Airborne schools are based on the one here at Fort Benning; often British students attend this school which really is the finest in the world. If they can't make a paratrooper out of me, nobody can. Boy, this shit is really something to be proud of!

"Love, Tony. (Airborne all the way!)"

Tony got his wings. He sent them to Mum with the message: *"Here it is, the Badge of Courage. There is a tradition in the Airborne that you mustn't wear the wings they give you, but send them to someone you love and buy some more, so here they are, earned the hard way!"*

Most of Tony's fellow paratroopers received more than their wings at Graduation. They got their Vietnam orders too.

CHAPTER FIVE

With the award of his Airborne wings, Tony was for a short while on Cloud Nine, and eagerly awaited his assignment to the 101st, but was disappointed to find that he was to be sent instead to Fort Bragg, North Carolina, home of the 82nd Airborne Division. With no alternative but to accept this sideways step in his plans, Tony was quick to praise the 82nd, which had acquired such an outstanding reputation for itself in WWII in Sicily, Salerno, Anzio, Normandy and Holland and had on many occasions distinguished itself in the same campaigns as the 101st Airborne. Besides, he told us that the 82nd was a division less likely to go to Vietnam en masse, and that was all we cared about.

In May 1966 he wrote, *"Well here I am in the 'All Americans', the famous 82nd Airborne. It was chosen as the crack American Division to march first through Berlin and was subsequently christened 'America's Guard of Honor' and led the victory parade through New York."*

But that was then, and the 82nd's past plaudits did not alter the fact that Tony had become once more *"a troop"* and was bored stiff. After the excitement, achievement and relative élitism of Airborne School, he now found himself taking his turn working in the mess hall as a member of the Kitchen Police from 4 a.m. to 8 p.m. without a break. *"I hate kitchens at the best of times, and spending the day doing KP, scrubbing, washing and mopping, not to mention chipping potatoes and cleaning sinks is not my idea of fun."* Always wanting to be active and facing new challenges, he realised that even as an Airborne trooper he would still be just one in thirty thousand. As his application for Special Forces could not be considered until he had become an American citizen, he cast about for an exciting alternative and wrote home that his next ambition was to join the SEALS or Underwater Demolition Team (UDT), a little-known but 'crack' unit of para-frogmen demolition specialists. Looked upon as supermen in terms of their fitness, *"they start the day by running ten miles and swimming two. They walk around the Navy base in shorts and sneakers, never salute anybody and nobody messes with them. That is exactly the kind of small, tight specialised outfit (with no KP!) that I wish I was in."* Garrison life was definitely getting to him.

My pre-occupation with my boyfriend, Mike, was clearly dominating my letters to Tony who, bored stiff with what I had to say, felt compelled to put me down. In a letter to Mum and Dad he said, *"I'm getting to hear about every phone call she makes to him now. I've got a crush on the 1ˢᵗ sergeant myself. He never even speaks to me. Beast. I wonder what I could do to attract his attention. Maybe I should shave my knees, or wear a rose on my steel helmet. I could shorten my trousers an inch or two"*. And so on. Okay Tony, very funny, point made.

"Depression and boredom are my two worst enemies as you know, and the frustration of being a soldier training and training and training to fight yet never fighting, is very real indeed. You see, no matter how awful the war is in Vietnam, it doesn't help at all me not being there! In fact the more I hear about villagers being mistreated, the more I wish I <u>was</u> there, because I know I would probably be far more considerate and kind than the GI I replaced.

"Oh dear, the old subject again. You see how boring it is, there's nothing else to think about. Anyway, OCS is still foremost in my mind except for my yearning to be in the Navy SEALS (always want something different) so let's hope things happen soon. Love, Tony. P.S. Piss, shit, fuck, balls"

The boredom of barracks life, whether on duty or off, caused Tony to look for ways in which to fill his spare time and make the rest of his stay at Fort Bragg, some six months, bearable. He was short of money and hated KP. Furthermore, he was not jumping but was instead working on drop zone detail, which entailed clearing up all the equipment after jumping operations and folding and bagging enormous parachutes weighing 250lb. It was monotonous and very tiring work, which made the war veterans on the post wish they were back in Vietnam. To cap it all, at the last minute his Company was restricted to post on what was supposed to be a free weekend which included the Memorial Day holiday. Memorial Day was to be no holiday for Tony two years on either.

He felt there was nothing to look forward to. But of course he had a plan:

"Next month I'm going all out to try and do something in the evenings. The State University is running courses on post and I am going to enrol and take subjects like Psychology, American Governmental System, Criminology, Political Science, Sociology. There is also a karate club here and I think I'll join that too. With all this to try for, things should get a little better, but it still won't take the place of a bit of crumpet off post. When I think of the fun I used to have with Ronnie, going to the Lake District and everything, I feel like hell. I can picture myself 94 years old and still without a girl. Why is it I seem almost destined to go through life without the thing I really need most? It's enough to drive you crazy when you have nothing to do but think, and feel sorry for yourself. Just think, I'll be 27 when I get out of the army and still poverty stricken! Then I'll go to college for four years, that means I will be educated but still poverty stricken at 31. Still, it's all my fault. I chose to be a bum instead of an E-type-Jaguar-owning man-about-town. I always did want my cake and eat it. Actually, I never should have turned down a job I was offered with the BBC."

By the beginning of June, however, Tony was beginning to feel more like his old self. He had had a couple of jumps *"the first one was a bad one. I was awfully sick in the plane. Imagine what*

it's like sitting in the aircraft listening to the Jumpmaster begin his commands:
"'Ten minutes' - '6 minutes' – 'Get ready' - 'Stand up' - 'Hook up' - 'Check static line' - 'Check equipment' - 'Sound off for equipment check'. At this point the count starts from the back of the line and each man shouts 'Okay' and hits the man in front of him until everybody has sounded off. Then: 'One minute' (gulp - this is when we are all so nervous that we rattle our static lines and make as much noise as possible yelling Go-Go-Go!') - 'Stand in the door!' (oh no!) 'GO!!' (Aaaaaarrrrrgghhhh!) and we shuffle out of the door in quick succession, pausing momentarily to grip either side of the door and spring out into the prop blast. It was a bumpy ride and I sat there heaving into a plastic bag almost until the moment to jump. The winds were very high and we never should have jumped, but some fat-assed General was out there to see the drop and couldn't <u>possibly</u> be disappointed. I think I've done more praying in the last three weeks than the Archbishop of Canterbury has done in the last 20 years." And there was good news on the rifle target practice front.

"The other day I at last fulfilled my ambition to fire EXPERT with a weapon on the range. We qualified with the new M-16 rifle and I shot about 73 targets down out of 84. 50 is expert! It seemed so easy, I just couldn't go wrong, the silhouettes kept falling! So now I can wear an expert badge, the one with the laurel wreath around it. A lot of people just buy them and wear them anyway, but I have always hated that and swore I would never wear one until I earned it. Yippee!"

By June Tony had started his evening classes and was immediately captivated by the course on classical civilisations. *"You would love the course I am taking, Mum, it starts with a study of the Egyptians, the Mesopotamians and the Minoan civilisation on Crete. Right now we have got as far as Greece and it's fascinating to learn all about the great philosophers who contributed so much to Christianity and our present-day thought, like Socrates, Plato, Aristotle,*

Pythagoras and Archimedes. Tomorrow we move on towards the Roman Empire and the whole course covers the period from about 3,000BC to AD1600. I am finding it hard. I have to write a book report soon, something I haven't done before, then a term paper called 'History is trapped in the past'. We have to either prove or disprove this theory and imagine ourselves living in AD1600 making no reference to anyone or anything written after this date. Boy, I just don't know where to begin!"

A weekend pass with his buddy Rick to the seaside resort of Myrtle Beach was a welcome break, but once again Tony failed in his attempts with the girls, but he was not alone. *"We met one rather sweet girl but I think she mistook us for a couple of sex-starved paratroopers instead of a couple of sex-starved paratroopers!*

"Seriously though, our intentions were entirely honourable. Service life, being so devoid of tender things like peace, quiet, privacy, beautiful scenery and being alone with a nice girl, makes you want the simplicity of a girl's company in pure contrast to the hustle, bustle and noise of barracks life with hundreds of other men. All we wanted was just a peaceful afternoon chatting with her, but as usual, how can a guy pick up a girl in a day and try to convince her of that?"

Returning to the post, the two men began preparations for an imminent five-week field training course during which time Tony would be unable to attend his evening classes, much to his regret. *"This Tuesday we jump in and attack some stupid hill shouting 'Bang' (you can't fire blanks with the new M-16 rifle). I hate these kinds of problems, as you have to go through all the bullshit as if there was a real enemy when there isn't. The other one we had was a lot of fun, as we were actually chasing guerrillas from the Special Warfare School. We had simulated airstrikes and everything to flush them out, and umpires decided on the resulting casualties and who won, etc. It was very realistic."*

His next letter was able to report that he was doing rather well on the training course: *"I captured two guerrillas on my own!*

Our patrol had captured two guards lying asleep and I had sneaked around looking for more when I found the other two. On bringing them in, the lieutenant was so surprised at seeing them approach he ordered the patrol to open fire. So I was deaded with them, AHA! Rotten swine, I think I'll play another game".

On a weekend trip with two buddies to the beach after the training exercise, somebody stole his travel bag from beside his head as he slept. Inside it were his camera and all his precious college notes and textbooks. *"After missing all those classes, what can I do now with no books?* A complete stranger, a lifeguard, helped to re-store his faith in humanity, however. The man gave him $5, took him back to his hotel and gave him a couple of stiff drinks and then offered to run Tony and his mates the 150 miles back after taking them out to dinner.

Having replaced his text books, Tony worked hard to get his notes up to date and began grappling with the Barbarian invasions of the Roman Empire at the beginning of the 5th century AD. Examina-tions were looming and he was once again seriously applying himself to his studies. In the event, he was given so much guard duty that he missed the final tests, something which angered him after all the work he had put in and the difficulties he had faced after losing his notes. Meanwhile barracks life was just as tedious as ever. *"Next week we go on IRF (Immediate Ready Force) which means about 5 days confined absolutely to the barracks, can't go anywhere at all. About the only time you go outside is for organised PT. Oh, that's going to be enjoyable."*

Planning a future in the US Army as an alien had many drawbacks for Tony. It seemed that the processing for some courses, such as Officer Candidate School, was so lengthy that if background clearance was held up, so was acceptance on the course, with months going by before the application could be satisfactorily resolved. Tony's experience in the 82nd was making him impatient to get out, get on. But bureaucracy's wheels would not be hurried just because a Limey Private found himself on KP duty peeling potatoes. Developments in the short-term seemed so unclear that Tony's fancy turned to what he might do at the end of his three years' military service.

"After getting out of the army (my immediate desire), I would like to finish off my travels and go round the world from Australia across the continents of Asia, India and Europe back to England with an accent on their history. This would take between six months and one year. I then intend to return to the States to settle down to college. Then on graduation I would like to try for the CIA. I know what you are thinking. Tony's chasing rainbows again! All James Bonds aside, I think it would be awfully interesting and might be just the thing to satisfy my hunger for a respectable profession. It would combine all sorts of talents and provide an occupation of great interest, mind taxing as well as providing a certain amount of physical and outdoor activity plus plenty of travel and a spot of danger (ADVENTURE!) Anyway, it's worth pursuing and who knows what might turn up between now and then? When I go to college I really want to just broaden my education for my own satisfaction. I don't think it matters a great deal what one majors in, but I'll go into that later on. I hunger for all the knowledge of subjects I missed at school - Psychology, Sociology, Economics, History, Theology, Political Science, maybe I can even take Music after all this time. Of course I'll only be ninety four when I get out, but still...."

Shortly after tossing these largely unformed plans about in his head, Tony was surprised and delighted to learn that his background clearance had come through. He hastily re-applied for OCS and very soon went before the board (*"I charmed all the colonels so I am sure I will be accepted!"*) and was able to look ahead to some home leave, his first since leaving England eighteen months previously. He needed thirty days 'in the bank' in order to apply for overseas leave, and felt optimistic about being able to finesse enough to make the trip. If successful, *"I will be on my way in a flash of light, a cloud of dust and a hearty 'Hi Ho Silver'!"*

It wasn't a flash of light, it was a thunderclap. My diary for 21 September 1966 records: *"TONY is home!! For 5 days! We'll have some job trying to live down the grenade simulator he let off in the drive. We had the police round."*

The grenade simulator was to announce his arrival home, an event we were expecting but the timing of which we were not at all certain. It went off in our quiet little cul-de-sac after dark one evening. We – and neighbours up and down the road - rushed outside to see what on earth had happened and discovered Tony, standing grinning in the dark in uniform, arms folded, legs apart, wreathed in smoke. Having had the circumstances explained to him, the local bobby decided not to press charges, swung his leg over his ancient bicycle and slowly pedalled off down the road, shaking his head. Things like that didn't happen in Datchet.

Five days was all the leave Tony could manage because he had, at long last, been accepted for OCS and needed to get back to Fort Benning. Oh how quickly those days went by. We went out as a family and with Tony's friends; we went to the Harvest Festival service at church where Tony proudly wore his uniform and looked so smart. On it had been pinned his recent trophies, so hard come by – the Airborne wings and the marksman rifle badge. On his shoulder was sewn the patch of the 82nd Airborne, with its distinctive 'AA' insignia standing for 'All American' and on his cap was the parachute badge. He looked wonderful. He was relaxed, happy and excited at the challenge of OCS ahead. Mikey the dog was in seventh heaven having his master back and was allowed to sleep on Tony's bed. The household was all smiles (including Mikey who really did grin in a ghoulish sort of way when requested).

Time was so short, but Tony managed to meet and take out a girlfriend of his friend Brian's. Brian was dating two girls at the time and was happy for Tony to see Dee. They had a lovely day out in London and a picture of him, arm around Dee's shoulder while they fed the pigeons in Trafalgar Square, shows him handsome and laughing. He was falling in love again.

Chapter Five

All too soon it was time for him to get back to Mildenhall US airbase in Suffolk to hitch a free flight back to America. On 29 September 1966 he signed on the dotted line and became a raw recruit again.

The Infantry Officer Candidate School at Fort Benning, Georgia, came into existence in July 1941 after it was recognised that the United States Armed Forces were short of officer material. Tens of thousands of officers were subsequently commissioned in the following few years but the programme was suspended in the late 1940s, only to be revived in 1951 in response to the Korean crisis. By the time OC Tony Harbord began his training, the school comprised 66 companies organised into five student battalions, with a yearly commission rate from the school of more than ten thousand men, all of whom had demonstrated to the board that they had leadership potential and sufficient academic development to qualify them as officers. The mission statement of the school was:

"To develop selected personnel to be Second Lieutenants of the Army of the United States who will be capable of performing duties appropriate to their grade in Infantry units, and who, with a minimum of additional branch training, will be prepared to serve as Second Lieutenants of other branches designated by the Department of the Army. The secondary mission is to serve as a basis for mobilization as the needs of the service require." That, of course, meant active service.

In an exciting breakthrough after months of stalemate I obtained a photocopy of the 1967 OCS yearbook containing some two hundred officer candidates' head and shoulders photographs, all looking very much the same. On the page featuring the men from the 83rd Company's Fourth Platoon (nicknamed 'Popken's Pumpkins' after their Tactical Officer, Bob Popken), there was Tony's picture, the slight smirk on his face I knew so well betraying both excitement and a little embarrassment. As most, if not all, of these men would have gone on to see action in Vietnam, I checked each one against the names of the dead engraved on the Washington Vietnam Memorial Wall. Out of the platoon of thirty men, Tony's was the only name. Harbord's luck. I felt quite numb.

At the back of the yearbook were all the candidates' 1966 home addresses including ours in Datchet, the only overseas address out of two hundred. On a wing and a prayer I fired off several letters, hoping that at least one might land in the mailbox of a long-resident family. I also did a 'people search' on the Internet for those with unusual names and off went a few more letters.

I was well rewarded. An ecstatic Vince Laurich emailed me saying that my letter had been delivered to his old address where his mother still lived after all those years, just as Mum and Dad had stayed put in Datchet. She had read the letter and had got straight on the phone to him. "YES YES I'M VINCE!" yelled his email to me. "Who have you found? How? How long have you been trying? How did you get the yearbook? I've got a million questions for you!" And I had a million for him. It was a lucky break that really turned the tide for me, for very soon after that another and then another contact came up trumps and all of a sudden I had seven or eight middle-aged American Vietnam War veterans ringing, emailing and writing to me, all wanting to talk about Tony and to see who else I had found. I began putting them in touch with each other and two years on (and, I suspect for many more to come) they continue the contact. *"The last three days have been an extremely emotional experience for me,"* wrote Lew Paulen to me. He had suffered a serious back injury soon after graduating and was never called to serve in Vietnam, becoming instead a TAC Officer with the 83rd Company at Fort Benning. *"Vince and I were on the telephone for over two hours last night and I am so wildly enthusiastic about this that I feel like I'm going to jump out of my skin. The old memories are flowing back and I thank you for being the person who started this whole thing. I was devastated when Vince told me about Tony. I just wish he was one of the guys we could see and reminisce about the old days."* Vince, who had heard about Tony's death fairly soon after it happened, told me, *"Gay, know this. Every year, since its inauguration*

Chapter Five

in 1982, Tony is remembered when I stand at the Wall in front of the panel with his name on it and his name and story is retold to people standing there with me." So now I had found another who, like Tom Coffey, had paid his respects to my brother in Washington long before I ever got there myself. Again I felt humbled and desperately saddened. And so, so grateful for such love.

Tony, Vince, Lew and Tom duly began their course in the 83rd Company at OCS that September. It was divided into three distinct phases, Basic (12 weeks), Intermediate (6 weeks) and Senior (also 6 weeks, when the candidates were almost officers), a total of six gruelling months. What sort of a figure did OC Harbord cut amongst his all-American colleagues? He hadn't grown more than half an inch since his late teenage days in the Royal Marine Volunteer Reserves, his OCS acceptance papers showing a final height of 5' 9" and a weight of 155lbs, much of which was the result of relative inactivity in the 82[nd.] Lew Paulen recalls, "What I remember most about Tony was his stature. He wasn't tall, but the first image that came to mind was of him standing around in his tailored uniform with the OCS helmet, his arms crossed, speaking so self-assuredly that you were sure he knew most of the answers, if not all of them. One of the first things we were taught was to make a decision. Tony invariably made the right ones. He was physically able to do more than most of us and practically all of the younger guys looked up to him." The grim determination to improve his physique, stretching back to the chest-expander days, had honed his body into one of firmness and strength, capable of quite extraordinary endurance and performance. Paulen continues, "His leadership qualities always struck me. You simply wanted to follow him. And his bearing was always ramrod straight." That was a legacy from the Royal Marines, and one about which he would be greatly teased whilst in OCS.

The 12-week Basic phase was one in which the Tactical Officer (Tac) supervised anything and everything the Officer Candidates in his platoon did. The emphasis was on detecting and encouraging leadership potential rather than demonstrated leadership itself. It seemed, however, from Tony's early letters, that there was precious little opportunity for anything other than staying awake and avoiding harassment. He had chosen yet another tough assignment.

After just one week he wrote home, *"We get up at 5 and are on the go all day until 11 at night. On coming in at night we immediately have to start shining boots etc. and even the floor has to be spit shined. We run everywhere and catch hell all the time. The schedule is so tight that we have a job getting to and from different areas on time, even though we run everywhere.*

"Last night the Blues [the senior candidates] came back and screamed and yelled and harassed us for two hours. I caught hell because I was previously Airborne and they tore me to shreds. I was exhausted by the time they left, my mind was a whirl and I still had so much to do before lights out. There is nothing to look forward to except bed and graduation. As soon as you finish for the day it's time to jump into bed and wake up again. There is never time to go anywhere except for a few minutes. We are not allowed to buy candy or cokes or anything like that and weekend passes are a long, long way off. Basically all our rights have been taken away, to be given back as privileges over 23 weeks. The days are so long I feel I have been here for weeks, forgotten by the outside world.

"I have to present a little talk next week on Wilson's Vietnam policy, and the opinions of the British people. Please send some newspaper articles that are relevant as I am very out of touch. Also send some of those amusing 'This is America' cuttings from the Express. Love, Tony.

P.S. Mum, give me your opinions, and I will read them out to the class"

Harold Wilson essentially supported President Johnson's policy of continuing the war in southeast Asia, whilst condemning any prolonged bombardment of Hanoi and Haiphong. It was the infiltration of North Vietnamese into the South that he felt should be curtailed, either by bombing or by diplomatic arbitration. Being fairly newly elected, Wilson was always keen to seize opportunities which might improve his personal standing in Foreign Affairs, and he spent much time visiting both Washington and Moscow, to little effect. Johnson's throw-away request to Wilson for even a few British pipers to be sent to Vietnam was apparently not felt worthy of a response – Wilson had no intention of supplying any forces to this conflict. He had problems enough in Malaya and Rhodesia where thorny Commonwealth issues were raising the issue of military deployment. As far as British public opinion generally was concerned, American involvement in Vietnam was viewed with a great deal of disapproval, particularly amongst the youth culture who shared the "Make Love, Not War" principle held by so many of their peers across the Atlantic.

Despite the calls on his time, Tony could never stop himself planning ahead. His next letter put the idea of joining any kind of intelligence corps out of the frame *"as I might get stuck at a desk analysing photographs. I cannot give up the old jumping routine, so I have decided to take my commission in infantry and apply for the Special Forces. I'm not a pencil pusher. Special Forces operates 12-man teams of experts, to advise, train, aid and lead local bands of guerrillas."* Special Forces was the one recurring theme in his letters. The US Army's élite force. Of course.

"I'm so glad you and Dee got together. I knew you would discover, as I did, what a delightful person she is. Poor old Brian really got a shaking. He thought all these women were kissing his boots and he could play the big Casanova without losing one. It was extraordinary how we got on together so well in just two days. I certainly won't hold any claims to her. Now Brian has woken up she will probably go back to him." Was he recalling his bitter experience with Ronnie in Newcastle? That affair must have seemed a million light years away yet, deep down, it still ate away at him. *"Anyway, what sort of relationship could we carry on 3,000 miles apart, with me coming home every six months for two weeks? It's wonderful to have someone to think about and write to, but I don't want to be selfish and try and take her away from Brian. In two days it was*

impossible to tell whether we had just a good friendship or something more serious. She may be out here for Christmas, which will be nice, and then we will get a chance to talk and get to know each other better.

"I am not settled yet either. I don't even know where I really belong or what it is I am really looking for. I'm still a lost soul in a sea of uncertainty, concentrating on the immediate future rather than the ultimate future. Maybe I'll never find what I am looking for, or even find out what it is I am looking for. I'm getting an old man now, and still can't see any signs of settling down like a normal person! I dunno, I really don't. I suppose you could say I seek truth and peace of mind. I think peace of mind must be the key, because it would encompass all things, strength of character, maturity, happiness, truth, satisfaction, love, knowledge and a complete sense of fulfilment and contentment. It's a lot to expect, but I think everybody needs these things basically, and the trouble with the world is that few people realise it or attain them.

"Maybe I'll find my slot one of these days, but until I do, I can't really start thinking seriously about anybody. It would be unfair to them more than to myself. But there again, one can only follow one's own feelings honestly and take it from there, but right now I don't even know what they are."

What tender words from a man whose 7-day week began with rough waking long before dawn and ended with a few hours' exhausted sleep late into the night.

"Yesterday the Blues came again, harassing us, creating the usual chaos and scuffing up my floor I had just shined on my hands and knees. They caught one candidate coming in with a bag and found it to contain about 3 bags of chocolate chip cookies. 'Pogey bait' as tuck is called, is strictly forbidden, though ' what the eye doesn't see' etc., and so this man was certainly in for it at the hands of the senior candidates. We knew what was going to happen, and watched as he was forced to open all the bags and start gobbling. They surrounded him shouting 'Eat 'em Wales, eat 'em Wales',

'Shove 'em down Wales' until he had eaten them all, about 40 cookies! I always have a supply of candy, have done from the beginning, but haven't got caught yet!"

He was taking a big risk, for everything was inspected, day in, day out. And everything had its place in cupboards, lockers and also on the beds which were checked for geometric excellence. Attention to detail was paramount and all the time the Tacs were bawling out their men, insulting them, creating chaos, often making the candidates feel and look ridiculous, pushing them ever onwards to the brink. Many men quit the course because they couldn't take the constant mental and physical torture. Indeed, much of the early weeks of training was designed to purge the weak, marginal and non-committed. The army did not want to waste time and resources upon them. Others had to drop out through injury but were often given the chance to be 'recycled' at a later date. Tony, however, seemed to be in his element and, in Vince's words, "was certainly the best and most prepared in the Company. He focussed on being good at whatever he tried and when he spoke or shared his opinions – and he didn't say much or waste words – we all paid attention."

By November, Tony was celebrating having completed almost a third of the course. He had also been chosen for a place on the Battalion Staff. Vince describes these candidates as "the sharpest troops, best at marching, drill, precision movements, looking good in the formal ceremony situations such as parades and advancement exercises. Like the Color Guard they were out front of the OCS Company during all such events. In other words, they were figureheads representing the 83rd Company." So, despite Tony's tendency for a truly British high-arm swing, he had learned to temper it and had been chosen for what was quite a prestigious post and had also found precious free time to practice sabre drill. But he was in a moral quandary about his Christmas plans.

Brigadier General F A Hoghton, shortly before his death. Mesopotamia 1916

Vivien in the saddle. America 1935

Chapter Five

Vivien 1937

Bill & Tony, 1942

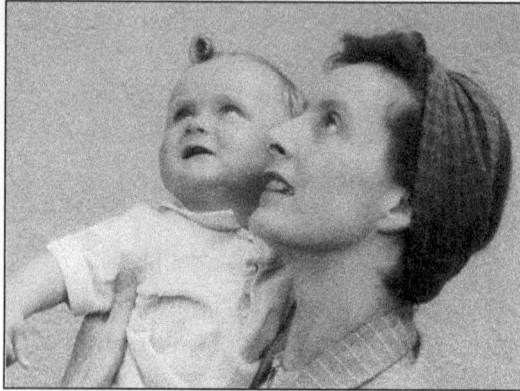

Watching the RAF bombers, 1942

Tony in his grandfather's cut-down uniform

Tony and Gay c.1951

Supervising the shrimping at Bexhill , 1952

Tony arrives in New York, March 1965

Fun in the sun, Florida

First days at Basic, Fort Polk, Louisiana

Squad Leader, Basic Training

Officer Candidate Harbord

Tony (left) - Graduation with Honors!

Jump Tower, Fort Benning, Ga.

Airborne students boarding a C-119 "Flying Boxcar"

Ranger trophies

Tony and Dee, Trafalgar Square, London, September 1966

Chapter Five

The Godfather - to Todd Anthony Marmontello

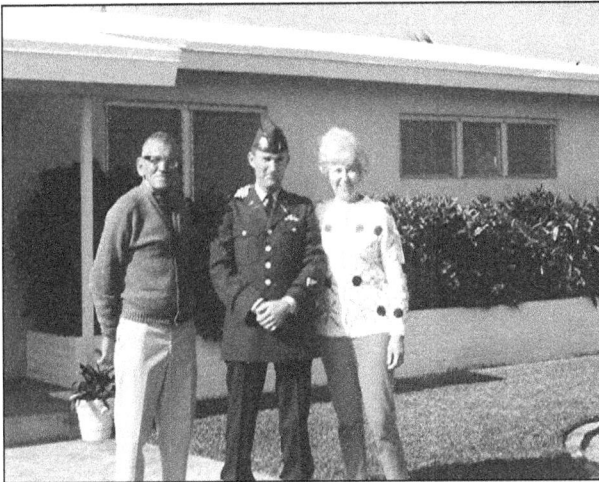

Leaving Jack & Betty's, Ft. Lauderdale, for Vietnam, January 1968

Young Rick Knight

Ernie 'Weasel' Flores

110

Soldiers celebrating Mass in the jungle

The Hawks' hilltop bunker

Rick cooling himself under his waterfall

Tony opening his dehydrated C-rations – dreaming of strawberries?

Zingen preparing to launch the lizard into space

Training the South Vietnamese, Saigon, January 1969

Memorial Service, Binh Trung

Vivien at the Vietnam Memorial Wall, September 1992

Ernie & Rick meet again, in Bisbee, Arizona, February 2001

'Anthony G Harbord'. Top row of The Wall

"As you know, Dee is coming over for Christmas which will be fun as I didn't really have any plans or anywhere particular go to. Old Jack, the fisherman from Fort Lauderdale, has had two operations which is rather sad. I'm sure the old seahorse will pull through, but he has had one operation on his eyes which was successful, then it was discovered he had a malignant tumour in his bowels. Poor old boy, his wife wrote to me to ask me to write and cheer him up. She also mentions selling the 'Amigo' which I can hardly bear. Jack has chartered out of Lauderdale since the beginning of time, and I had planned to buy his boat myself in a few years' time. If he needs any help I may have to go down at Christmas time. The 'Amigo' has been in the yard for months, and Jack will be missing out on all the winter fishing crowd. Don't mention a word to Dee, but I told Jack if he needed me to work for him at Christmas for nothing, I would go, and if he wants me I'll have to. I couldn't let him down. I only wish I could go back down and help him out full time. I doubt if he will need me, as his wife really does seem to think they will be selling the boat, but I had to offer anyway.

"Last weekend we were allowed out on post for the first time after a 12-mile forced march with full field gear, rifle and bedroll. I was exhausted afterwards but my blisters weren't as bad as some other people's. This weekend we were restricted again, as the barracks were not up to standard. All I've done is paint and clean up. Every weekend all we seem to do is paint and clean up, and I hate painting."

A hastily written letter followed with news that for the next two weeks Tony would be training in the field with the Ranger Department: *"We won't be getting much sleep and it's getting colder than a witch's tit so promises to be hell. This afternoon we actually have a river crossing – we will walk across a river twice and it's freezing here, without the help of the Chattahoochee River! I can hardly believe we will actually be doing it this afternoon. Rangers are the US Army's Commandos, who trained with the British during WWII. They have a tough school here with tough instructors, and*

116

apart from their own 9-week Ranger course, the Ranger Committee also runs the OCS field training program.
"Pretty soon, 17 days in fact, we will be leaving for our various Christmas destinations. By the time we get back we will be more than half way through the course, whoopee!"

The last letter of 1966 betrayed a certain degree of tension and exhaustion.

"Everything is set for Christmas. I leave here on 17th December for Ohio till 23rd. I then leave there and fly to New Jersey to meet Dee. We just got back off our bivouac, 5 days of patrolling through woods in the middle of the night, sleeping little, wrapped in a poncho and are now restricted again. We all felt sure we would be let out on post this weekend, but the bastards have kept us cooped up again. I am so tired, having only got two or three hours of sleep a night, freezing my balls off. I led an ambush patrol that was pretty good. Only five days to put up with until we get the hell out of here. I am going to sleep my ass off all Christmas!

"I was all pissed off today. I started off tired and in a bad mood, and a Tac jumped all over me in the mess hall and sent me out for push-ups. It mushroomed through my 'daggers' expression, to quite a shouting, unpleasant scene. I think it will blow over though. I need to let my hair down, there is just no way to do that when you are cooped up all the time, and I am afraid I will do something I will regret in the wrong situation. I think my Tac understands though. Happy Xmas."

Tony's high hopes of a happy Christmas with Dee were not realised. His next three letters revealed himself as being a disappointed, unhappy man, full of tension and self-doubt:

"I don't know what the hell happened, but things went wrong. Dee told me I had changed and was nervous and tense, which only made me more nervous and tense. Anyone would have been after what I've been through down here. She was the one who was different. She seemed cold and distant at times, which of course

only worried me more. I wanted so much to have a nice relaxing time, and tried so hard.

"What a disappointment after counting off the days for three months. I felt like hell on the way back and thought I was going to die when I finally ran through the pouring rain and entered the barracks. I looked at those lovely pictures of Dee in the front garden at home and was convinced the same person did not come over here.

"She is still in New Jersey and I thought I would write so as to let you know the position before she gets back, so when she comes round to see you, don't let on that I have written. It's not her fault, I suppose, it must be me.

"I wish to hell everything had been different. I think if we had been completely alone together down in Florida or somewhere, it would have. As it was, we were staying in a small flat with two other people and I had to erect a bed in the living room every night, so it was a little crowded.

"Just before I left here for Christmas I was jumped on by a little shit of a lieutenant and I fought back in my usual way showing my dislike for the man quite openly. This always makes it worse for me, but it's my way. I refuse to take it lying down. As a result I was like a cat on hot bricks when I left for Cincinnati en route for New Jersey. Tom Coffey and I drank like hell to try and calm us down. He is the number one candidate here, an ex-sergeant with four years in the army, and he was as bad as me. I had been sick in Cincinnati; caught some bug or something, didn't know whether to vomit or shit and did plenty of both, and never fully regained my appetite. I didn't eat for nearly three days, so by the time I met Dee my stomach was in knots. There I was, with my first time off in 3 months, meeting someone I had known for two days and who was flying 3,000 miles to see me, and I was supposed to act charming and relaxed like I was at home. Being awfully sensitive to things that go wrong, one day I just cracked up completely. A combination of worry, exhaustion and fear of dramas I suppose, and I just went absolutely quiet, never spoke a word, never ate, my stomach wouldn't take a thing and I wasted a

whole day. This was what really did it. Dee thought, 'Oh Christ, I can't stand any stress' and so everything was ruined and she never lifted her invisible screen the rest of the holiday. I must be fated the way I fuck up every single time. It seems I'm never going to have things go my way. Inside I must be a completely immature inade-quate person who is discovered only when I am known better. Something must be wrong – everywhere I go I seem to be well liked and very popular, and yet give me a girlfriend and I'll guarantee to have her turn against me in no time flat. I wish I knew what the hell was the matter with me. One of the reasons I joined up and went Airborne, etc. was to try and develop my character more, and maybe harden me a little. Seems I'm just the idiot I always was. I think when I get my commission my confidence should come back. I hope so anyway. It's funny, in some ways I have quite a lot of moral cour-age, and in others I am weak and gullible.

"Well, I must drive on. Say 'Hullo' to Dee for me, but don't let on about any dramas, she has plenty of her own. I hate to admit it but Brian has won."

This was a hard letter for our parents to read. It had been a hard one for Tony to write. The disappointment and despair he had felt upon returning to the post after the pre-Christmas anticipation, high hopes and planning was crushing. And he had lost another girl. We all wrote to him, knowing not only that he needed our support and understanding, but that right then he felt so very far from home. To stand in the mail line and for his name not to be called was not something we wanted to happen to him at this tough time. We imag-ined his delight and relief when his name was called, when he saw our familiar handwriting on the envelopes.

By mid-January 1967 Tony was still smarting. He had had time to talk to others about their experiences on leave and did, at least, take some comfort in what they had to say insofar as it enabled him to understand his own behaviour better.

"Since my last letter I have talked with some of my best friends, all of whom are outstanding candidates here at OCS. Ap-

parently they all had the same trouble. They were tense and nervous, and couldn't relax for a minute. They quite upset their wives at first, but fortunately they understood and there were no real problems. Unfortunately for me, Dee didn't understand and when I sensed this reaction to me and she told me I had changed and all that bullshit, I just got worse until I just snapped inside completely. I was valiantly put up with but was dubbed a dramatist and a martyr and a brick wall was built between us. " But Dee was upset too. On 13 January I recorded in my diary that Dee was very worried about Tony. Yes, she had flown all that way to see him. Yes, it was Christmas, and there she was at immigration laden with presents from us and others. And, yes, she must have been terribly disappointed to find Tony diffident, taciturn and tense, so different from the happy, charming young man she had spent a lovely two days with just three months previously. But Tony's self-analysis went on.

"Sometimes I think 'what the FUCK am I doing here?' God, how I hate myself and this course for messing me up yet again. I have taken a whole lot more harassment than the average OC here, because of my accent and everything. It's mostly good humoured but still upsets your heart action."

He was by now embarking upon the six-week Intermediate phase of OCS, during which time there was less stress on direct supervision by the Tacs over the candidates. Command responsibility was proportionately increased and the candidates were required to demonstrate a greater degree of leadership potential and performance. It was just as hard, if not harder, going than the Basic phase. At regular intervals at the post other companies would reach their senior phase and their ultimate goal, graduation. The end was in sight.

"Today we watched another company perform their senior status review, or Blue Day parade. It was very impressive and all the families and girlfriends of the candidates were there. I have a very important part as Adjutant on the Battalion Staff and I do so wish

you could all be here to watch our parade. It's going to take hours of practice out there on the parade field freezing our balls off!"

Unfortunately, Tony's spirits were still flagging. His introspection was causing him continued pain and sadness. *"Thank you all for writing and trying to cheer me up. I am of course getting better every day – the world hasn't come to an end. I guess I am more depressed and confused about myself rather than Dee. I simply cannot figure myself out. I go for long periods without meeting girls or sharing their company and even longer periods without an actual girlfriend. For this reason, when I meet one that clicks, which is so seldom, I must show them too much attention. There is almost nothing I won't do for them and they've got me where they want me. Dee is just another Ronnie. I never would have married her, nothing was further from my mind, and yet I was so attached to her. I guess I like perfect relationships that never end but aren't permanent! It's just a deficiency in my character. A hole that needs to be filled by somebody. But it's actually not that negative. I am too much of a giver, although that sounds pompous. I need somebody to give to is what it basically boils down to. You would have thought I was the ideal 'catch'! That's what Ronnie and Dee both thought at first. What I can't understand is that while I'm getting even fonder of them, they are doing the opposite. The main problem this time was not any inattention on my part, rather that I had seemingly changed from a cheerful young paratrooper and adventurer to a nervous, tense, serious-minded individual running away from the world. This impression was caused by the effects of the course and the environment we found ourselves spending Christmas in. What really finished the whole thing was this:- one night Dee and I met an OCS buddy of mine and went to a small party in New York. He had failed to bring a date and spent most of the evening looking at Dee. It seemed to me that she spent most of the evening smiling back. She being the person she is could have simply been being friendly to a friend of mine, which is what she said, but after the experiences I had had you can imagine how I felt. I found myself getting so tensed up inside it was like a knife in my stomach. I shut up like a clam and tried to fight myself – a big mistake.*

"So that's it. I'm too sensitive and too bloody soft. It's enough to drive you round the bend. One minute you're wonderful and the next you're an ass-hole. I'll always be a loser because I haven't got the strength to turn away and say 'Okay, if that's the way you feel, fuck you'. I get too sentimental, and try to argue and explain and hang on. If only Dee and I could have gone down to my beloved Florida on our own, instead of staying with two people in that little flat in freezing New Jersey, things would have been much more like they were that day in London. I could have relaxed down there I know. I wish to hell I had gone down there anyway. Poor old Jack is still seriously ill in hospital and his wife says he is very fond of me and likes to get my letters. I could have done the world much more good had I gone down to see him and I would have avoided all dramas. BLAST!

"Someday I will overcome myself, but it might take a tour in Vietnam to do it. Love, Tony"

It was so hard for Mum and Dad to read of Tony's despair, so intimately shared. And then there was that last comment, almost uttered as a challenge to himself, which set us back on the edge of our seats and prompted Mum to take the only action she could think of. She began to scour the British press for news and views on Vietnam, this time for features heavily biased against the war to try to counter what she probably quite justifiably believed was pro-Vietnam propaganda being fed to her son.

Almost before she had had a chance to get started on her task, Tony wrote home in great spirits. Was it our fervent prayers that had wrought some miraculous cure for his despair? Was it that his period of introspection and self-analysis had borne fruit? Was it simply that the depressive black cloud to which many in our family were prone, myself included, had spontaneously lifted? Whatever the reason, something caused a sea-change in Tony's attitude and it seems now, looking back, that he suddenly became more focussed, positive, more at ease with himself and others and more determined than ever to achieve the goals he had set himself in the army. His extravagant use of exclamation marks was evidence enough of his high spirits.

"This letter is actually intended to inform you of an extraordinary change of attitude on my part! Allow me to explain, pull up a bollard and sit down. The stupid way I acted at Christmas time was a complete freak. I remember getting a depression about a week before my leave started that I couldn't figure out. It must have continued subconsciously, showing outwardly as nervous tension. I snapped that night at the party under the strain and the depression came back. But about five days after I got back, I woke up in the morning and felt better than I have ever felt before. I didn't give a big old hairy rat's ass whether I ever saw Dee again! The whole thing which I took as love for her actually had little or nothing to do with her at all. Extraordinary, really. I thought I would be all depressed at the Company party because Dee wasn't there, but I was glad she wasn't actually, because I had a ball. I rushed around hustling all my buddies' girlfriends! I switched on the British accent and the charm and had a blast observing the effects! It was a great party with us candidates dancing out on the floor along with the lieutenants and their dates (that we had fixed them up with!). It was the kind of party that would never happen at a British Officers' school. The Colonel said it was the best one he had been to. We all thought it was going to be stuffy and boring but it was great. The 18th-week one will be more formal, but will probably be even better.

"We are working hard for our parade. I am going to try and get pictures and a tape recording of the ceremony to send you. It really is a pity you can't be here. It's an awfully good parade, not one that drags on and on for hours, and it will probably be the last one of its kind I shall ever be in in the army. They are cracking down on wasting valuable time practising for parades and have even taken our sabres away. We now just wear 45 automatics and salute in the normal way. This pissed us off, I can tell you, but it's still go-

*ing to be a good review. As the battalion staff pass the reviewing
stand, the narrator introduces them over the loudspeaker; my buddy
Tom Coffey is the narrator and I told him he had* <u>better</u> *say my name
louder than everybody else's!*

*"Last week we went to the field and froze our balls off. I
had a recon patrol with a scout dog that was very useful. They are
being trained to detect enemy patrols and also are being used in
search and clear operations to detect trip wires and booby traps in
VC villages.*

*"I was made platoon leader on a heliborne search and de-
stroy operation. Somebody fucked up and we were set down in the
wrong place. We ended up in a swamp! We crossed a freezing cold
stream thigh deep and continued slogging through the gooey mud
until we reached the other side. Then I received an order to go back!
For this some members in the platoon christened me Swamp Fox!*

*"On Friday we had hand-to-hand combat training and
learned two judo throws, both of which I already knew. I threw my
partner all over the place. I eat that hand-to-hand shit up, it's the
only kind of sporting activity that ever really appealed to me. TaTa
for now, love, The London Scrambler (my other nickname)"*

By the end of January 1967 Tony's thoughts had happily
turned toward buying a car and he wrote home asking for help with a
deposit, such a loan to be repaid by him in stages. There was never
any money spare in our house, and if such a loan was made to Tony,
I cannot conceive from which pot it might have come. I can imagine
Dad, sitting in his armchair smoking his pipe saying, "What does he
need a car for? Does he think we're made of money?" while Mum,
the letter in her lap, racked her brains for a way of sending Tony
something. It wasn't that Dad was mean, he just didn't move with
the times, didn't understand the American car culture and didn't see
why his children should have things he had managed to do without.
He also had a short memory. He had conveniently forgotten that
when he was a young man in his twenties, he had owned a sporty
little number, which had thrilled him to bits. But then perhaps it had

been a bit of a wreck, cheap enough for Dad to buy outright for a few pounds.

But Tony wanted a new car. *"'Fuck it' I thought, 'I'm twenty-five years old with nothing but the uniform I wear. Why shouldn't I buy a nice car?' After all, I will be making quite good money as a lieutenant and will need a decent car, plus the fact I think I've earned one. And – I have ordered a <u>gorgeous</u> American sports car called a Cougar, which is $3,000, or approximately £1,000. Now, although I am in a profession that I can neither quit nor be fired from and won't have any trouble making the payments, I would <u>still</u> like the payments to be as little as possible. To do this of course one needs a good down payment. In OCS it's pretty hard to save anything out of $170 a month and I haven't got much of a deposit. I have no credit over here and nobody will loan me money. As soon as I get my commission and get back my extra Airborne pay I will be able to save quite a bit and pay off my debts, but right now I need a little assistance. If you can't help, it doesn't matter. I just thought I would ask."* The car was due for delivery in time for graduation.

Undeterred by the unhappy Christmas he had spent with Dee just a few weeks previously, Tony reported that he had recently had a date and would be *"all right for a week or so"*. He borrowed a car and took his girl Dolores – also known as Dee - to a pizza parlour, which had an old time banjo band and sing-along. *"After an hour or so of singing and eating pizza we went to a place called the Chickasaw Club to do some diddley-bopping. We had a table right by the floor and pretty soon two Senior Candidates asked if they could sit down so as to have a ringside seat for the show. I vaguely remembered about some show they had there, but paid no attention to it. As soon as the blonde cavorted on to the floor I remembered what kind of a show it was – a really gross striptease! After the usual slinking about, the girl threw off her brassiere and advanced towards my table. 'Oh no!' I thought, 'Here we go!' She came right up to this senior candidate until his bowed head touched the centre of her chest and then proceeded to do the shake so that we was severely beaten about the ears by her two breasts! There I was, sitting with this charming girl who neither smokes nor drinks and goes to church two or three times every Sunday, thinking 'I've done it again'. Luckily, she being 23 years old and no prude at all thought the whole thing was as funny as I did. I phoned her the next night and she had told her family and they had all had a good laugh (thank goodness for that!)*

"If you see the 'old' Dee, tell her to drop me a line. I have written three times but have received no reply. All I want to know is how she is getting on, as I hate to break off completely and lose track of people I have something in common with. Be sure and tell her that is the only reason that I want her to write, no underlying dramas whatsoever."

Tony had by now received Mum's newspaper cuttings. Predictably, she had collected those that were particularly biased against the Vietnam War although, in her defence, she would have found it hard to put together much in the way of pro-war reportage. Realising that her action had been prompted out of deep concern for his safety rather than blind criticism of his intentions, his reply was again gentle and his argument well thought-out.

"I think you exaggerate a little about propaganda and brain-washing. All the information put out here is strictly of a military tactical nature, and totally non-political. In other words the Infantry School says 'Regardless of whether our country is right, wrong, or in-between, our leaders have ordered us to do a job and we will do it to the best of our ability'. If one wants to get an accurate picture of the situation over there, all you do is talk to a soldier who has been there. You can't tell me that a private or a sergeant who has served a year in the jungles and swamps being shot at and seeing his buddies killed is going to deliberately fabricate some sort of patriotic propaganda.

"You forget we (British) did the same things in Malaya for 12 solid years. My immediate concern is for American lives. Many of my friends here will leave the USA forever and die trying to do a

good job. Many will probably be killed while engaged in one of the massive civic action and aid programs organised by the US Army, because the Viet Cong can't stand to let the US do good. We have had extensive classes on this type of work and know what goes on. The mission of the entire US Forces on all their operations is to destroy the communist guerrilla, secure the area and help the people to improve their standard of living by protecting them and showing them how to develop their land. One never hears about this side of it, the papers only print the spectacular things like artillery errors.

"I do not particularly want to go to Vietnam with a line unit. If I go it will be with a Special Forces team, which operates in one area from a well defended base camp, and whose mission is entirely to train, advise and equip the Vietnamese and Montagnard tribesmen to fight for themselves. The VC hate the Special Forces, also known as the Green Berets, because they are so effective and at one time they placed a bounty on the beret." Information overload, Tony.

"I have put in for Special Forces and indicated the 10th Special Forces Group, Germany, as my first choice. It will be great if I get it, as my new car would be shipped over there and I could hop home on the ferry!" Now that was more like it

By early February 1967, Tony and his fellow Officer Candidates were gearing up for their 'Blue Day Parade' on 17th, after which the men would become Senior Candidates or 'Blues'. He had hired a suite at a motel for the party on Blue Day and wished he could have had his car by that time, but its delivery was delayed.

"The time is gradually slipping by, all the companies around us are graduating and living it up and we are impatient to get it all over with and see what comes next. I am hoping like hell that I get Special Forces and not a line unit. If I do, I stand a good chance of getting foreign language school."

With just days to go before 'turning Blue', and a mere six weeks before graduation, Tony was showing signs of sheer exhaustion from the course, yet was proud to report that he was well regarded and liked by his superiors. *"I'm so tired I can hardly think of anything to say. I ran the mile yesterday in a little over six minutes, which once again was far ahead of the rest of my group. I think there was only one other man in the company of 200 that was faster.*

"The Company Commander is always taking the piss out of me. Every time he sees me he starts singing 'There'll be blueboids over the white cliffs of Dover'! He is a great guy, with an informal manner and a great sense of humour. I play up to their harassment and they get a kick out of me. One day the C.O. said 'Don't you think I look smart in my dress greens, Candidate Harbord?' I replied 'I think you look positively charming, sir'. He just about cracked up. They are always making me salute British style and once they even asked my opinion of the course, which shows I am held in fairly high esteem, which is why they are always messing with me, to see if I can take it. They know I can, and knock themselves out over my retorts.

"When they choose five candidates who are the smartest and the best marchers to carry sabres, I think I am going to be one of them. I am being considered for the S1 or adjutant, who has to do a ridiculous walk just as fast as his legs will carry him, and call the battalion to attention (about four companies)."

However, not everything in the garden was lovely. He was caught for having some forbidden 'pogey bait'. *"I am sweating at being punished for having lemonade in my canteen which was discovered by an officer last night. Earlier in the week I was caught with peanuts in my footlocker, and am supposed to do 55 laps of the field outside, one for each peanut. Unauthorised foodstuffs are supposed to warrant disciplinary action, but I know they don't want to mess up my chances of graduating. However, they have to do something, and I bet I am restricted this weekend when everyone else is off."*

He was right on both counts – his misdemeanour did not harm his chances of graduating, and, yes, he alone was confined to barracks for the weekend. There was also still one more hurdle to be cleared before receiving the coveted infantry blue helmet. Each candidate had to find his own helmet in an exercise of light-hearted degradation, which had become an established rite of passage at Fort Benning.

"The night before the parade we were awoken at 12.30 and taken on a mad, pitch-dark run through the woods dressed in ponchos, everyone screaming as they flitted across the countryside in search of their helmets. Our tactical officer had been thrown in the creek early that day and was getting his revenge. He led us an exhausting chase, and finally climbed through a garbage dump, up a man-made cliff and secured our headgear. When we got back to the billets we all stood inspection, stark naked except for our blue helmets, standing on top of our dressers! Our Tac then announced there was one more thing to be done before we turned blue, which was baptism. We immediately surged forward and dragged him into the shower with us, giving him his second ducking! We got to bed at 1.30 and then up at 5 ready for the parade."

<u>Senior</u> Candidate Harbord was jubilant about the ensuing ceremony.

"The parade was a great success! The colonel arrived and all sorts of officers and dignified birds and our knees were knocking. The band took their position on the field and I marched out to take my position (the commentator was saying 'notice the battalion adjutant...!') After a signal I commanded the band to sound 'attention' and adjutant's call and we were off. They kicked in with the River Kwai march and the company came marching onto the field, their blue helmets flashing and white gloves swinging. It was really great. The review lasted about 25 minutes while we were inspected briefly by the colonel who then fixed a blue streamer to our guidon (unit flag) and finally we passed in review with the battalion staff leading. Everything went well and later we were complimented on an outstanding review. It was a proud day that we had worked hard for and I was sorry that no one I knew was there to see it.

"The party started around seven and I picked up my date (Dee) who was dressed in a fabulous yellow long evening gown. I

didn't really enjoy the party too much, as those kinds of do's aren't really my scene. One had to make sure that no officer was left alone for a minute and all that bullshit.

"During the dinner our singing group provided entertainment. They sang 'The White Cliffs of Dover' in my honour and made me an honorary citizen of the United States! The colonel's wife loved it and said it brought back memories.

"My car comes in today but my bloody licence hasn't arrived yet so I can't pick it up. BLAST! BLARST!!

"On Thursday I was fastest miler with a time of 5.54, 3 seconds better than my old best. Funny thing is, we haven't done any running or PT for ages and I have a really thick chesty cold. Must be Blue magic! Extraordinary how I can run like that, beating men who have run in college. I was never that good at Long Close School! I run the first lap so fast that all competition gets demoralised. Of course I can't keep it up, but no one ever catches me up again although they get pretty close to it.

"I have ordered my blue uniform for graduation, the old cavalry blues. Dark blue jacket and light blue trousers with gold stripe. You will have to make sure there is a posh do I can go to when I'm home, otherwise I will probably never wear it. Don't rigidly expect me home right after graduation as it so depends on my school or duty assignment as to what leave time I will get. If I only can get Special Forces Germany it would solve everything. Time will tell.

"I got my first salute on Friday before the parade, and chewed out my first Junior Candidate for not saluting! Hee-hee! I love it! I love it!"

There were just six more weeks to go. The Senior phase was the culmination of all efforts to create a high quality Infantry Officer. At this level, supervision by the Tacs was minimal with the Senior Candidate assuming greater responsibilities with emphasis on demonstrated performance. He could still fail the course. As well as completing the course, each man was eagerly awaiting his alert noti-

Chapter Five

fications which were not final orders but were notification of what the army had planned for each candidate based, sometimes all too loosely, upon what had been requested. Meanwhile the course dragged on.

"Just a line during a boring class on supply and property and forms and receipts...boring boring BORING! In a few days we should get our alert orders and these are dominating my thoughts at the moment. Put a few words in to the 'Big Ranger' for me. It means everything to me that I get assigned to the US Army Special Forces." It meant a lot to us, too, to have him just across the English Channel in Germany, out of harm's way.

"Tomorrow we have our last field problem here at the school. It is an overnight problem (freezing cold here at the moment) and encompasses all the things we have learned. We have tanks, armoured personnel carriers and the lot. Next week will be our last week of training YIPPEE! The following two will be devoted to out-processing etc. and we should have plenty of time off to harass new candidates just starting!

"The car is going well. Last Saturday I washed it and waxed it. I have only done 225 miles so far and am still babying it and driving ultra carefully. In the glove compartment they have put a very thoughtful item. It's a folded cardboard sign that says 'Send Help' on one side and 'Need Gas' on the other in bright fluorescent red. Knowing me I'll probably use the 'Need Gas' one."

Inside the envelope Tony had placed a cutting from an American news magazine. A black and white photograph shows South Vietnamese villagers being rescued by a US Army helicopter and bears a quote by Paul-Henri Spaak, former Premier of Belgium, "If I were an American, I would not give up at this time. I would defend people who want to be free from Communism". It is not clear whether it was this pro-Vietnam war statement or something else that provoked what must have been a bitter attack in a letter from our mother. Heavens, Tony was doing all he could to avoid Vietnam, placing all his hopes on the Germany assignment. He received both

131

Mum's letter and his orders on 13 March 1967 and made a rare telephone call home to express his bitter disappointment at not getting Special Forces. He had clearly lost his temper during the phone call and wrote a contrite and explanatory letter home immediately.

"I guess it was the strain of anxiously awaiting my usual disappointments that caused me to get so annoyed and fly off the handle that way. It has been murder waiting and waiting for news of our orders. I guess it was because I knew I wouldn't get what I wanted that made me so frustrated and tense. At my age and in my present environment, all I want is nice newsy letters not moans and groans, so I must ask you to forgive me for being so harsh.

"Today it finally happened. Two upsets in one day. Your letter and my orders. After all my hoping and praying for Special Forces, and Germany, so that I could get home, I find I am to be assigned to the Ranger department here at Ft. Benning as some sort of instructor. I am so disappointed about everything, especially staying here. No jumping, probably supervising OC classes taking their PT tests. BLAST! I will re-apply and re-apply till I eventually get out of here. I wanted SF so bad I could taste it. Now I certainly won't be able to get home for a while. Why do I always have to fight tooth and nail for everything? Nothing ever works out first time. Still, there is a possibility that it's just a holding-over slot until there is a vacancy in SF. There are 18 of us altogether assigned to the Ranger department, all have applied for either Airborne, SF or flight school, so there is still hope. If I get a leave on the 30th I think I will pop down to Florida and see Jack.

"Looking on the brighter side, I will be a fully-fledged lieutenant in 16 days! Whoopee! Today we brought smoke on the new candidates in 82nd company. I really pulled some shit on them! Sorry, Mum, if I seemed bitter. I'm not bitter, I just wanted you to stop criticising me. Much love, Tony." If only he had got his Special Forces assignment my parents might not have lost their son, or I my brother.

Tony went on to complete the final stage of Officer Candidate School. Describing his feelings on completing the course Lew Paulen recalls, "They tear you down and rebuild you, but it was a fabulous experience and the day you graduate you feel that there isn't a lot you can't do. You've accomplished minor miracles and there is a camaraderie that you have for the other guys who made it through with you. You become a group of people who want to see everyone in the platoon succeed. You all worked toward the same end, graduation day. Tony was a big part of all our lives for those six months and we were a big part of his." Tony's hard work and dedication paid off. A document from the Headquarters, United States Army Infantry School, Fort Benning, dated 30 March 1967, informed the new graduate, Second Lieutenant Anthony G. Harbord, that he had been placed 14th out of 164, thus ending up in the top 10%. He was designated a Distinguished Graduate, and the citation went on to say:

"Your superior grades in examinations concerning both academic subjects and leadership, together with an average aggregate score of 90.29 per cent out of a possible 100 per cent, fully substantiate an outstanding performance. On behalf of the Commandant and the Infantry School, I congratulate you on this exceptional achievement and wish you continuing success in your future military career."

Tony went to Florida. He had just over three weeks to prepare for the hell of Ranger School for which soldiers, given the chance, spent months toughening up. He needed a break.

CHAPTER SIX

The blue sea and sky of Fort Lauderdale embraced Second Lieutenant Harbord that April of 1967. And so did Jack and Betty Weygant who were thrilled and touched to see him and instantly invited him to sleep on Jack's beloved boat, the *Amigo*. Jack, older than the century, had fought in two World Wars, enlisting in the second at the late age of forty-two after news broke of Japan's bombing of Pearl Harbor and America's subsequent entry into the conflict. 'Captain Jack' had battled the sea's greatest fighting fish from Nova Scotia to Peru and had fished out of Lauderdale since 1927.

Tony, back in the arms of his 'surrogate parents', reported on Jack's physical condition. *"He has had a hell of a time. First of all he had a cataract removed from his eye. Then he had this malignant tumour in his intestines and for the last nine months they have been cutting his ass-hole right out, shoving instruments up his penis and God knows what else. He is 67 years old and now that his ass is sewn up he shits through a hole in his stomach. What a tough old bastard he is. He had only been out of hospital a week when I first got down here, and already he is back down at the boat, sanding and painting, trying to get his strength back. He took me shooting one day (trap shooting) and he broke more birds than I did! He is a wonderful old man, and Betty his wife is so nice too. She is a little like Peggy but not so highbrow, more sort of a sporty woman, with pictures of her in their albums holding up ducks and enormous fish."* Despite the seriousness of the cancer which had plagued him for the past year, Jack was to live for another twenty-five years. A quote from a fishing mate in Captain Jack's obituary summed up the old sea-dog, "He smoked two packs of Camel a day, drank rum and could bring in a 600-pound tuna before the sharks had time to smell the blood. Yet he was the kind of guy who'd recite poetry from the bridge in 10-foot seas".

Not for the first time Tony begged our parents to make the trip to America. *"I do so wish you could all come over for a holiday one year. If you start saving now, maybe I would have enough to help out. Jack and Betty are about the best friends I've got over here, real people, which is exactly what they said about you when they saw the pictures I took. You would really like them and I do wish you all could meet.*

"Johnny, my old fishing buddy is still here, now married with a baby. Bill, the dark-haired captain I first worked for is also here. Everybody was so interested and thrilled by my OCS achievements and I thought how lucky I am to have people like that reasonably close. Do you know, I have made more real friends here in America in two years than I got in England in twenty-three! As Jack put it, 'You know whenever you are in Florida you won't go hungry or sleep outside, that's what friends are for'. Indeed, I ate lunch and supper with them almost every day, even though Jack hasn't earned a cent in almost a year.

"I am really able to relax, recuperate and take plenty of exercise for the forthcoming Ranger School. Every morning I do exercises on the beach, go for a run along the sand, and finally have a vigorous swim. It's said that Ranger School is ten times as tough as OCS, less than 50% of each class making it through, so I have done my best to be prepared."

It was not until 1992 that Mum, aged eighty, made it to Fort Lauderdale. She and I had flown there after our visit to the Vietnam Wall in Washington, DC, just missing Hurricane Andrew, which had devastated enormous areas of Orange, Dade and Broward Counties. We visited the newly widowed Betty who welcomed us with open arms; we walked along the lovely Bahia-Mar Yacht Basin and looked at the view which would have been so familiar to Tony; we bathed in the sea on the beach where he had made his last-minute physical preparations for Ranger School. After the stress and strain of the emotional pilgrimage to the Wall, Fort Lauderdale was a wonderful haven in which to relax and feel close to Tony. But our stay did not pass without drama and could have ended in utter tragedy, for my mother at least. Had the thunderbolt landed just a few inches closer to me I would not have known anything about it. As it was, I was silhouetted against the flash as Mum and I began to run along the street towards Betty's house in mounting panic as the clouds above us suddenly began to boil. Betty, anxiously looking out for us from her window, saw the bolt land and thought at least one of us must have been hit. Mum and I, always somewhat excited about thunderstorms, never felt easy about them again, something Tony found out for himself in Vietnam.

Ranger School had not been on his wish list. Famed for its brutal regimen of physical exercise and high dropout rate, it would make Airborne and OCS seem like the Teddy Bears' picnic. Rangers are the US Army's equivalent to British Commandos and Tony clearly anticipated a tough time ahead on the nine-week course. *"I am back at Benning as a lootenant and there are a dozen of us doing odd tasks such as book store inventories until our class starts on April 24th. It's going to be a bastard. The idea is to push you to the breaking point of your endurance and then make you do more. Hand to hand combat, no sleep, vigorous physical training, patrolling for days, no food at times, mountain climbing, rappelling down cliffs, swimming rivers in full equipment.*

"I have met a cute little bird in the bookstore and I actually kept her for four days before I said something that pissed her off, and I haven't seen her since. Quite a record, Harbord's done it again. Round about the middle of June I should be making love to the snakes in the Florida swamps, so keep your fingers crossed. We get

mail dropped in once a week, so don't stop writing. I'll need it to keep my sanity."

Units specifically designated as Rangers and using Ranger tactics were employed on the American frontier as early as 1670 but it was not until 1756, under New Hampshire Militia Major Robert Rogers, that they were formed into a permanently organised fighting force prompted by the French and Indian War of 1754-63. Moreover, Ranger strategy was based on the guerrilla-style tactics used by the Indians. Their method of hitting hard and fast, running, regrouping and attacking unexpectedly again somewhere else had proved extremely effective. More than 250 years on, Ranger tactics are little changed from Rogers' initial Standing Orders, which ran thus:

- Don't forget nothing
- Have your musket clean as a whistle, hatchet scoured, 60 rounds powder and ball and be ready to march at a minute's warning
- When you're on the march, act the way you would if you was sneaking up on a deer. See the enemy first
- Tell the truth about what you see and what you do. There is an army depending on us for correct information. You can lie all you please when you tell other folks about the Rangers, but never lie to a Ranger or officer
- Don't never take a chance if you don't have to
- When we're on the march, we march single file, far apart so one shot can't go through two men
- If we strike swamps or soft ground, spread out abreast so it's hard to track us
- When we march we keep moving till dark to give the enemy the least possible chance at us
- When we camp, half the party stays awake while the other half sleeps

- If we take prisoners, we keep them separate till we have time to examine them so they can't cook up a story between them
- Don't ever march home the same way. Take a different route so you won't be ambushed
- No matter whether we travel in big parties or little ones, each party has to keep a scout 20 yards on each flank and 20 yards in the rear, so the main body can't be surprised and wiped out
- Don't sit down to eat without posting sentries
- Don't sleep beyond dawn. Dawn is when the French and Indians attack
- Don't cross a river by a regular ford
- If someone's trailing you, make a circle, come back on your own tracks and ambush the folks that aim to ambush you
- Don't stand up when the enemy's coming against you. Kneel down, lie down, hide behind a tree
- Let the enemy come till he's almost close enough to touch. Then let him have it and jump out and finish him up with your hatchet

Any Ranger or Commando today would identify with Rogers' Standing Orders. Only the weaponry has changed; instead of musket and hatchet Tony carried the standard issue of M14 rifle and bayonet plus a personal knife. The course was not focussed entirely upon killing, for the men also needed to be taught how to stay alive under the worst possible conditions. That included not only physical torture but mental torture also. The nine-week course was carried out under conditions as miserable as war itself and is today little changed from the one followed by those trained at the height of the Vietnam War. 75% of recruits now drop out due to fatigue, injury or failure to demonstrate the high criteria needed to win the coveted Ranger tab which admits them to the most élite fraternity of trained killers. As front-line commandos they must be prepared to attack day or night with lightning speed across land, sea or air. Indeed the Rangers were there in the vanguard of the Normandy invasions of D-Day in June 1944 when, in the first moments of the offensive to liberate France, a team of Rangers scaled a hundred-foot cliff at Pointe du Hoe to capture and destroy lethal Nazi gun emplacements.

The early weeks of Tony's Ranger course were harder than even he had imagined. Given that the candidates were constantly challenged by seemingly impossible obstacles, and survived on little food and minimal sleep whilst at the mercy of tyrannical Ranger Instructors (RIs) taunting them to quit, it is not hard to see how even the most committed man must at some time have been tempted to throw in the towel. Each Ranger was teamed with a Ranger Buddy, a student, like him, who would not only share two-man jobs such as rope exercises, but was a backstop as far as safety and problem solving was concerned. If you were lucky, your Ranger Buddy would have skills that you yourself lacked – and vice-versa – making your two-man team that much more effective. Another advantage of the Buddy system that Vince Laurich appreciated was the psychological aspect, especially valuable when one or other felt under particular strain, "A man could bitch and complain to his Buddy who would do his best to straighten you right up."

Six days into the course, Tony wrote home on 2 May 1967, *"It is really tough. We have done nothing but run, march, PT, hand-to-hand combat and bayonet training. The PT increases every day (starting at 4.30 in the morning, up at 3.30). The mile and a half run gets quicker and the forced marches longer. Last week we took a swimming test, in clothing and equipment, to include walking the plank off the top board blindfolded. Yesterday we force marched 8 miles to a big lake to take a fear test. We had to climb this enormous 75' tower and slide down a long cable on a pulley suspended over the water. When you reach about 50 mph and are zooming close to the water level, a big sergeant commands 'Drop' and you let go,*

*crashing into the water. The whole thing is called the Ranger Slide
For Life. It really is great, but awful climbing the tower. Next week
we go to a place near here called Camp Darby for patrolling instruction - long weary patrols through thick vegetation and swamps. After
that we are committed to simulated combat in the mountains of
Georgia for conventional-type action and then down to the Florida
swamps for counter-guerrilla operations.*

*"They say that if you get caught by the aggressors you get a
bad working over in the POW compound. You trudge on for days at
a time hungry and exhausted. It's going to be hell, and all for a little
tab that says RANGER, which you wear above your unit shoulder
patch. A lot of people drop out on the runs and fail to climb the
ropes in the PT area (suspended over water, and you have to leap for
them) but I was in pretty good shape when I got here and am striding
out quite happily. I am eating like a horse and drinking three car-
tons of milk with each meal."* He was soon to be on hunger rations
having to kill to eat.

*"I might go to another school immediately after this one. I
intend to put in for the Jungle Survival Course and the Airborne
Pathfinder Course. Love, Tony*

*P.S. I have lost my rank already and am now Ranger Har-
bord until the completion of the course."*

A letter to Dad at the end of May 1967 expanded on the
Camp Darby exercises and, given the circumstances, was an admira-
ble effort to commemorate his 59th birthday.

*"A typical day begins at 4 a.m., then we spend all day plan-
ning a patrol, leave on night patrol at 8.30 p.m., spend the whole
night thrashing through the undergrowth in the dark, up hills, across
streams, through swamps and return back to camp about 8.30 a.m.
the next morning about to fall down. No sleep, get your gear ready
for inspection at 11 a.m. Stand in the sun for two hours waiting to be
inspected. After lunch 2 hours of bayonet training with pugil sticks.
After that, run through the obstacle course and then classes until
about 7.30 p.m. You make a feeble attempt to wash in cold water and*

flop into your tent dead beat to be awoken at about 4 a.m. for the same thing all over again. Well, those were two typical days at Camp Darby, the playland of the south. We have continued like this every day including Saturdays and Sundays.

"The last night there we packed our rucksacks and slept in ranks on the ground. At 1.30 a.m. we were awakened and marched 17 miles into Victory Pond, Ft. Benning. Here we ate a hearty breakfast before negotiating the rope drop confidence test, the second of our fear ordeals. This consisted of climbing a 40' pole and walking a horizontal log out across the water upon which is set an obstacle which you have to climb over, forty feet up. It seems easy, but felt like a scaffold walk and was terrifying. Four men quit, two of them captains. They just could not go. There were snakes in the water too! After crossing the log with your whole body shaking and wanting to cast itself off, you had to monkey-crawl a horizontal rope and drop into the water.

"After this we had our first time off, just a few hours, and at 2 a.m. the next morning we had to be up to get ready to move to the mountains. Today was our first day of mountain training. We were up at 3.15 a.m. and have been learning how to rappel down cliffs, make rope bridges, etc. Pretty soon we are in for 3- and 6-day long range patrols over mountainous terrain and I hear that you get so tired you can't believe it." He was right. The three weeks' mountain camp at Dahlonega, Georgia, was another make-or-break test of young manhood. Utter exhaustion, brought on by punishing physical exertion and an average of one hour's sleep per day caused men to hallucinate. Mentally affected by the extreme fatigue brought on by round-the-clock simulated warfare, men could be fooled into believing that an inanimate object such as a tree was in fact a telephone at which they would make imaginary phone calls, or maybe a vending machine which inexplicably refused to yield a can of Coke. But these men were all bound for the jungles of war-torn Vietnam where the enemy felt at home in mountain, forest and swamp. The Ranger

students had to go through it to stand more than a faint chance of surviving their imminent postings.

During this testing time in the Georgia mountains, Tony had to put behind him any sympathetic feelings he might still have nurtured regarding his love for animals. 'Flying' cats, which had caused him to throw in his job on the Walt Disney film back in safe old England, would now have been a source of food for the starving Ranger, had he chanced upon one. On his trip home at Christmas later that year he told a friend that bitter cold had forced him and his fellow Rangers to trap and kill wild animals, slit them open, and plunge their frozen hands inside the warm, bleeding bodies. Dahlonega was no place for sentiment, nor would Vietnam be a place for thinking twice before doing what had to be done. Vince Laurich remembers clearly the freezing temperatures in the mountains of Georgia and recalls a Ranger survival class where an instructor killed a cow with a blade through the throat. He then filled canteen cups with warm blood, which all the students had to drink. They were taught how to subsist on the available food sources such as plants, roots, snakes, rodents and other creatures. Together with his Ranger Buddy, each two-man team was given a live chicken which they had to kill, pluck, clean, cook and eat "under dismal conditions", recalls Vince. "We had no utensils, no matches, no dry wood or tools and very little time. My Ranger Buddy and I got a fire going and still had to eat the chicken raw – but it was warm, and I remember it was not good, but then again, most never even got a fire going."

Throughout the course, as at OCS, each man's immediate superior was his Tactical Officer. Tacs were chosen from among the Captains within the Ranger Department and were assigned to accompany each Ranger Class through its training cycle. Their job was similar to that of a commanding officer and apart from ensuring that the students were in the right place at the right time and in the right uniform, they were responsible for evaluating each student's daily performance and counselled him concerning his attitude, adaptability, durability and leadership characteristics. Because of this interaction

with his men, Tony's Tac, Millard 'Mike' Peck recalls Tony, his student of thirty-three years ago, very clearly. "He stands out
particularly in my memory because he was British and had volunteered for all the difficult schools in the American Army, although he
could have avoided it all by simply climbing aboard the next flight to
England. Because of this, and his unique personality, he was quite
popular with everyone. As his Tac Officer, I was impressed by his
quiet competence and physical and mental toughness. Since he was
British, I often felt his drive to over-achieve was motivated by a desire to uphold his personal sense of national honour and project the
proper image in difficult situations. As I remember, he was exactly
what I would have imagined and expected of a classical British officer in an American uniform: quiet, dignified and competent, with a
very dry sense of humour – excellent both as a team-mate and a
leader. In addition, adding to his appeal, there was also a trace of T
E Lawrence in him, which is probably why he elected to go through
Airborne and Ranger Schools and later to Vietnam. We all liked
him." Peck's analogy with Lawrence is interesting and astute, for
there was a great deal of the altruistic, very English, adventurer about
Tony. Sadly the resemblance did not end there, for both he and Lawrence met almost identical, untimely deaths, sustaining the same fatal
injuries in avoidable situations.

Ranger School marked a crucial stage of Tony's development as a soldier and as a man and, unexpectedly, the mountain
phase tested to the limits the relationship he had with our mother.
Since he had set out for America that snowy day in March 1965,
Tony had written home regularly, averaging one letter at least every
ten days, and he continued to do so to the end of his life, except that
there is now a three-month gap in the record. For although his letters
continued to arrive on our doormat at regular intervals, Mum chose
eventually to destroy several of them because of a stormy incident
that blew up between them. The episode upset her deeply and after
his death she found it too painful to recall, even though her actions
had been in his interests, as ever.

Tony, being an Englishman and proud of it, apparently came under extra pressure from the Ranger Instructors whose job it was to seek out those who might break under the strain of the course – and, by implication, ultimately under conditions of jungle warfare or enemy imprisonment. He had already reported while at OCS that he had taken more harassment than the average candidate because he was English. Considering the high dropout rate at Ranger School, it is not difficult to imagine how inhumane was the general level of hazing to US citizens, let alone an Englishman. Whatever actually happened seems to have escaped the notice both of his Tac, Mike Peck, and Vince Laurich who recalls that every Ranger student "took heat and verbal abuse from the cadre. Certainly the students didn't give Tony a bad time". Despite having his own Ranger Buddy, knowing now the stuff of which my brother was made, I have no doubt that he kept any hurts close to himself, to be shared only with his family several thousand miles away.

His letters at this time were as honest as ever and he was probably utterly unaware of the effect their content was having upon us in general and Mum in particular. It was enough for him in his exhausted state that he could download his bruised feelings, stuff them into an envelope and send them away. He was not asking for help. However, the fact that her only son was being victimised and bullied mercilessly was too much for Mum. Never one to take a back seat and expect things to work themselves out, unlike Dad, she went into action. She recalled a letter of Tony's written a year before when he was finding things very hard to bear in Advanced Individual Training. He had written of the instructors *"It's amazing they get away with it, when all you have to do to get a Federal investigation into a complaint of 'ill-treatment in the army' is to write home to Mom who contacts her Senator"*. We had no Senator, and requesting help from our Member of Parliament would have been pointless, so Mum addressed her plea for help for her son to the Army Chaplain at Fort Benning, informing him of the situation and begging that something be done. Appropriate contact was subsequently made

Chapter Six

with the Ranger powers-that-be and Tony was sent for. The outcome
was far removed from Mum's original, reactionary intent. Her action
seriously backfired, for Tony wrote home in great anger and distress,
mortified that she should effectively have humiliated him in front of
men and officers at this crucial period of his training. Judging by the
fact that she destroyed letters over a three-month period, the acrimo-
nious exchanges were clearly both painful and prolonged.

    Looking at the situation from her point of view, she believed
that her beloved son's spirit and morale were being broken by an
alien war machine which, with now almost 250,000 GIs in Vietnam,
was more than likely going to swallow him up too. The ties that existed between them were torturing them both.

    Tension between mother and son persisted for some time,
and no letters now exist of the last three weeks of the course which
took place in the North Florida swamps around the Eglin Air Force
Base, but it was clearly as unpleasant as the previous six. Any minor
injuries such as blisters or insect bites that had been sustained during
the previous two phases were now disproportionately exacerbated
due to prolonged immersion in the murky swamp waters. Vince recalls that being hot, tired, hungry and wet was the normal state of
affairs, further aggravating the now constant state of stress and fatigue. The Florida phase focussed largely on water operations,
thereby training and preparing the men to function effectively when
they faced similar conditions in Vietnam. Vince has vivid memories
of one particular exercise, "During the last week there I recall we had
a major operation that involved a very brutal escape and evasion task
including realistic PoW experience if captured. It was an attack that
included a co-ordinated Company-sized night crossing of the Santa
Rosa Sound in small rubber boats. That delightful week ended with a
grinding 25 mile timed forced march."

    As if wading through deadly snake- and alligator-infested
swampland day and night, soaked to the skin, covered in mud and
deprived of food and sleep were not enough, Tony also had to cope
with the mental agony of the situation which had blown up between

him and our mother. Nevertheless, he graduated on 26 June 1967 and the precious little Ranger tab was his at last.

Tony's impressive performance on the course, and in the Florida phase in particular, attracted the attention of officers at the Florida Ranger Camp. They were faced with a shortage of suitable NCOs to become Ranger Instructors, due to Vietnam requirements, and began to hand pick 2nd Lieutenants from the graduating classes. When Tony arrived at the Camp to take up his post as an instructor he was an immediate hit with the Camp Commander, the then Major Charlie Beckwith, a colourful character who later, as a full colonel, led the US's abortive Delta Force raid into Iran in 1980 to try to retrieve 52 American hostages.   Standing six feet three inches, 'Chargin' Charlie' was an avid Anglophile who had been to a British Airborne School as well as to Malaya with the British SAS.   Mike Peck recalled an incident between Tony and Beckwith who was much taken with the young Englishman.   Tony had just returned from a patrol in the swamp and Peck took him in to meet Beckwith who was highly amused when Tony referred to the Major's black Ranger beret as a 'berry' rather than the American pronunciation 'b'er-ray'. They chatted back and forth, with Tony's accent becoming more and more pronounced, once he observed the effect it was having upon the Major. Prior to Peck dragging him away, Tony extracted a prickly thistle from his own uniform, one of many that he had acquired during his sojourn in the swamp, and stuck it on Beckwith's beret.   Hamming up his English accent, Tony said, "Theyah's a proppah Rangah het bedge fowah yowah berry, Mayjah."   Beckwith laughed uproariously and, taking his leave, Tony affected a British Army salute, palm outwards, stamping his right foot in place.   That cost him fifty push-ups. It probably also forged his destiny.

Life was at last becoming more comfortable.   No longer a student, Tony discovered the benefits of being an instructor.   He rented an apartment at Fort Walton Beach with a view over the sea and made friends with the family who ran the complex, often being invited into their home for meals. In return he would invite them to graduation days where he would play the perfect host. Although the work was hard it was enjoyable, with time to relax with new friends made at the Camp. One of them, Harvey Watson, was also a new instructor and recalls that Tony had immediately passed what he called the 'Flank Test'. "Each of us would size the others up by asking ourselves the question, 'if we were in combat, would you want this person to be leading the unit on either your right or left flank?' A 'yes' answer to the question meant that you had a respect for the other person equal to or greater than the respect you had for your own combat skills. I guess that Tony and I passed each other's Flank Test because we went on to become very good friends".

Life after the Ranger School continued to improve. Not only was Tony a 2nd Lieutenant, enjoying privileges such as the officers' beach club, he was Airborne again after nine months, this time making jumps into the sea. More importantly, he was learning how to train men, something he found intensely interesting. But he was still under scrutiny. *"I am soon to be put in charge of the quick reaction live fire lanes. They were a great success last cycle. A student has to track an enemy through the woods by following footprints or other indicators, and fire at targets which pop up in front of him from time to time. Up until now I have done well and have got a good reputation for doing a good job. All new 2nd lieutenants have been observing other officers this cycle, walking with the students to see how the grading of the platoon leader is done. Next cycle I hope to be grading instead of observing. I have also got to give a class! Can you imagine giving a 50-minute period of instruction on a subject you don't really know too much about, to a class of officers and NCOs, with most of the officers outranking you? I have never given a class before, nor had any experience as an instructor. My subject is the handling of POWs and techniques of interrogation. I have a couple of weeks to work on it, but I just know all the staff here will be watching to see how I do."*

His birthday, August 1ˢᵗ, was celebrated with his new friends and colleagues Harvey Watson and Ron Stetter. It had become a ritual amongst the three men that the two others take out the birthday boy for dinner and drinks at a favourite restaurant. Writing home to thank Mum for his birthday cheque, he commented, *"Twenty fucking six! I'm getting to be an old man! You know, it's funny that I should have started off in such casual professions as filming and music, and ended up a military nit like your dad, ain't it? It's a ridiculous sort of love-hate profession, but I think it's the best thing I've done so far. It makes a change to work alongside men I admire and respect. There is no fancy socialising or putting on airs here. All the 1ˢᵗ lieutenants and senior officers here are returnees from Vietnam, mostly captains, and they are all <u>men</u>, which is the best thing I could say about them. They all work like hell to help the students benefit from their experience, and <u>raise</u> hell when they're off! I'm learning an enormous amount from them, I'm proud to serve with them, and it's nice to know there are still people like this left, in this age where it seems the thing to do to be as effeminate looking as you can. (Here endeth the gospel!) Lots of love, Tony"*

Sitting by the pool at his apartment block one sunny September afternoon, he began another newsy letter home, which unexpectedly contained the news we had for so long been dreading. *"I ran my live fire problem with much success again, improving it a little each time. This last time I contacted two USAF spotter aircraft (Birddogs) and had them swooping over the Rangers' heads to add realism to the problem. Everyone seem impressed with the way I run things, and I must say I enjoy doing it almost more than I enjoy my off time. Next week I am walking in the swamps on a search and destroy operation, during the grading phases of the course."*

And here it came. *"Now I have to say a few things which will have to be said sooner or later. Have no doubt in your mind, I will be going to Vietnam. As an officer, I volunteered to fight for the United States, and I have received much training in the art of counter-guerrilla warfare. Before, I decided not to volunteer, but now I do not intend to shirk my duty or try and hide behind some excuse while all my contemporaries go out to do the job they were trained for. I have gone too far now to turn back. I am a professional soldier of my own choosing and when called upon to lead 30 American soldiers in combat I will definitely go and do my level best for them.*

"Some of my NCOs the other day paid me a tremendous compliment. They indicated that they thought I was an outstanding officer, which is most unusual. Generally NCOs hate young 2nd lieutenants. I am older and more mature than many of my peers, and have decided that the time is rapidly approaching when I will be ready to do my bit. I think you always knew that I would. It won't be quite as glorious as having a troop of lancers in India, but reports are coming back that the American GI is the finest soldier that the United States has ever seen. Given good leadership he will attack anything, with complete disregard for his own life, and is capable of extraordinary acts of heroism. The young private is never ceasing to amaze his old NCOs and officers who thought that he was an undisciplined sloppy no-good.

"I know that I am better qualified to lead a platoon than most of my friends who have already left, and as an officer I have a definite responsibility to those privates fighting against one of the most efficient, dedicated and fanatical enemies the world has ever seen. The other day I put in an application for assignment to the 101st Airborne Division, the Screaming Eagles, the unit that I have always wanted to serve with. You will be pleased to hear that the camp commander turned down my application for one month as he says I have not been here long enough yet for the army to have had its money's worth out of me as an instructor.

"On October 10th I intend to apply again and see what happens. I also put in for Pathfinder school before re-assignment, but it's touch and go whether I would get that." His application for the Pathfinder course gave two main reasons why he wished to be considered:

a)   "During my entire period of military training, to include both OCS and Ranger School, all airmobile operations had to be cancelled due to non-availability of aircraft. I feel strongly that it is vital for today's combat leader in Vietnam to have a thorough knowledge of airborne, air movement and airmobile operations.

b)   I am both Airborne and Ranger qualified and strongly desire any additional training that will help me to be a more knowledgeable and effective small unit leader."

His application ended:

"Furthermore, I respectfully request that upon completion of the Pathfinder course I be granted a 30-day leave prior to my subsequent duty assignment. This will allow me to visit my family in England before my deployment to a combat zone."

His plans were clearly far more advanced than we could possibly have imagined and he set about explaining to us at length the reasons he had made the most serious decision of his life.

"An infantry platoon leader in combat has the most responsible job in the world bar none. Not only does he have to know how to lead men, but he has to have an excellent knowledge of small unit tactics, be able to call in and adjust artillery fire, call for and adjust mortars, call for and adjust Aerial Rocket Artillery (helicopter gunships), call for and adjust air strikes, call for and direct the landing of Medevac choppers, at the same time be issuing orders and directing the fire of his machine guns, M-79 grenade launchers and automatic rifles, constantly inform his company commander of what's taking place, see that his wounded men are seen to, do all this at once while under fire, keep a cool head and defeat the enemy. I wonder if all the civilians who say 'He's only in the army because he can't do anything else' could handle it. I think not, but the big ques-

Chapter Six

tion is can I? If I can, maybe I'm half way towards being the man I want to be. Either way, I have to find out.

"Whatever happens, I'll keep you informed. It will probably be two to three months before I go and I will get a leave to come home first, probably 30 days.

"Please try to understand. Love, Tony"

'Please try to understand'. The plea behind those words was overlooked, certainly by me, for a very long time. Now, as I re-read the letter, I sense the mixture of excitement, apprehension and anguish Tony must have felt as he told us of the biggest decision of his life. His handwriting, always bearing the influence of those italic pen and ink lessons, is especially fluent. I can imagine him thinking, "There. I've said it." He was free.

Again Charlie Beckwith stepped into Tony's life. Towards the end of their time at the Florida Ranger Camp, Beckwith called some of the instructors together. Among them were two young Captains, David Bramlett and Jim Daily, both of whom had already done one tour in Vietnam and, although senior to Tony, had become friends, and would meet up again in-country. Harvey Watson remembers that day clearly, "Charlie was sort of a crazy guy and it was possible that he had had some liquid fortification prior to his appearance. But we all looked to Charlie as if he were God. The reason for the meeting was for him to announce to us that he was leaving to go to the 101st Airborne Division which would soon be deploying the remainder of the division from Fort Campbell, Kentucky, to Vietnam. Charlie looked at all of us after praising us faintly and said, 'Any of you sons of bitches that want to go where I'm goin', let me know.' By this he meant the 101st in Vietnam."

In October 1967, Tony received his orders from the Department of the Army.

"Dear Lieutenant Harbord,

This is in reply to your letter of 20 September 1967. Assignment instructions have been requested assigning you to the 12th Combat Aviation Group, Vietnam, with an availability date of 30 January

1968. You will attend the Pathfinder Course, class 68-5, in a temporary duty status en route. You will receive your orders in the very near future.

Best of luck in your new assignment."

Tony wrote home with the news and took the opportunity to explain something of what his Vietnam assignment might entail. *"I will be working extensively with helicopters and advising infantry units on their landing zones and their employment of choppers. It is a good assignment, and an excellent way of getting my feet on the ground and finding out exactly what goes on. From there, if I really feel I want it, I can later apply for a field platoon. As a Pathfinder, however, I won't be spending too much time in the field, so there isn't much to worry about. I expect to learn a hell of a lot about airmobile techniques, which will stand me in very good stead. I am to attend the Pathfinder course at Fort Benning Airborne school on November 18th for five weeks. After Christmas I will come home and be in Vietnam on 30th January.*

"The other day I parachuted from a helicopter with a Long Range Reconnaissance Patrol team. It was a fabulous jump, I thought I was going to stay up for ever. This week I have been helping out at the local fair, showing snakes and weapons. I met two delightful girls, two in one week! Both were married with children of course, so that was that as usual. Thank God I'm going to Vietnam, this shit is driving me up the wall.

"While on patrol I caught two snakes. A water moccasin (cottonmouth) and a coral snake, both deadly poisonous. We use them in our snake classes and shows. We have two very big eastern diamondback rattlesnakes that as yet I haven't had the guts to touch! See you after Xmas, love, Tony.

"P.S. If it means anything, I am very pleased about my assignment."

It meant everything to us, but for a very different reason.

With his mind now crowded with the most exciting plans of his life, Tony was somewhat distracted by the attentions of one of the girls from the fair. *"Remember I told you I met a couple of married girls at the Fair, and you wrote back saying you wished you could wave a magic wand to conjure up a beautiful babe for me? Well the day you waved that wand one of those girls came back to see me! A sweet girl called Nancy, 22 years old, married (unhappily) for four years, with a little boy of three. She falls madly in love with me and leaves her husband for four days to come down here and stay with me! Everyone here wondered where the hell I found such an attractive girl, and the funny thing is, I just can't seem to get worked up like I used to. She cried when I took her to the airport, and yet I seemed to take everything in my stride. I really don't know what the hell to do! I can't seem to decide how I feel. (She's a bit of alright though.)"*

By mid-November 1967 Tony's time at the Florida Ranger Camp was drawing to a close, and he and Ron and Harvey went out to celebrate at a favourite restaurant, the Blue Room in Destin. By this time, Harvey had met and proposed to Dixie, the girl he was shortly to marry, and she had been accepted into the group. When the band began to play, Dixie took turns dancing with the three young officers. As Tony was dancing with her he whispered in her ear that she should not marry Harvey. When asked why, he replied, "Because all three of us are going to Vietnam and none of us is coming back." Dixie laughed it off but inwardly shuddered, and later shared her fears with Harvey. Tony was to be two-thirds correct in his prediction.

With one day to go before starting the Pathfinder course, he wrote to tell us that he had been paid a great compliment by the Eglin Air Force Base Camp Commander, Major Getz, who congratulated him on having done an excellent job. Moreover, he received an outstanding efficiency report from his Committee Chief, Captain Jim Daily, who was also one of the men hand-picked by Beckwith. Tony was presented with a plaque and an engraved fighting knife, which he was to bring home with him on his last leave for safekeeping. There then followed more news about his girlfriend:

"Nancy came down again and stayed with me during my last week. I am still utterly confused about her. She is so attractive and appears to be in love with me. It seems extraordinary that things seem to have got turned around and I am the one being chased. Anyway, I have enough to think about for the next year. Do you realise I make 1ˢᵗ Lieutenant on March 30 1968, and Captain a year later! Due to the war, rank is very fast now to fill the need for small unit leaders, platoon and company level. (Captain 'arbord, I like that!)

NEDDY SEAGOON: "Major, this is no time to think of women"

BLOODNOK: "Ohhhh! Well I'll just go to sleep, wake me up when it is, will you?"

The three week Pathfinder course was rescheduled to finish on 22 December, allowing the men the chance of getting some home leave just in time for Christmas. The primary mission of a Pathfinder (motto 'First in, last out') is to provide navigational assistance and advisory services to military aircraft. To accomplish this mission, the Pathfinder student is trained in:

- Air Assault/Pick-up zone planning and operations
- Marking and operating of day-or-night helicopter landing zones
- Rigging and inspecting slingloads for external air movement
- The essentials of air traffic control and ground-to-air communications
- The marking and operating of day or night drop zones for Army or Air Force aircraft for the paradrop of equipment or personnel

Modelled on the Pathfinders of the British 6ᵗʰ Airborne Division in World War II, US Army Pathfinders have been used in all subsequent major conflicts, most recently during Operation Desert Storm in 1991. With the Army's increased use of helicopters in the 1950s, the Pathfinder's role was broadened to include this new form of military transport, which was to play such a huge role in Vietnam. In addition to the establishment of landing zones (Lzs) and drop zones (Dzs), the men who joined Tony that winter of 1967 were also taught how to assist in the recovery of downed aircraft and the moving of entire fire bases rapidly by air. It was an exciting time and reinforced Tony's desire to put all his knowledge and experience into practice. With days to go before the end of the course he reported that he was neck and neck with two other officers in his class for Honor Graduate. *"I would love to get it, be No.1 just once! Our academic and field grades are averaged out and the highest score wins the trophy. We are all scoring in the 90s on both field grades and examinations.*

"The 23rd is the day I head for the nearest base. I do hope there won't be too much of a problem getting a flight home. I shall stay till the middle of January. I don't want to stay for a whole month, as it will be all the harder for all when I finally have to leave, and there won't be anything to do after you all go back to work. I am going to come back Stateside and spend a week in Florida with all the old gang, Jack and crew, possibly take Nancy along with me, and then head for California and spend a few days with Peggy, before heading for San Francisco. It's going to be a hell-raising month! I'm going to start by blowing up Lawn Close and I don't give a damn who likes it or not! Balls to all civilians! AIRBORNE!! RANGER!! EEEAHHH!!!

"See you all soon. You better call Scoop Bluebottle on the Express for my exclusive story, or he'll be furious! Love, Tony"

He made it home on Christmas Eve, landing once again at Mildenhall in Suffolk. Mum was racked with severe toothache and had resigned herself to a Christmas of pain now that the dentist's surgery was just about closed for the duration and had no available appointments. But within minutes of arriving home, Tony was on the phone demanding that our dentist see her as an emergency. It had never entered our heads to make a fuss. We were the sort of people who, on holiday, would never complain about bad food, dirty cutlery or questionable bed linen. However, Tony was practical, assertive and successful; Mum's abscess was lanced, drained and treated with antibiotics, enabling her to enjoy this precious time with him which we all feared might be our last.

But although pleased to be home, Tony was strained and tense. He seemed to go out of his way to court attention and criticism. If this was his aim, he succeeded. Dressed provocatively in his GI uniform he visited the familiar pubs and clubs of his youth with his friends. It was just three months before the terrifying anti-Vietnam War demonstration in Grosvenor Square of March 1968, and Britons were far more *au fait* with – and against - the war than they had been on Tony's previous leave. There was, therefore, a great deal of antipathy felt towards someone – particularly an Englishman – showing his political and military colours so overtly. Rising to any kind of bait, Tony displayed some of the dangerous skills he had learned over the previous 18 months. Taunted by one young man with British naval experience, Tony laid into him, showing him no mercy and had to be dragged away by his friends who did not recognise this side to him.

There was no excuse for what he did, but in his defence I can understand how focussed he was on the job he was going to have to do, the job for which he had trained so desperately hard. He had to believe in it. He did believe in it.

The Christmas holiday was over all too soon for us, but Tony was anxious to be on his way. After saying his goodbyes, he returned to Mildenhall to wait for a plane that would take him on the first leg of his journey back to the States and from there to Vietnam. We never saw him again.

CHAPTER SEVEN

A New Year and a new adventure. Impatient to get back to America as soon as possible, all Tony could get in the way of free transport at Mildenhall was an uncomfortable seat on a C-130 transport plane which took its time getting across the Atlantic. After six hours' flying it touched down in the Azores, only one-third across, from where he sent a card home. *"We take off tomorrow at 5 a.m. It seems like I'm never going to get there."* It took another eight hours to reach Dover Air Force Base in Delaware, gateway to his new life. Tragically, it was to be the point from whence his body would be flown back to England just over a year later.

Catching a flight from Dover AFB to another base in Georgia, Tony eventually picked up his cherished car and began the drive down to Florida, hoping to see Nancy in Jacksonville along the way, but it was not to be. Nevertheless he made the most of his brief visit to all his old friends in Fort Lauderdale and was delighted to be asked to be Godfather to Johnny's latest arrival. *"Johnny and Shirley christened their youngest baby last night in a Lutheran church, just before we all went out to dinner together with Jack and Betty. They christened him Todd Anthony Marmontello. Harbord held the baby, which started to cry of course, while the minister, dressed in a rather sporty check jacket, performed the short ceremony.*

"The five of us all went out to dinner at a restaurant called the Moonraker and had a wonderful time. Jack said how wonderful it was to be together with his friends again, and I must say it is amaz-

ing how close we all are, considering our widely different environ-ments and ages. After dinner we went to the Pier Top lounge atop the fabulous Pier 66 Hotel. This glass-walled, circular bar-cum-lounge rotates continuously so that one can observe the whole of Fort Lauderdale while sipping a cocktail and listening to a swinging little trio. It is particularly fabulous at sundown, watching the sun sinking over the sea and the lights of the city beginning to come on."

Then a final plea for our parents to visit. *"It's an absolute necessity that you all come over next year. Maybe one at a time if necessary. Say, Mum gets off school in February and Dad another month. But both together would be best. There is an association in Manchester called Overseas Family and Friends. It's an Anglo-American association and members get plane fare reductions. Dad could tour the golf courses of Florida while Mum and I go sport fish-ing with Jack.*

"I am leaving my car with Johnny who is going to start it up for me a couple of times a week. I leave from Miami airport tomor-row at 5 p.m. and arrive in LA at 7 p.m. I will spend Sunday with Peggy and leave again on Monday for San Francisco and Travis Air Force Base."

His letter went on to harangue the government of North Ko-rea which had tried to assassinate the South Korean Prime Minister and whose forces had begun attacking the border with the South. *"What a filthy, deliberate attempt to make us commit more men to war, and then call us the aggressor if we do anything. Poor old Johnson, what worries he has. It's about time we hit those Commu-nist bastards and taught them a lesson. They are so jealous of the success of the Republic of South Korea, which is doing so well eco-nomically under a democratic government. It will never end until we smash them. I hope to God they do before you read this. Thousands of poor reserves have been called away from their jobs and families to beef up our forces. When will it end?"* 'Poor old' President John-son would soon tell the world that he had had enough.

Chapter Seven

Tony left the Sunshine State on Saturday 27 January to fly west and Jack Weygant promptly wrote to our father telling him of the time they had spent together.

"We drove Tony to Miami where he boarded his plane for California. We just made it, so we didn't have time for a long farewell speech. We don't have to tell you how we felt when the time came for him to leave. We are very proud of Tony and are looking forward to his return. When Tony came to Lauderdale he was alone and in a short time he had earned the respect of many friends. I also think Tony is trying to prove something to himself.

"We always have fun when he is here. There is never enough time to do all the things we plan. He sailed with me a couple of times this trip. The fishing was poor but we did hook a few fish. As Tony gaffed a kingfish he remarked 'I haven't lost my touch'. He seems to enjoy the boats and the fishing a great deal. I told him that the boats and the fishing are not going anywhere and will be here when he gets back.

"A cruise ship docked here from Southampton yesterday and I was thinking how nice it would be if the Harbords could be aboard. Tony mentioned that before he left. That will be the day!

"The best of everything to you and yours, always, Jack"

Arriving in Los Angeles, Tony made his way to Peggy's home in Beverly Hills where he stayed that weekend, departing on Monday morning for his flight to San Francisco. Peggy lost no time in writing to Mum. *"You have been in my mind and in my heart so constantly during the last days that I wouldn't be at all surprised to have you materialize right here in the room! I don't know how you found him at Christmastime: probably tired and a bit tense from the strain of the past months of training. But when Tony arrived here, he had had a fine relaxing week in Florida and he was tanned and happy and handsome.*

"The big difference I see in him since he entered the army is his maturity. Two years ago he was an impressionable and highly

159

romantic boy – today he is far more assured, more down to earth, and without losing his sense of fun he is more serious.

"He is determined to finish his education – and quietly confident he can do it. It did him worlds of good to compete in those officers' classes and find out he could finish in the top group. Now he knows that nothing can stop him! I can't tell you how impressed I am at his growth. He seemed so much more thoughtful, more aware of others – I feel that his army experience has acted as a crucible and that he has emerged from all that slogging through swamps and jumping from planes, refined into steel. One would think it must coarsen a spirit – but it seems to have had just the opposite effect on him. He's a fine man and you and his Father must be so very proud of him.

"We fed him hugely, and saw that he had enough sleep for two nights – and now he has gone – and I pray that the war will be over before he gets involved. Surely Johnson must see that he must come to terms with Ho Chi Minh if he wants to win his election!

"I must stop and go to bed – but first I must tell you that Derek [her son, Derek Bok, one of Vivien's charges back in 1935] *has just been made Dean of Harvard Law School – the youngest Dean they have ever had. It is the most respected Law School in the country and I believe he can do a good job. Can you believe that little Dek could be so grown up!*

"Goodnight, dearest Vi. It's no use telling you not to worry: how can we help it? Just hang on to the fact that he is highly trained – and pray.

"All my love, Peg"

Events in Vietnam were at this moment escalating alarmingly and the realisation that the US may not, after all, be victorious, had dawned both upon the military and civilian population. Just four days before Tony's departure for Vietnam, 40,000 North Vietnamese Army (NVA) troops had laid siege to the American military base at Khe Sanh. The Americans had responded with great force, and claimed a communist body count of 10,000. However, these massive losses were seen by the NVA as a necessary evil in order to draw attention away from their main objective, a huge offensive in the South during the festival of Tet, violating a week-long truce called to celebrate the new lunar Year of the Monkey on January 30.

The famous Tet Offensive exploded on 31 January. Tony was drinking cocktails in Honolulu awaiting a flight to Guam, whilst in Saigon, a crack Viet Cong commando team pierced the underbelly of the American presence in Vietnam by mounting an audacious assault on the compound of the US Embassy. By the time the compound was secured several hours later, five Americans had died, and the world could judge for itself whether or not to believe Washington's propaganda any further.

Tony's arrival in Vietnam was delayed. He was enjoying life on the lovely Pacific island of Guam, east of the Philippines and Vietnam, blissfully unaware of the events occurring at his destination.

On 4 February 1968 he sent a postcard saying, *"We have just heard we leave tonight at 8 o'clock. The Bien Hoa airfield must be clear."* However, two days later he was still there, most likely unaware that Bien Hoa airfield had been seriously damaged by a VC attack four days earlier, as part of the Tet Offensive. He wrote of his wonderful time on the island, *"Today is our last on Guam. We have been staying at the air station ever since we were grounded six days ago. We have had a fabulous time here. Five of us rented a car and toured this beautiful but poor island. The beaches are fantastic and the weather gorgeous. I have a tremendous tan again. Yesterday we went skin diving after hiring some masks and flippers. The fish are really amazing, just like the ones in exotic tropical aquariums.*

"We visited the village of Umatac where Magellan landed in 1581, and talked to the nun who teaches in the little school. We also found some of the fortified caves and tunnels that the Japs used to defend the island when the US Marines stormed its beaches in 1944, liberating the island after two years of Japanese occupation.

"Tonight at 11 o'clock our flight to Vietnam continues, stopping briefly in the Philippines, I think. Heaven knows what's been going on in Vietnam, it sounds absolutely ghastly. Thousands of civilians wounded and homeless, many ruthlessly executed by the VC, like six missionaries and a Vietnamese army officer's wife and children. The family was machine-gunned and the father beheaded. I hope things are quietening down for my arrival so that the brass bands and reception committee awaiting me will not be disappointed! The first week of my 'Vietnam tour' has been very pleasant, nothing but an extension of my leave, so having got off to such a good start, let's hope the remainder of my tour will be something less than unpleasant."

The day after his arrival, Tony was already writing home. *"Last night we arrived apprehensively in Vietnam. As the plane touched down we could hardly believe we were finally here. We heard some artillery in the distance, but so far no close incidents at all. We were bussed to the 90th replacement battalion at Long Binh for processing."* Long Binh had not escaped attack during Tet, for the VC had destroyed an ammunition dump there just days before. It would not have taken the new arrivals long to learn into what chaos they had landed - and to realise that they had had the good luck to miss an offensive that had claimed 2,000 American lives. *"It's dusty and terribly hot, and it's clear that mod. cons. are going to be a thing of the past. From now on it's cold water and piss in a hole in the ground.*

"This morning I resigned myself to shaving in cold water, not at all pleasant. I went to the PX and bought myself a new watch. For $42 I got a fabulous Japanese watch called a Seiko. Stainless steel, waterproof, shockproof, etc. with the date and the day and also a little alarm bell. The little Vietnamese girls that work in the PX are <u>delightful</u>. Very petite with long split dresses over trousers. One tiny thing was lugging great bundles of laundry and I couldn't resist helping her carry them."

Chapter Seven

The next day he wrote to say that his assignment to the 12th Combat Aviation Group had been change to the 101st Airborne Division at Bien Hoa, *"a miserable, desolate, hot, dusty place with practically no facilities, except believe it or not a <u>swimming pool!</u> What an oasis in a sea of swirling dust! I am to go through jungle training, 8 days, before I know what my assignment will be."*

Remembering Charlie Beckwith's comment to his Ranger instructors "Any of you sons of bitches that want to go where I'm goin', let me know", Tony duly despatched an appropriate and prompt message. He wrote home exultantly, *"'Charging Charlie' Beckwith, the big, tough Lieutenant Colonel who used to command the Florida Ranger Camp, has just got an infantry battalion in the 101st. I let him know I was here, and he just about dragged me out of the Finance Office where I was seeing to my pay, threw me in a jeep and took me out to his unit which was, until today, operating outside the Bien Hoa airbase. Instead of giving me a platoon right away, he is putting me to work in the battalion tactical operation centre (TOC) for two or three months. This will give me a good idea of what goes on, and I man operational maps, monitor all unit radios and make a written log of everything that happens during my watch."* At least that sounded a relatively safe posting.

"Today I rode around in a helicopter as escort for a truck convoy. We swooped all over the area looking for 'Charlie', in case he was sneaking up to ambush the convoy. I spent last night at the base, kept awake by artillery all night long, as they fired their 'harassing and interdictory' fires on suspected targets in our area of operations. This morning we pulled out, unit by unit, in the hot sun and swirling dust, the helicopters covering everything when they came in.

"In a couple of days we go up north to join the Marines near the DMZ. The weather up there is nearing the end of the monsoon season. We will be joining the rest of the 1st Brigade, which has been over here since the first US troops came to Vietnam. They have

been chosen to operate up north where the big offensives seem to be coming from.

"Last night one company spotted 4 VC near their perimeter through infra-red scopes and called artillery on them. A helicopter with a chemical 'people sniffer' device picked up two on a sampan and sank it." After two and a half years of hard training, Tony was now actually in a real war situation and he was in his element.

Within a week he was on his way to the 2/327 Infantry battalion headquarters which were located in a very hot spot. "We left Bien Hoa on transport aircraft and landed south of Hué, where all the fighting is going on. We are presently occupying a big Marine base camp waiting for the rest of the Brigade and eventually the Division to get here. We do not know yet what missions our battalion will receive. At Bien Hoa we had to dive for bunkers at night as the VC mortared the airbase, but we were never hit ourselves." The relative joy of using a flushing lavatory was something he had had to leave behind at Bien Hoa, for his current camp had more primitive facilities: "a hole in a plank into an empty oil drum leaves a lot to be desired, especially when it starts to fill up. In the morning, the drums from all over the base are dragged outside, gasoline poured in and set alight. The whole beautiful morning is thus shrouded with a haze of burning shit!

"The feeling here is that the recent attacks on Saigon, and the build-up in the North (where we are) are the last attempt by the NVA to secure a major victory with which to bargain from a stronger position at the peace table. If we can hold them through the next big offensive, we could have them whipped. The VC have been reduced to terrorising people into joining them and murdering those that won't. The Navy medics here have had to cease their civic action and medical help to villagers because the VC murder all the village officials who help them." This US policy of Pacification, which was introduced to gain the confidence of civilians, had backfired tragically. For when the Americans returned to their bases at night, the Viet Cong visited the villages and searched for US collaborators.

Chapter Seven

The resulting mistrust of villager for villager (and even between family members) defeated the US' charitable objective of bringing aid to the civilian population.

Tony ended his letter with a plea for small items, which could accompany mail from home. On the list were razor blades, camera film, packets of powdered soft drinks, little packets of non-melting chocolate sweets and dehydrated food or soup *"of any kind, just to make a change from C rations"*.

By 28 February mail from home had begun to arrive and Tony was enjoying himself immensely in the TOC. Moreover, it was very good training for the assignment which was shortly to come his way, courtesy of Chargin' Charlie. His fluent description captured the sense of frenzied urgency and excitement that was generated when the radio traffic was thick with reports and requests for assistance or orders from the field. *"The battalion has been operating south of Hué for over a week now. I have been working in the tactical operations centre with all the maps and radios etc. It's been hectic. I have an NCO with me, and all transmissions of any importance have to be written down. When a company gets in contact it's* really *hectic. You try to find out what is happening, the Company Commander in the field has plenty on his mind without giving you a running commentary, so you go crazy trying to get his location, what kind of contact has he got, does he want gunships, does he need a Medevac, is he calling in artillery, and so on. Then you get on the Brigade net and let them know what's happening, request gunships and Medevac (giving details of wounded personnel), give location of unit, radio call signs etc. Spot reports have to be written on the incident and called in by telephone to Brigade, the maps have to be brought up to date and by this time another unit is in contact and they have a wounded man! So everything goes on at once, with the radios about to burst with all the people talking and cutting in on the same frequency. Suddenly I get a call from Brigade that the weather isn't clear enough for the gunships to take off. I inform Colonel Beckwith who goes mad and says 'What the fuck are they, fair*

weather flyers?   Tell them there is a war on and I need them right now, the weather out here is clear as a bell'. So back I go and relay this, and Brigade says they will check again. This goes on all morning until finally the choppers agree to fly. 'Trojan Dodge 33, this is Eagle 18, over'. Now the Medevac is calling me and I give him information and who to call when he gets out there. 'Trojan Dodge 33, this is Scarface 51, over'. Now the gunships want information, what's the weather like, what kind of targets are they to fire at. I tell them as much as I can and inform them to contact 'Charger' when they get into the contact area. Phew! Somehow I managed to keep on top of everything, but I was worn out at the end of the day."
Every contact between the six companies and the TOC at Battalion Headquarters was recorded and typed on to the log sheets and covered a twenty-four hour period.   Communication with the radiotelephone operators (RTOs) in the field went on around the clock and a typical daily journal at around this time would have well over one hundred entries. They reflected in cool, detached and abbreviated form the frenetic activity that was taking place and which Tony had described so vividly.

Commenting on something he had read in one of our letters to him, he witheringly wrote, *"Tell all those worthless bastards who threw eggs at the US Ambassador in Brighton* [England] *that if they really want to do something worthwhile, and they have such high principles, which I doubt, there are thousands of refugee children over here that would greatly appreciate a little food, clothing and medical care. I don't see too many hippies out here working among them. This morning I saw a little girl picking lice out of another one's hair and eating them. They all went wild with excitement yesterday when I brought in a helicopter with hand and arm signals, all standing behind me copying my actions. (Actually, they get on your nerves after a while, they just won't leave you alone.)"*

The 'two or three months' he had been told to expect in the TOC were, however, becoming more like two or three weeks, due to the enormous Tet Counter-Offensive launched by the US forces. *"I*

Chapter Seven

have just heard that I am to take over the Reconnaissance platoon (Hawks) in a couple of days. Wish me luck. Love, Tony"
He was ready, he was prepared, he was flattered, excited and probably apprehensive. It was a sought-after job, but no amount of training or watching war films could measure up to the real thing. Now men would depend upon him to lead them safely through the horrors that jungle warfare held for them over the next few months. They were his responsibility. There would be no more simulated fire, no feigned casualties; the next bullet would be live and the next casualty would bleed. Moreover, he was joining a unit whose men had already been in the field for varying amounts of time. In terms of combat experience, he was a tenderfoot and they were veterans whose tight-knit team was going to have to accommodate a new leader. And an Englishman at that. The men were going to have to adapt to their new lieutenant, tolerate his mistakes and likely initial adherence to doing things 'by the book'. Such disruptions to units were, of course, inevitable, but the integrity of a team was a key to its successful operation and any changes at the top were likely to be met with dissatisfaction by the men.
The 2/327 battalion had six companies, A to E, each with about one hundred men. The 'Hawk' Reconnaissance Platoon, part of E Company, was a specialist platoon whose job it was to carry out reconnaissance and surveillance although, as it was soon to transpire, the platoon would engage the enemy when and where it could. Tony wrote home again the next day, giving an idea both of what was happening in the area and also what he might expect in his new assignment:
"Tomorrow morning I go to the field to take charge of the battalion recon platoon. All units are presently sweeping the area capturing prisoners and equipment. They just brought in some 'detainees' a few minutes ago, including four tiny little children clutching cans of C rations that GIs had given them. The men were captured in VC territory without weapons and are to be interrogated to determine their true status. I gave the kids some chewing gum,

167

and they just sat there rather bewildered, but blankly accepting what was happening to them, rather awed by the helicopter ride no doubt. They didn't seem to have any parents.

"Anyway tomorrow I start my big challenge and command a platoon of twenty to thirty men in combat. No more showers or sleeping in a hut. My rucksack and web gear, complete with rifle magazines filled with ammo, grenades, smoke pots and five days' canned food weighs a ton! My bedroll doesn't lighten the load either, nor do six full canteens of water! For a couple of days I'll be in bad shape until I get used to it.

And again: *"Wish me luck"*.

The environment into which the new platoon leader was dropped was very different from the harsh Ranger training grounds of Florida. South Vietnam is another 15° or so of latitude further south than Eglin. Not only is this equivalent to the distance between London and Tunis in North Africa, but being that much closer to the equator as Vietnam is, 15° made the desperate discomfort of Florida seem like a Sunday School outing. In the monsoon it rained relentlessly and there was no way of keeping dry. In the dry season the heat could be intense. Reconnaissance patrols carried enormous packs, which had to sustain them for five days at a time before new supplies could be dropped and because of the nature of the unit, easy routes had to be avoided for fear of ambush. This all too often meant taking the mountain path rather than the valley, and a look at a relief map of the area shows just how tough the terrain is and how exhausted the patrols could become. This was what Tony had been training for. The hunger, lack of sleep and physical exhaustion of Ranger Camp was about to be played out for real.

As is the case in any war, it is a time that those who were there and survived will never forget, try as they might. For the career-minded, it was an opportunity to advance up the military ladder; David Bramlett eventually retired a highly decorated four-star General, latterly commanding the US Army Forces Command. For others, particularly the very young recruits, it signalled their rite of passage from youth to manhood. For all too many it left physical and mental scars so deep that all these thirty-odd years later they cannot leave the past behind them and move on. Unlike the First and Second World Wars and Korea, America lost the Vietnam War and its men were not welcomed home, a bitter experience for those who, in putting their lives on the line for their country, would carry the horrific images of that conflict in their minds forever.

*

I had a problem. I desperately needed to find even one Hawk, not only to be able to flesh out the sparse knowledge I had of Tony's time in command, but most importantly to talk to someone who was there with him in the jungle, who saw him in action, took orders from him, lived with him in that violent environment like the brothers in arms they all were to each other. I needed that knowledge so badly, yet I had absolutely nothing to go on. How was I to find men from the Platoon when Tony only ever referred to two of them and even then used their nicknames? I had found Vince Laurich by writing to a 1966 address and I had struck lucky. I had found David Bramlett, not that difficult as he has an extremely high professional profile. I had found several other men who had trained with Tony, whose full names and possible whereabouts were known to me through documentation, but no Army personnel records of who served with whom could be divulged to me. Backwards and forwards went the correspondence between me and US Government departments, all to no avail. They had a policy whereby they would forward any letters on to Vietnam veterans' addresses, but I did not even have names, so that was a dead-end. I had even visited the National Archives & Records Administration headquarters at College Park, Maryland, during my second visit to Washington DC, to trawl through boxes and boxes of daily journals relating to Tony's time in the jungles of Vietnam, but there were no names.

I reckoned without the Vietnam Veterans' organisations. A large part of their modus operandi is to put people in touch with each other, but they cannot work miracles. Many people do not want to be found, and others would prefer to put their experiences behind them. Some are too ill to be asked to revisit the past. The more I searched, the more it became clear that the way ahead lay in my writing a short piece for publication in one of the many Airborne-dedicated veterans' periodicals. A newspaper called The Static Line (named after the line on to which paratroopers are hooked prior to jumping from the aircraft door) has a column dedicated to the 327th Infantry and that was my breakthrough. The piece from me requesting information on men who had served with Tony was duly sent to the column's editor and he contacted me the day the paper was published, confirming that my article was in print. I was so excited and expected the phone to ring, the letters and emails to arrive. But nothing happened. For three long months. But then it came, a letter from Tony's radio operator who had been the closest man to him in all that time. Rick Knight, 100% disabled due to post-traumatic stress disorder, had at last got round to dictating the letter to his girlfriend Kelly at his home in Bisbee, Arizona. And he had an original copy of E Company's roster for June 1968 containing names, service numbers and social security numbers. Moreover the list was classified into platoons and there were all the Hawks. Including Tony. I could not believe my eyes. Between us, we found Ernesto Flores, one of the Hawks' M-60 machine gunners, living in California. The excitement these men felt at being put in touch with each other again after thirty-three years matched the thrill felt by Vince Laurich when he spoke to his old buddies from OCS and Ranger School.

Ernie and Rick had had a bad time after Vietnam. Drink, drugs and failed marriages had all taken their toll. As late as 1990, Ernie woke up one day on the garage floor he was reduced to sleeping on and knew he could not go on living from one fix to the next. He went to his brother-in-law, just out of rehabilitation for drug abuse himself, and asked for help. "If I go to rehab, will you take me?" asked Ernie. "Nope," came the reply, "you gotta go on your own." And he did. It was a nightmare process that only those who go through it can possibly understand. He came out the other side whole, free and healed, although rebuilding a shattered life has not been easy and more recent events were soon to cause him a severe setback.

Rick, so heavily dependent upon medication and other sources of comfort to his soul, has yet to take that giant leap and admits to being unable to let go of the past and move on. "The first thing I think about in the morning is 'Nam," he says, " I think about it all day and my last thought at night is 'Nam." To him it was and is his life.

These two men badly needed to see each other again. And I badly needed to see both of them. I flew out to Los Angeles from London in February 2001 and, exhausted from the journey, I wondered if I would have any trouble in spotting a very tall, dark man sporting a goatee beard. I need not have worried, for standing conspicuously at Arrivals was "the tallest fucking Mexican I've ever seen" as Tony apparently exclaimed when he first set eyes on Ernie. He enfolded me in a bear-like hug and, driving back through the dusk to his home in Menifee, with the biggest full moon I had ever seen hanging in the sky, it did not take me long to realise that this man had loved my brother.

We were both in a state of high anticipation for the next stage of my trip, the visit to meet Rick in Arizona. In the couple of days that I had spent at Ernie's I had noticed that he was not looking or feeling totally well. Nevertheless we left early next morning, with Ernie driving us the several hundred miles to Bisbee, a fascinating copper-mining town where horses really had been ridden into the bars in the days of the Wild West. Its rapid rise as a wealthy town in the nineteenth century resulted in a stock exchange being established there and the old stock market boards are still in situ in the dealing house. The journey to Bisbee took nine hours, with just a couple of short breaks; we were anxious to get there knowing that Rick and Kelly were eagerly awaiting our arrival in one of the town's most famous bars, St. Elmo's, a watering-hole for some of the world's most eccentric and warm-hearted people. We approached the town through a tunnel, which we soon imagined must have been a time tunnel for it seemed to have transported us back a hundred or more years. The winding streets, old hotels with verandas, men sporting drooping moustaches and wearing cowboy hats and boots and appeared to be from another century. Pulling up outside St. Elmo's I turned to Ernie, my heart in my mouth, and asked, "how are you feeling?" "I can't breathe," he replied. We walked in through the swing doors and Rick and Ernie fell into each other's arms and wept. All around us people stood, the tears falling down their cheeks. They knew how much this moment meant to their good friend Rick.

Holed up in one of Bisbee's oldest hotels for that weekend, the two men talked and talked and Kelly and I listened and listened. The two men, both in their early fifties, bearded and well over six feet in height, were unstoppable as the stories came pouring out and every so often Rick would release one of his infectious, slow, deep chuckles as anecdotes and schoolboyish platoon pranks were recalled. In stark contrast were the brutal horrors that these two men, then barely twenty years old, had also faced.

On the few occasions that we ventured outside the hotel, the townspeople of Bisbee stopped and greeted us warmly. They bought us drinks, they gave us presents. It seemed the whole town had heard we were coming and knew of the circumstances. On our last night a surprise party had been arranged for me at the American Legion where I was honoured to receive several mementoes and gifts, but my abiding memory of that evening is the impromptu speech Ernie gave. In a moving tribute to our hosts and to his brothers in arms Rick and Tony, he described the pain he had gone through to release him from the captivity of drug and alcohol addiction, beginning his address with the startling words, "I went to Vietnam in 1967 and I 'came home' in 1990". The poignancy of what he had to say touched us all very deeply as it did his father, the former US Army Scout at the Battle of the Bulge, the siege of Bastogne, when Ernie showed him Kelly's videotape of the evening. Father and son embraced, and forgiveness, understanding and love passed between them more strongly, more unconditionally that it had ever done since Ernie's return home from Vietnam.

Not so fortunate is Rick, whose own father was also at Bastogne. Wanting only to follow in his footsteps as a paratrooper and have his father be proud of him, Rick became Airborne and went to Vietnam. "But it was 'the wrong kind of war' and he has hated my guts ever since," he says, slowly and painfully, believing that – unlike Ernie - he can never achieve reconciliation. Like countless other Vietnam veterans, Rick carries an intolerable burden of sadness and psychological pain and he has suffered from insomnia for thirty years. It is small wonder he prefers to live in the past. Despite the horrors he encountered there, he says gently, "I learned to love in Vietnam. I knew, from the way I was treated – the way we treated each other – my buddies would move heaven and earth to rescue me."

Saying goodbye was so hard. It was not as if we would never meet up again, it was just the realisation of what that meeting had meant to all four of us in our different ways. Ernie addressed himself to our punishing nine-hour drive home, and back through the time tunnel into the twenty-first century we drove, deep in our own thoughts and memories of the weekend.

I flew home a few days later, laden with video and audiotapes of the trip and a bulging notebook. Buoyed up by my trip I was totally unprepared for Ernie's bad news, which broke just a few days after my return home. The reason he was suffering moments of forgetfulness and disorientation was because he had a brain tumour. The powers-that-be were attributing it to the long-term effects of being exposed to the lethal Vietnam chemical defoliant, Agent Orange.

It is thanks to my two brave new-found friends, Ernie and Rick, that I can now tell the rest of Tony's story the way he would have wanted it.

CHAPTER EIGHT

Chargin' Charlie Beckwith's handpicked Ranger Instructors continued to arrive in-country. One of the Eglin threesome, Ron Stetter, began his tour on 2 March 1968, just a few days after Tony, and joined him in Beckwith's battalion. The third member of the gang, Harvey Watson, arrived in April and, as Beckwith's complement was by then complete, he joined another 101st Airborne unit. Jim Daily and David Bramlett followed on later, taking command of Beckwith's B and C Companies respectively.

The job of a Reconnaissance Platoon Leader is not only to seek out the enemy and pass that information on, but also to take care of his men and not to make decisions that would compromise their safety. Beyond that, in Vietnam at least, there was the added mission of direct action taken against the enemy and the desire of the leader to perform his duties in a manner that his men had a right to expect from him. In the small recon units of Vietnam of some 18-20 men, whilst the leader was separated by virtue of his rank, he was almost always directly involved in the action. Moreover, the giving and receiving of trust between all of them was vital both to the success of the missions and indeed each man's survival.

The environment in which the Hawks (motto 'No Slack') worked, ate and slept was hostile in more ways than one. The NVA had a bounty out for members of the 101st Division in general and the Hawks in particular. The 101st patch, the 'Screaming Eagle', was prized by the NVA but its name did lose something in translation. Rick Knight gives one of his long, low chuckles as he remembers friendly Vietnamese pointing to his shoulder and exclaiming "Chicken Dai! Chicken Dai!" "Yeah," he drawls ironically, eyes twinkling, "Beware the men who wear the chicken patch!" However, being prized as a trophy by an enemy who was naturally accustomed to jungle conditions and almost always moved in greater numbers, was not so funny for the members of the Hawk platoon. Strict noise discipline was enforced at all times, and when it came to taking turns to sleep in their hastily dug 'foxholes', the men slept noiselessly, having learned from necessity how to do so for fear of detection. Their ability to awake fully and lethally alert in an instant was to prove difficult for many of them – and dangerous for those waking them - in the civilian lives to which they returned. Many family members found the safest way of waking their returning veterans was to prod them with a broomstick from a safe distance. That is, for the lucky ones who could get to sleep in the first place.

The jungle, too, held its own discomforts. "Everything either bit or had thorns," recalls Rick, with enduring memories of his head distended by enormous swellings and puffiness forcing his eyes tightly shut. Apart from the stinging and biting insects that were a constant plague, there were the leeches that managed to crawl into every anatomical crevice possible. To knock them off an accessible part of the body while they were latched on was to risk tremendous loss of blood due to the natural anti-coagulant the creatures emitted. To lose a leech in an inaccessible orifice necessitated a Medevac helicopter being called to extract the casualty who would receive more sophisticated treatment than could be provided by either of the platoon's medics. Back at HQ, the 'No Slack Quack' had that unenviable task. Diseases, too, took their toll, with malaria the most prevalent, followed closely by hepatitis. Sandwiched in between the information radioed in to HQ of contact with the VC and requests for air strikes were the daily reports that all companies were up to date with their malarial prevention.

The new Hawk platoon leader, whilst no stranger to the privations of Ranger training, was nevertheless inexperienced. Tony

was taking into his charge men who, for the most part and for varying periods of time had been out in the field, had seen and done
unimaginable things and would undoubtedly be watching his every
move closely. "He was learning too," recalls Ernie, "and he hung
around the vets picking up information". But they would take time to
get used to him, particularly as he was something unexpected, an
Englishman. Changes in command were not welcome to men whose
lives depended upon the reciprocal understanding and confidence
forged between them and their immediate leader. It was less difficult, perhaps, for the platoon leader, who had a say in who should
thereafter join the platoon which, like its Long Range Reconnaissance Patrol (LRRP) counterparts the 'Tigers' in the 1/327 and
'Recondos' in the 2/502, was considered an élite force in which to
serve. He would, however, need time to get to know them, to win
their trust and to give them his. But time was not something in abundant supply and Tony was given just three days to observe the
platoon sergeant running the unit before taking over himself. Using
the co-ordinates from the daily journals I obtained from NARA and a
contemporary military contour map - accurate to within 100 metres -
supplied to me by General David Bramlett, it was possible to plot
every move of Tony and his men

On 11 March 1968 he wrote home from his position some
fifteen miles south of Hué to describe his early days in command.
Some of the information sent our pulses racing. *"I fucked up a lot at
first, but I am getting the hang of it now. The second day I took over,
we crossed the river and headed south. We don't operate like a line
company that moves around by helicopter. We move quietly and try
to find out where Charlie is at before he spots us. Then when we find
where he is located we call in artillery and air strikes on him, and the
line companies can move in. We were the first unit across the river
and moving south in our area of operations. Just as we came over a
hill we saw a man run down a slope and two mortars started firing at
the battalion base camp across the river. We had surprised them.
They had probably decided to wait until dark but when they saw us*

176

*coming they got off as many rounds as they could and then fled when
I called in artillery and air. A chopper flying overhead received fire
and the door gunner opened up on us as he thought we were Charlie.
(We wear floppy jungle hats instead of steel pots.) Luckily no one
was hurt and we contacted the helicopter by radio.*

*"Since then we have been moving further into Charlie's
area, quietly and slowly trying to find his base camps. When we find
a good place to set up, we form a perimeter and send recon teams out
from this base. If the teams find any used trails or travelled areas we
put out ambushes at night.*

*"We carry five days' rations on our backs in a rucksack,
and move to a fairly secure area every five days to be re-supplied by
helicopter. Of course, every time we do this Charlie knows where we
are so we have to pack up and sneak off somewhere else again. As of
this date we haven't killed anybody yet. I wish we could get the drop
on a small group. It's nerve-racking never knowing where he is.
Morale would improve 100% if we could knock a few off."*

As a young teenager, Tony had served as an altar boy in our
local village church in Datchet. He still had deep-seated thoughts
and convictions about religion, which he was able to air on the occasions when army chaplains visited the men in the field. Not all the
men who went to these field services were believers, but they still
went. "It helped ward off bullets," chuckles Rick who, like his fellow soldiers, was highly superstitious. From attending Mass
conducted by the chaplain (call sign "Sky Pilot") to putting the left
sock on before the right, ritual played a very big part in the game of
odds and percentages. Tony's faith was, however, more traditional.
*"On Saturday the RC and Protestant chaplains came out by chopper
during resupply to conduct services. This is really meaningful, living, simple religion. I went to the service, where we sat on the
ground while the chaplain in his jungle fatigues donned a black scarf
and placed a small gold cross with a base on the ground in front of
him. We prayed and then he took the 23rd Psalm and explained how
David, being a field soldier like us, had written it for us and not for*

the people back home having breakfast after church. The chaplain had been through Ranger School too, to get the feel of the infantry. After the short and moving service I asked him over to my position, put a canteen cup of water over a heat tablet and we talked over a cup of coffee – My team has just made contact - back later –"

The letter was resumed five days later and contained the worst shock yet. Of course it had been inevitable that Tony would see real action, would use the weapons with which he was so lethally expert, but it was his reaction to the encounter with the NVA that was both unexpected and hard to equate with the young man we thought we knew. The Daily Journal of 11 March 1968 at 11:45 logged the report from the Recon Platoon leader that the Hawks had engaged an unknown size NVA force. Tony's letter took up the story. *"While snooping around in the jungle we killed two NVA coming down the trail. This trail was apparently their main route down from the mountains. It's hair-raising sneaking around in Tarzan-type terrain, wondering if there is a gook behind every tree and waiting to hear the ear-shattering burst of automatic weapons fire to break the eerie silence. So far we have suffered no casualties in my platoon, but we really tore up the two enemy soldiers with machine guns. My first action! Even though the first one was dead, I shot him again myself to see what it was like. His arm raised up and fell again. I didn't turn a hair."* Too much information. But there was more.

Daily Journal, 18:55: "Recon Plt Ldr reported hearing grenade go off where contact was made earlier today." *"My platoon sergeant booby-trapped one body with a grenade and later that evening we heard it go off. Two days later we went back down into the area, and the carcass was blown in two. Both bodies reeked and were covered in big buzzing bluebottles."* In the jungle climate decomposition of bodies was rapid. The dead could be crawling with maggots within hours; after a day they had turned black and become bloated. *"The NVA had tried to drag the bodies off the grenades with rope from a distance but I think they were wounded as everything had been left."* Booby-trapping bodies was common practice, as more often than not the VC would attempt to retrieve the bodies of their dead comrades. Designed to kill the body retrievers, the plan did not always work. Rick ruefully recalls an incident in C Company before he joined the Hawks. "We saw a woman in a hootch [native house] with hate in her eyes. Then we saw Charlie approaching with a Mauser. We shot him up and booby-trapped the body so it would get *her* when she recovered it. The bitch stole the body *and* the grenade. And there we were, waiting for an explosion that never came."

"The reason we went back down to the area was to take a rifle company there. My platoon led the formation and my two point men, Rat and Twiggy, were opened up on by two more soldiers in hiding. Both quickly hit the ground returning the fire and hitting one of the NVA soldiers. They were lucky, but good too. This was my first tactical decision under combat conditions. I took another team and manoeuvred right, trying to get on the enemy's flank while the point team continued to lay down a base of fire. We assaulted through the jungle but found they had fled. The day after, we were lifted out by helicopter to the TOC area on top of a hill. 'Charging Charlie' Beckwith seemed pleased with us, which is unusual as he gave all the rifle company commanders a bollocking for fucking around not doing much!

"P.S. I was right. There is nothing quite like being a platoon leader in combat. The relationship between me and my men, people I would probably never meet or bother to talk to, is something no civilian could ever hope to understand. I hope to hell I never lose any of them, especially Rat and Twiggy, my point men. What a great bunch they are, and what they have to put up with --- we haven't seen a girl or a can of beer or a juicy steak or a nice room for quite a while, and won't for a hell of a lot longer. In a way I like it, it makes you appreciate things others would consider less than nothing. Love, Tony"

Back in the United States President Johnson was taking momentous decisions. The disaster that had been Tet had destroyed much confidence in America's ability to win the war. Johnson was having to rethink his country's involvement in the conflict and, contrary to military requests, vetoed a massive troop expansion. On March 31 he announced that bombing was to be scaled down to a point of almost virtual cessation and continued his address with the now famous declaration that he would not seek, nor would he accept, the nomination of his party for another term as President. His announcement did nothing to boost the morale of the half a million Americans in Vietnam. If their Commander-in-Chief was getting out, what on earth were they doing there?

At the beginning of April Tony took on two new Hawks, both experienced in fighting with the line companies. Ernie Flores, "the tallest fucking Mexican" Tony had ever seen was one. Ernie had survived the almost total annihilation of two line companies and was looking for a job and was offered one of the two posts of M-60 machine gunner. The other, Rick Knight, had been headhunted by one of Tony's men Tony Chavez ("Flipper"), as a future Hawks Radio Telephone Operator (RTO), for which post there was now a vacancy. The loads the men carried were heavy enough without the addition of radio paraphernalia; their rucksacks weighed around forty pounds and added to that were the many canteens of water, weapons and ammunition. Rick, who carried eight canteens and a half-gallon water bag, could not lift his radio pack above his knees. He had to strap himself into it, roll over and then stand up. The field radio needed five batteries, each weighing five pounds. They came wrapped in large plastic bags, which were at a premium in the jungle and were much sought after by the men who used them to keep spare clothing dry. Rick came up with a plan. Whoever wanted a plastic bag should carry a battery. That way he could spread his load amongst the platoon members. But at one point all the men who wanted a plastic bag had got one. "Are you *sure* you don't need another one?" begged the overloaded RTO, buckling at the knees. He ended up carrying the full twenty-five pounds of batteries himself. Ernie spread his weighty bandoleers of machine gun ammunition around and, though it was not expected of him, Tony carried extra ammunition and medical supplies.

On 2 April he was preparing to move north with his men to guard an installation north of Hué. A year had passed since graduating from OCS and he was now a first lieutenant. Although he saw the task in the north of South Vietnam as a chance for a rest, he was also planning to use the time to work and train with his men who were *"getting pretty good now at snooping and pooping, and 'Charging Charlie' seems pretty impressed with us. The rifle companies go crashing through the jungle like elephants, that's why they get into all the big fire-fights by stumbling into Charlie. We flit through the undergrowth like ghosts, nobody speaking and conscious of every twig, so Charlie never knows where we are. Because we are better than he is, we beat him at his own game and always detect him first. He has one bad habit that gives him away every time. He thinks he always knows when US soldiers are in the area by the noise, and when he thinks no one is around he yaks away loudly. We are not out there to fight, just report what we see and hear so we seldom make contact with the enemy, we just get in there and hide!"* This last comment may have been written to allay the fears the family had at the degree of danger in which Tony was finding himself. He was not fooling us. Reconnaissance was one thing, but making contact seemed to be just as large a part of the platoon's remit.

"I put Rat and Twiggy in for a medal the other day, they deserve one for the dangerous job of walking point and they have done an outstanding job more than once in contact with a couple of Charlies. I have three Negroes that are always getting together and singing and bobbing about. I put on a straight face and pretend to be cross and tell them no diddy boppin' during working hours. One is a terrific machine gunner and the other a great medic. The third is a very quiet, reserved rifleman. They all bend their floppy hats down over the ears and tie the string at the back of their heads." It is only through the recent reminiscences of Ernie and Rick that it has been possible to put names to some of these men who formed such an im-

portant part of the Hawk platoon. The black medic referred to was Doc Jesse Brown, or "Voodoo", and the man Ernie joined as co-machine gunner was Luther Smith, a man he would dearly love to trace. But Browns and Smiths are just as abundant in America as in Britain, and those particular needles remain firmly planted in hay-stacks for now.

The journey north past the once-beautiful eighteenth-century city of Hué began. Once Vietnam's capital, the city sits on the east coast of the country's narrow waist in its wettest region. Taken during the Tet Offensive by the NVA who massacred thou-sands of civilians, the city was all but levelled in the Counter-Offensive with the loss of many thousands more troops and civilians.

"We are now loaded on trucks ready to go north. Twiggy has the shits and wants to know if he can stop the convoy when nec-essary. I told him to shit off the back of the truck! It's a cool, damp, misty day. We are now 7 miles south of Hué and are passing paddies with Vietnamese paddling sort of paddlewheel affairs and children riding water buffalo.

"We just passed through Hué which is quite a mess. Across the flat paddies to our right we can see tanks firing and trees on fire. All along the road are old women carrying poles on their shoulders with two baskets, one in front and one behind, and grubby children waving at us. Must go, love, Tony"

He did not mention the fact that the convoy was shot at, but Ernie and Rick remember it well. Tony was sitting writing his letter in the truck's cab with the driver while the Hawks, smoking pot and drinking whisky, were piled into the open back. As the sniper's shots rang out the convoy dispersed, men dived for cover, but not the Hawks. They sat tight. "Wasn't nothing gonna move us, man," says Ernie. The pot smoking was a fact of life and was done all the time. Marijuana grew there and the men used it. Some used hard drugs if they could get hold of them and many of the Hawks, Rick and Ernie included, suffered hideous consequences in later civilian life but sur-vived. Others died. But how could recon teams, on the alert all the

Chapter Eight

time, be smoking something that is used as a relaxant? And did Tony not only tolerate this but also do the same? I wanted some honest answers. "We smoked on the trail, yes, but it had the effect of increasing our state of alert," explains Ernie. "We could hear a pin drop in the jungle. At stand-down it had the opposite effect. We smoked to relax." Tony knew his men smoked. He also knew that it did not seem to impair their performance and tolerated it for the most part. I eventually managed to drag out of the two reluctant men the fact that Tony had been known to smoke occasionally himself. "But never in the field," Ernie and Rick firmly assured me, "only at stand-down."

The convoy arrived at its destination. Quang Tri, up near the Seventeenth Parallel which marked the Demilitarised Zone (DMZ). The Parallel had been decided as the separation point between North and South Vietnam under the Geneva Accords of 1954 with the intention of a reunification pending elections. These never took place and the DMZ with its strip of no-man's-land either side of the Ben Hai River became the accepted border until the end of the war in 1975. As a border it was ineffective, for the Ho Chi Minh Trail, just a few miles to the west on the Laotian border, provided all the communications needed by the NVA to infiltrate and supply the south with forces and arms.

With the job of guarding the military installation over, the Hawks returned to the jungle, or the 'boonies', as they were known. It was April 15 and just five weeks away from my wedding, a fact which had not escaped Tony despite all he had on his plate. *"When is Gay's wedding again? I lose all track of times and dates. Yesterday was Easter but I didn't know it. I have absolutely nothing to send her and no way of getting anywhere to buy anything so I am sending this bullet that my machine gunner made for me to wear around my neck, just as a souvenir. Maybe James Walker* [the jewellers] *could shine it up and put some more silvery-type wire into the melted lead. The bullet is a 7.62mm Nato round, taken from an M-60 machine gun belt and made into a charm while out in the field one day."* The bullet did not make it back to England. It probably never left the country, for mail was censored and, unknown to Tony, ammunition was strictly forbidden in the mail. But, as they say, it is the thought that counts.

Ten days later, some fifty miles from Tony's position, the 101st's C Company made early morning contact with a heavily reinforced NVA platoon. Withdrawing into a tight defensive perimeter, C Company received continuous small arms fire and grenades. At 17:20 the perimeter was breached by the NVA, resulting in heavy casualties on both sides. With the perimeter once again secured, ammunition was running low and helicopters were called in with emergency supplies. Throughout the evening the helicopters came and went, escorted by gunships. The toll at the end of the day was 22 NVA killed, 10 US wounded, one US missing and one US killed. The dead GI was Ron Stetter, Ranger Instructor friend of Tony and Harvey Watson. He was twenty-one years old and had been incountry less than two months. Dixie Watson wrote to her husband with the news and Harvey, sitting on his steel helmet by the Song Dong Nai River reading her letter, recalled Tony's prophecy that all three of them would fail to return alive from Vietnam. It was a sad and chilling moment for him.

On April 27 Tony wrote a newsy, cheerful letter home.

"Dear Folks, I'm writing from out in the woods again (never seem to get out of them). I have set up a little base and sent two recon teams out to check the area for enemy activity. The terrain is extremely rugged, just like the Lake District without the lakes and every inch covered in jungle. We push on day after day with our rucksacks, getting re-supplied every 5 days or so by helicopter, continuously looking for Charlie. I am fit as a fiddle with all this walking, but rations are getting rather boring.

"The line companies have been making contact quite frequently and employing artillery, air strikes and gunships against the enemy. Gunships are terrific. I used two from the 1st Cavalry Division on an ambush we had. The Cav. calls it Aerial Rocket Artillery.

Chapter Eight

Each helicopter has about 90 rockets plus machine guns. They hover around like dragonflies pouring rockets into targets you point out to them. We were lying in the bushes on a riverbank watching the VC move up and down the other bank and in and out of a hut. 'Blue Max 490' was the gunship radio call sign and I told him to destroy the hut which I described to him. Suddenly whoosh-whoosh-whoosh-whoosh, he put four rockets right in the open front door! What a pee-bringer! Rattled Charlie's teeth a little no doubt. I watched the bastards come down the trail in NVA uniform, go into the hut, change clothes and hide their weapons then come out innocently in civilian clothes holding a little girl by the hand for protection and continue up the trail. They never had any idea the Hawks were watching them for two days, and one morning we opened up with rifles and machine guns at first light, just as an old woman was ferrying four VC with weapons across the river. We soon put a stop to their caper! Blue Max 490 came on the scene and finished the job. I really enjoyed that day, it was the most exciting thing I have ever done and my people didn't get scratched. That's the way we operate, not charging in like the infantry and taking casualties.

"The NVA is as thick as thieves down here in the northern quarter of South Vietnam. They hide out in the hills and jungles and wait for the US Army to try to clear them out then fight from trees and bunkers. The guy that is waiting under cover has always got the drop on the guy who is moving and searching and the line companies are taking casualties.

"It poured with rain yesterday and we all got soaked, but used the weather to move to a new area. We put up shelters and are just about dried out now. Keep your eyes open for any little light articles of food to send airmail. Anything that would give my diet a different flavour. Soups are good, little cubes of beef or chicken to add to dehydrated meals would be good but anything would do. When is Gay's wedding again? I keep forgetting and I lose all track of times and dates out here. I have been here almost 3 months already! One quarter gone! Only another 3 months on line and then I

185

will get a soft job back in the rear, like company executive officer. I
am looking forward to R&R. I might go to Australia or possibly
Hong Kong or Tokyo.

"Keep everybody writing. Mail coming in through the trees
by helicopter is quite something to look forward to. Nancy has decided to try her best to patch up with her husband, for the child's
sake, so that's that. The best thing really, but I'm nearly 24 and no
girl friend again. BLAST! I'll just have to start from scratch when I
get back.

"Oh well, I must put some water on and make a Long Range
Patrol ration, BORING dehydrated beef and rice! Lots of love, Tony.

"P.S. I don't suppose there is such a thing as dehydrated
strawberries is there?"

Strawberries. Just one of the little luxuries the men dreamed
about when faced, day after day, with C-Rations and LRRP-Rations.
C-Rations were canned foods ("Yeah, canned in 1943!" says Ernie
wryly) and Rick recalls with disgust cans of chopped ham and eggs,
"They were BLUE!" LRRP-Rations, on the other hand, were dehydrated and, with the addition of sauces sent from home, could be
constituted into an acceptable meal. "But the biggest treat was
peaches and pound cake," says Rick, savouring the memory, "and
canned fruit of any kind was really thirst quenching."

Tony had begun writing to an old friend, Kay Rouselle,
singer in the Don Smith Orchestra back in the Newcastle days. His
first letter to her, written the same day, came out of the blue. *"This
letter is straight from the Vietnam jungle!"* he began. She had not
heard from him since he had left Newcastle in December 1964, three
and a half years previously. *"Yes, I am over here now, a first lieutenant with my own recon platoon in the 101st Airborne Division. We
are operating in what is known as I Corps area, the top quarter of
South Vietnam. Since I have had the 'Hawks' we have killed about
twelve Charlies and taken no casualties. This is because we sneak
around quietly and the enemy never knows where we are at. We recon by day and ambush by night when we find enemy trails. We*

never blunder around on search and destroy operations like the regular infantry line companies do. We pulled off a terrific ambush a few weeks ago, blazing away across a river at a bunch of VC who never knew we had crept up on them. I got my rocks off that day!"

The jungle telegraph had been working efficiently; he had heard of Ron's death just two days previously. *"A good buddy of mine was killed the other day. He was the second platoon leader in C Company. We had served together in the Ranger Department as instructors back in the States and had had a lot of fun in town off base.*

"So here I sit in my little shelter, on a hill in the middle of the jungle, wondering what will happen next time the Hawks clash with Charlie. I haven't had a bath for weeks. I stink like hell I expect, but am well used to living in the 'boonies' and find it quite acceptable.

"When the resupply comes in by helicopter it's a good day, because they bring mail too – drop me a line, Tony"

After more than six weeks in the boonies, the men were exhausted. They were driven to the limits of their endurance by the heat, humidity and insects. Water was a constant problem and operations were often interrupted because of the pressing need for fresh supplies. The terrain was so rugged that it could take several hours for a watering party, sent down off the ridgeline to the valley floor, to fill the canteens and climb back up the steep mountainsides. Watering holes and rivers were dangerous places to linger for obvious reasons and therefore only in extreme circumstances could water be airlifted in. Any water gathered from natural sources was rife with bacteria and purification tablets were issued to all troops. "They made the water taste awful," agree Ernie and Rick, who took their chances by not using them despite having seen what could float past in the rivers. Rick tells the story with some glee. "While I was in C Company, a particularly unpleasant officer stopped to take a drink from a river. He had not spotted the black, bloated body of an NVA

soldier a little further upstream. I decided not to warn him. Ha!
Was he sick!"

*

"To absent friends," was the toast at my wedding on May
18. We remembered Tony. And then he went out of my mind. Mike
and I left on honeymoon in his little sports car happily chasing the
early summer sun through France, Spain and Portugal. Half a world
away my brother was enduring a different kind of heat. Contact with
the enemy was becoming more and more frequent. The area in
which the Hawks were operating was a hotspot of NVA and VC activity and no prospect of stand-down seemed likely for some time.
Army rations were clearly not enough to sustain the men in the field
to peak fitness. On 29 May Tony wrote home begging for supple-
mentary nutrition, *"I am losing weight and these rations aren't
helping any. Even my men noticed it and that shows I must be, when
people who see me every day notice a change. I take vitamin pills
every day but I need something else. Any kind of high protein food
would do. I definitely need a tonic of some sort.*

*"Also anything that will make food taste different, soups,
gravies, sauces, spices, anything. These dehydrated rations day after
day are driving us crazy. What about some curry? Doesn't Vesta
make a light packet that is easy to cook? I am going frantic for
something different to eat, a new taste plus some nutritional value if
possible. What about some beef drink stuff, Bovril or Marmite or
Oxo or something, does that have any goodness in it?*

"How are things in the world?"

Help was already on the way, and how welcome it was.
Tony's next letter arrived just twenty-four hours later.

"Dear Mum,

*No sooner had I handed my mail to the door gunner of the
helicopter than in came our platoon mailbag with your soups and
sauces! I mixed some onion and mushroom together with some water
(it says milk on the packet, but I just didn't have any handy) and
threw in a can of chicken. It turned out pretty good, but didn't last*

188

me long. Peggy sends me boxes of canned fruit every once in a
while. Fruit is like heaven out here, OH HOW ABOUT SOME
STRAWBERRIES! Yes, aha hahaha strawberries strawber-
ries STRAWBERRIES – STRAWBERRIES
AHAHAHAHAHAHAHAHAHAHAHAHAHAH
Please
"There is nothing to look forward to except mail every five
days and the hope of something different to eat. I think I will have
my beef gravy with something tonight SMACK SMACK!
"Well, I guess Gay is married now. Pity I couldn't be there,
I was humping up a mountain at the time I believe. This terrain is
murder. It's nothing but hills and mountains, so you can imagine
walking up and down them in this terrible heat, with a rucksack on
your back. You live continuously in a state of sweat and exhaustion,
no escape from the heat. We haven't taken a shower for well over a
month now, but we change fatigues every five days on resupply. I
have had a couple of men completely pass out with heat exhaustion,
but right now we are just back from a five-day recon and are on the
top of a hill set up with a line company. The flies are murder. With a
bit of luck this operation, which has been going on three months now,
will be over in about 10 days. Then I hope we get a break and go
back south.
"I hope Gay got the cheque. Here is another cheque to
combine with Dad's birthday and to help with the cost of the wed-
ding. Go out to dinner with it.
"I am putting in for Germany as my next assignment. I
doubt if I will get it, but I might. Let me know about the wedding.
"Keep writing, I don't get any love letters these days! Love,
Tony"

By the end of May the Hawk Recon Platoon was operating
in an area of dense jungle a few miles from the A Shau Valley which
is close to the Laotian border. Days of intense activity and tension
were occasionally temporarily relieved by spells of frivolity. The
men needed to let off steam every so often but opportunities were

few and far between. Anything that would make noise was out of the question and so other diversions had to be created. It was customary for men in reconnaissance patrols to pierce their left ear. As only a couple of the Hawks wore earrings, several of the others decided to do something about it. They approached the medic, "Voodoo", to make sure he knew how to carry out the procedure and then sought permission from Tony who, with a huge grin, told them to go ahead but to leave him out of their plans. Voodoo gave Rick a list of the medical items needed and along with the usual resupply items such as boots and rucksacks, he ordered a 20 gauge needle, cat gut, a syringe with a tiny tip and some local anaesthetic for the earlobes. Sitting in a patrol base, deep in the jungle one day, the men decided to carry out the piercings.

As each man went through the process Voodoo suggested the holes be kept open with slivers of bamboo soaked in an antiseptic ointment to fight infection, since there were no earrings available to do the job properly. As the days wore on, the men's earlobes began to swell. They had failed to keep the bamboo slivers soaked in the ointment and their swollen skin began to turn all colours of the rainbow. "Voodoo" did his best, but jungle sores did not heal easily. The men still had a job to do and so there was nothing for it but to keep on 'humping the boonies' as usual, poisoned ears or no. One man, Pete Rossi, who had had his ear pierced, became very ill not from the piercing but from malaria. A Medevac was needed, but in an area of triple jungle canopy, finding a landing zone was no easy task.

Eventually an area was located where the saplings were only fifteen feet high, enabling the 'jungle penetrator' – a three-foot by six-inch device lowered from the helicopter which had pull-down seats for the evacuee – to reach the victim. Whilst waiting for the extraction, Rick and his buddy "Flipper" had a bright idea. Why not put the casualty tag for Rossi through his earlobe? Having done this, Rossi was hoisted up and the tag began to rotate in the rotor wash at about one thousand-rpm. Despite the dangers associated with helicopters hovering for any length of time, a crewman with a camera leaned out and snapped the malarial Rossi as he was hauled skywards, his ear becoming more and more inflamed and maddened by the rotation. As sick as he was, Rossi appreciated the humour of it, as did his audience both in the chopper and on the ground. The story quickly got around, reaching the ears of a livid Charlie Beckwith who gave Tony a piece of his mind when the men returned to Firebase Bastogne many days later. Rossi made a complete recovery. That is until hard drugs and a motorbike accident killed him years later.

At the end of May Americans remember those who have died serving their country in many different walks of life. Memorial Day is now something of a holiday weekend, but for the Hawks in 1968 it was anything but. The NVA were in the area in huge numbers and it was the Hawks' job to find them without being found themselves. All day, May 30, the Hawks trekked through the jungle, staying close to a curious row of telephone wires. That night they camped, posted sentries, and slept. As dawn broke on May 31, Hawk Recon were on 100% alert. The weather forecast was good, except for early patchy fog. At 08:07 Rick radioed in to HQ to report that they were about to move northwards. What neither the Hawks nor the NVA had realised was that they had both been camping less than fifty metres apart, the Hawks on the forest floor in their foxholes and the NVA in a bunker complex on a hill. "We'd slept next to 'em all night! We didn't hear them and they didn't hear us," says Rick. "We got up, moved about twenty-five metres and walked right into them. That's how quiet we were". They had made contact with a whole Company of NVA, about seventy strong, who were taking cover in the bunkers. "We finished breakfast before they did so we were just a few steps ahead of 'em. That's how we got 'em," he says, laconically.

The bunkers extended down through the earth with many inter-connecting areas, some containing surgical equipment, others with weapons, cooking utensils, propaganda leaflets and books. The topmost areas had overhead cover comprising three layers of logs and three feet of dirt with camouflaged firing ports giving a clear field of fire. Under heavy automatic weapon fire Tony, with Rick as ever right behind him, moved up to the front and motioned his men to follow and to get within a range that would enable them to flush the NVA out of the bunkers. The Forward Observer, call sign "India", was running close behind Rick whose radio antenna was visible to the enemy. Using the antenna as a reference point for its associated human element, an NVA soldier took aim and India was shot through the shoulder with an AK-47. He was short of his R&R by just one day and was swiftly Medevac'd to safety; as the jungle penetrator hoisted its casualty skywards, the Hawks opened fire with everything they had upon the enemy. Not so fortunate was John Bowden ("Bodine"), a twenty-one year old married Negro who was killed by a 500lb bomb. As his terribly injured body was being carried up a hill to safety he died.

Incredible as it now seems, Tony was still struggling to keep up with family birthdays. A few days after what became known as the Battle of Memorial Day Hill, he wrote an apologetic letter home. *"Dear Mum, sorry to be late for your birthday but we have been 'humping the boonies' rather hard lately and we had a little action on 31 May."*

This 'little action' resulted in Tony being awarded the Bronze Star Medal with "V" (for Valour) Device. The citation reads:
Reason: For heroism in ground combat against a hostile force in the Republic of Vietnam on 31 May 1968. First Lieutenant Harbord distinguished himself while serving with Company E, 2d Battalion, 327th Infantry, near Phu Bai, Republic of Vietnam. During a combat operation to clear a suspected mortar position in its area of operation, the Hawk Platoon came under intense hostile fire. The enemy was in bunkers securing the high ground and their mortar position. The platoon surprised a group of North Vietnamese soldiers sitting on their bunkers, killing three before the enemy could

react. After re-grouping, the enemy returned a heavy column of fire causing several casualties. Using his forward observer, First Lieutenant Harbord called in artillery on the enemy position until the forward observer was wounded by small arms enemy fire. With complete disregard for his own personal safety, First Lieutenant Harbord exposed himself to the murderous hail of fire while personally directing the artillery and tactical air strikes on the enemy position. First Lieutenant Harbord's personal bravery and devotion to duty were in keeping with the highest traditions of the military service and reflect great merit upon himself, his unit, and the United States Army.

That was his finest hour. But his tour was not over yet.

CHAPTER NINE

Life in the heat, humidity and danger of the Vietnam jungle had few redeeming features so pleasant surprises,
practical jokes and pranks such as the earring episode helped to break
monotony and tension, so long as they did not compromise safety or
the success of a mission. On patrol one particularly uncomfortable
day the men came to a small river, which was especially inviting.
Tempting as the water was, the area first had to be checked out thoroughly and sentries posted before, in turn, the men were allowed to
throw themselves, dizzy from the heat, into the cool, clear water.
Rick discovered a pool under a small waterfall and lay there, fully
clothed, radio in his hand, refusing to come out. It was a small taste
of Paradise for them all, for the terrain they were operating in was
punishing and after two months on full alert they were exhausted,
hungry, thirsty and dirty.

A little light relief came during re-supply every six days
when fresh uniforms, food and mail were dropped in, but these moments carried their own dangers as any NVA in a wide area would
immediately know exactly where the men were. They had to press
on quickly for fear of ambush and sometimes Tony was ultra-
cautious, moving his platoon several miles to a place of relative
safety. Rick, humping his enormous load, one day took exception to
what he felt was an unnecessarily long detour. He, like Tony, was
party to the information coming from HQ and knew that the area in
which they were operating was no NVA hotbed. In response to
Tony's request to obtain some painkillers from the medic for some

194

minor injury he had sustained, Rick had an idea. Seizing the opportunity for respite somewhat longer than a meal break, he gave Tony
seven tablets to take. "Are you sure I should take so many?" asked
Tony doubtfully. Reassured by Rick that it was a wise move, he
swallowed them down with several gulps from his canteen. The tablets were anti-histamines which, in a very short time, rendered Tony
virtually inert. The other men, in on the joke, began to take off their
rucks. As he lay on the ground unable to move, Tony muttered
faintly, "Knight, you son of a bitch".

Always looking for something to alleviate the discomfort
and stress they were under, one day some of the men decided to be-
stow the honour of being Airborne upon a lizard. Rossi - now
recovered from his malaria and rotating ear lobe - and his buddy Zingen, requested permission from Tony to conduct an experiment.
Permission granted, and with their highly amused Lieutenant looking
on, they strapped the creature on to a flare which contained a tiny
parachute for its return to earth. Up went the flare, a roar of 'Airborne!' resounded from the Hawks, and eventually down drifted the
parachute. Empty.

Tony's plea to Kay, the singer in Newcastle, to drop him a
line, was amply rewarded. Not only did she reply to his letter, she
enclosed two music magazines and a photograph of herself and Tony
on the bandstand in the Don Smith Orchestra.

Tony replied "*Ha Ha, Good old Kay! Thanks for the long
letter, 'Crescendos' and photo. I was tickled to death by it and
showed it to all the guys in my platoon. They couldn't believe that an
officer could be such a 'cool dude'! Well, it sure brought back some
memories. It seems like a dream now, something that never happened, but I'll tell you one thing, this war is real enough. I had my
first man killed a few weeks back when we ran up against some North
Vietnamese regulars on a hill. Would you believe, those bastards in
Paris are actually denying that the North Vietnamese are in South
Vietnam, when here we are fighting the bastards every day. Regular
uniforms, automatic weapons and all, in fact I picked up some docu-*

ments they dropped that designated their unit within the North Viet-namese Army and gave a personnel roster showing birthplaces, mostly Hanoi! Have you ever heard such bullshit? Bloody commu-nists. Make no mistake, we are doing the right thing. Those lying rats at the Paris peace talks are trying to deceive the whole world and what's more, it seems like many intelligent people are taken in by their carefully prepared propaganda."

The next paragraph came straight from the hip. *"Here I am in this bloody jungle, and to tell you the truth, I am doing better at being a soldier than anything I have done before. I love to kill these bastards, I really do, and I take pride in my unit being bloody good at it too. We are really starting to kick some ass over here.*

"I will make a point of coming up to Newcastle next Febru-ary when I finally get out of this son-of-a-bitch. I may extend, though, I don't really know what the fuck I want. Almost 27 years old and still not fixed up. What a hopeless twit, would you believe I don't even have a girlfriend to write to. The last one was another married babe – the old Harbord luck, 'everything he touches turns to shit'. I've always been curious about what happened to Ronnie. Have you ever seen her again? We were pretty tight at one time. I guess I let her fuck my mind up. Get ready to fix me up in February, love, Tony"

Not only was Kay a good friend from the days of the band, she was also unlikely ever to come into contact with our family and spill the real beans contained in his letters to her concerning the stimulating thrill which he got from killing the enemy. Writing to her gave Tony the safety valve he needed in order to express some of the violent and frightening things that were happening to him, things that he knew would upset us at home. We had, though, got the gen-eral drift.

Moving into the A Shau Valley which had by then been un-der Communist control for three years, the Hawks operated in the undergrowth along Highway 547, part of the Ho Chi Minh Trail, looking for signs of the countless NVA troops which used it as a link between the north and south and cutting a path for the other US companies to follow. Before the Tet Offensive earlier in the year, some 150,000 North Vietnamese had trekked down the Trail to prepare for and execute the unexpected and damaging attacks in the south and east. Stretching from Vinh in the south of Communist North Vietnam, it extended south close to the Laotian and Cambodian borders and, for much of its length, ran through them. As a result, Laos was heavily bombed by the US Air Force in an attempt to break this artery which was so vital to the NVA and Viet Cong. Two million tonnes of bombs, napalm and defoliant were dropped on friendly Laos, despite which the highway was never effectively severed, for after dark thousands of North Vietnamese men, women and youth workers worked feverishly to repair damage to its hospitals, ammunition dumps, food stores, fuel pipeline and to the Trail itself.

Back on Highway 547, the Hawks were getting too close to a heavy air strike for Rick's liking. He had had a particularly nasty experience with C Company the previous year when air strikes had been called for and he had been blown several feet into the air. "I suggested to Lieutenant Harbord that if we continued down 547 we would be in the thick of the attack and in some danger," he recalls. "Shrugging this off, your brother continued down the trail. Unknown to him I called battalion HQ, told them we were walking into an air strike and got the command to withdraw. Your brother never knew it had been my idea." It was not only aerial rocket artillery that landed its explosives in the A Shau Valley. A World War II battleship, the *New Jersey*, was sitting out in the bay off Da Nang, some thirty-five miles due east. Called upon to add its own fire-power to the engagement, the *New Jersey's* sixteen-inch guns opened up with massive projectiles which found their targets with astonishing and deadly accuracy.

Their superior firepower notwithstanding, the Americans took almost another year to make any headway against the NVA in the A Shau Valley. In May 1969 the Pyrrhic victory of Ap Bia hill – nicknamed Hamburger Hill because of the way the 700 dead of both sides were reduced to so much mangled meat – resulted in the NVA simply melting across the border into Laos. The valley was abandoned by the South.

The exhausted Hawks were overdue for a rest. They had been operational for four months without a break, half of which had been spent on the current mission. Tony wrote home expressing his eager anticipation of a long-awaited rest. *"In a few days we shall be going in for a five-day stand-down with plenty of beer and steaks and even a day at the beach! We are really looking forward to this, as you can imagine.*

"I shall be going on R&R on 1 September to Penang, Malaysia, that being about my halfway point and 'change jobs' time. Penang is supposed to be a real terrific tropical spot with loads of women of all nationalities and few GIs. How I am going to enjoy food again. When I get back from Vietnam I am going to do nothing but eat and drink and stare at round-eyed women!

"Got your news about the wedding, sounded like a smasher. Typical Harbord affair – everything starting to go wrong but turning out all right. The photo was really good. When I'm 93 I'll have an even better wedding!"

The stand-down was all he and his men had hoped for. Back in the base camp they built their own platoon club-hootch with a bar and stocked it with cases of beer. Each morning they drove into Hué to buy ice and spent the rest of the day drinking, smoking pot and going to the popular open-air movies. It was at one of these film shows that Tony, joining his men in smoking pot, had them all laughing helplessly. The soundtrack suddenly broke down and the audience was taken aback to hear a very English voice from amongst them begin to supply an improbable dialogue to match the action on screen. One by one, his men began to chip in, taking different parts and supplying ridiculous voices for the characters until the whole audience was in uproar. The Hawks were back in town.

As expected, the men also got their day by the sea. Tony wrote, *"One day we were even helicoptered to the nearest beach and then I took the men to a show over in the Navy area. We were the only army personnel there just about, so I gave the Australian girl singer a note to dedicate a song for us. When she said 'this next song is dedicated to the Hawks' we all went wild!*

"Back here on the forward base, life is back to normal and I am rather depressed and bored. There is nothing to do but guard the perimeter at night, train and hold classes during the day, nowhere to go and nothing to look forward to but going back out in the jungle in a few days. It is very hot at the moment and I feel like I haven't got the energy or the interest to do anything. I was paid rather a nice compliment today, though, one of my men, a Negro, had to go on emergency leave back to the States. When he left he said I was the best lieutenant he had ever seen in Vietnam and wished he could have spent longer in my platoon.

"I am now looking forward to my leave in Penang, Malaysia, but 2 months to go! Seems like forever. I shall stay in the swankiest hotel I can find, eat all the lobster I can eat, drink myself under the table and chase birds until I drop. That is an R&R, to cram one year of fun back in the world into five days. After that I should change jobs and become a rear echelon type, executive officer for a Company or something. Rather boring, rushing around with clipboards and doing all the paper work and administrative stuff. At least I can go to the officers' club and get stoned on rum and cokes every night and watch movies. I suppose then I'll be lonely as hell and miss my platoon.

"It's no wonder so many GIs take off after R&R and desert. My radio operator is a good soldier, intelligent, mature. Last year he extended his R&R in Australia from 5 to 50 days! He just couldn't bring himself to come back to this hell after sleeping with a different girl every night in Sydney, eating lobster and lying on the beach during the day. Filthy swine!" That filthy swine was, of course, Rick, who – as a result of his prolonged period AWOL - had lost any chance of promotion. Despite an otherwise impeccable re-cord, including a Bronze Star with V device for saving the lives of

two wounded men whilst under heavy fire the previous October, he was demoted from Private First Class to Private E1 where he remained. It did not break his heart. He saw the irony of the situation and speaks without sarcasm when he says, "I am proud to say that I never once saw a General in Vietnam."

It was now early July 1968, and the platoon found that it had been featured in an issue of 'The Screaming Eagle', the 101st Airborne Division's newspaper. Photographs showed the men wading through a mountain stream as they searched for NVA positions. Sending a copy of the paper to Kay, Tony wrote, with some humour, *"Here's a magazine to amuse you. My platoon is featured in two photographs. Maybe the Journal, or whatever that Newcastle paper is called, will pay you some cash for a story! I can see it now: 'Ex-drummer at the Oxford fighting in Vietnam!' 'I knew him well', says Kay Rouselle, well-known female vocalist, 'he used to goose me every time I climbed the bandstand steps!'"* Indeed he did. Kay recalls ruefully how the entrance to the bandstand was through a very narrow opening, allowing only one person through at a time. Inevitably, Tony would be standing behind Kay and as she stepped up to make her entrance, in her tight dress and high heels, he would poke her in whatever sensitive area he could find, thus often propelling her on to the bandstand in a less than ladylike fashion.

He continued his letter to her on a more sombre note. *"We had a bad accident recently, the hill we are occupying was struck by lightning, one killed and ten injured. Every one of us was knocked out by the bolt. What an experience, to come to after a shock like that and find men twitching and screaming in the mud, the rain still pouring down."* That wasn't the half of it. The twelfth of July had dawned overcast, with thunderstorms and rain forecast later in the afternoon and winds of twenty knots. The temperature was predicted to reach 101°, with 90% humidity. The Hawks were guarding a radio relay station for C Company and had been beginning to enjoy the assignment as it meant they could, for once, stay put in one place. It began to rain, and the men huddled under ponchos which had been stretched out over the front of the bunkers. Sitting in muddy puddles, their knees touching, they continued their task of filling sandbags. Ernie was keeping 400 rounds of gun ammunition dry by sitting on the box in which it lay. As he leaned back against an engineer's stake the lightning struck and he was blown fifteen feet into the air. C Company's RTO had made a fatal mistake, forgetting to earth his antennae and, with his headphones over his ears, was blown to pieces by the bolt, his bones ending up sticking out from the surrounding sandbags and his blistered flesh scattered across the mountain. One man had his eardrums blown out, another's leg was blown off and everywhere men were screaming and bleeding from ears and nose. Rick raced to the Command Post to call for a medic and radioed in to HQ at 15:25 to request a Medevac. By 16:14 the Medevac had extracted ten wounded men. The fragmented remains of the fatality were left to the men on the hill to deal with.

Tony's letter finished, *"Looking over my shoulder I see the clouds building up and it's starting to blow like a son of a bitch. I pray God we don't get it again. I was never scared of thunderstorms before, but I'm bloody terrified now."*

Ernie was unconscious and remained so for three days, his body badly burned down one side. Rick, for whom this was his last but one day in Vietnam, had had all he could take. In the past year he had heard too many cries for "Mother! Medic! Morphine!" from the injured and dying. But at least he was alive and in one piece. He returned home a few days later, still in shock. To this day, he hesitates when putting a plug into a socket, recalling the nightmare on top of that hill in Vietnam.

By July 30, two days before he turned twenty-seven, Tony could almost taste his imminent R&R in Penang. *"Tomorrow we go in again for a three-day stand-down (we haven't really done anything since the last one). After that it will be almost time for my R&R and a change of jobs.*

"Goody goody, I'll be able to booze up on my birthday instead of being out in the field, quite a stroke of luck! Boy it's hot

today. I am sitting in my bunker with no shirt and the sweat is just pouring off me continuously. I am very darkly tanned again, so am in good shape for my R&R. Some of the time I have been running around in my green undershorts trying to get my knees brown. One day a chopper came in, and because I had got tired of jumping into my trousers in case it was an officer, I didn't bother. This time I was almost caught. A whole load of colonels got off! I rushed around the side of my bunker and scrambled into my trousers and just about made it, though I looked a bit of a sight, because I had no time to tuck my trouser bottoms in my boots and just rolled them up a bit. Phew."

By the end of August he was out of the field for good. Although he had known that he would soon have to leave the Hawks, he – and they – were unprepared for the summary way in which it was executed. A helicopter had flown in to the Hawks' position carrying not only the usual re-supply equipment and mail but also, unannounced, a new Hawk platoon leader. Tony was ordered to climb aboard. His time with the Hawks, the men with whom he had shared everything, was suddenly over. As he boarded the chopper he waved at all the old faces and the tears welled up in his eyes. It was a painful leave-taking from men who had all shared so much together for six tough months. The camaraderie and fellowship that had existed between Tony and his men who, day in day out, had carried out their dangerous mission with only one fatality in some of the most hostile conditions on earth, left him empty and deeply saddened. Ernie recalls the event with disgust. "When your brother left the Hawks, a part of me was lost. He kept us alive. He knew what he was doing. He asked our opinion of situations and discussed them with us. The new guy was such a dick. He was all 'Do what I say'. 'Fuck you', we said." Fresh out of West Point, the new lieutenant's attitude from the start was to do everything by the book and not to take advice from the veterans in his command. Ernie was intensely irritated. "He arrived with gold bars, crossed rifles and West Point ID on his uniform. He even had a gold bar on his fuckin' hat! I said

Chapter Nine

'You gotta take that shit off, sir, you're Recon'". Not only was it bad form to advertise your rank or achievements in the Hawks, Tigers or Recondos, it was plain survival common sense that jungle fatigues should carry no flashy tabs. Meeting with resistance from the new platoon leader, Ernie walked away muttering, "Just keep away from me, like at least ten paces!" The new mix just did not work and soon Beckwith had no option but to - reluctantly - pull the plug on his daring, unorthodox recon team.

Tony wrote home in distress at the beginning of September. *"An awful thing happened which depressed me very much and has caused me to try and get out of this battalion. When my old platoon came on to this hill that the TOC is on, they were assigned a new platoon leader. They did not like him and unanimously wanted me back. The battalion commander just got pissed off and disbanded them. So the guys that were like my family for six months and wore the floppy jungle hat of the Recon platoon were all split up, handed steel helmets and thrown into the four rifle companies. It sounds silly, but it meant a lot to all of them and especially myself, to see what we all felt was the élite outfit of the battalion suddenly destroyed after so long.*

"The Colonel suddenly decided the Hawks had a bad atti-tude, and without giving them a chance, organised a complete 'changeover for the better' so the new platoon leader won't have to overcome the resentment of the 'old hands'. Just imagine what it was like, friends splitting up after going through so much together, but who the hell cares about that at battalion level? I just hope none of them gets killed in one of the line companies after we stayed alive together for six months. Every time I see one of the new 'cherries' who call themselves 'the Hawks' walking around the area in a floppy hat it makes me sick. Nobody really understands how I feel, they just think I am too sentimental and 'got too close to my men'. Fuck 'em.

"I hate this bloody job inside a bunker full of maps and ra-dios, but it's all part of the 'career pattern' of an officer. I am trying to find another home. I might be able to get into the Pathfinders like

I was originally supposed to do. I have applied for Special Forces on Okinawa after Vietnam. I am also considering transferring to Military Intelligence." It was clearly a very different job from the active, dangerous and exhilarating one he had been doing in the jungle. Special Forces would provide that excitement and fulfilment again, if he were accepted. They certainly were the élite force of the US Army, known for their expertise in infiltrating by air, land or water, sometimes penetrating deep into enemy territory for the purpose of attacking strategic targets, rescuing friendly troops or collecting intelligence. He wanted to wear the coveted Green Beret next.

September 1 came and went, and the promised R&R still appeared to be some way off, but Tony's spirits seemed to have been restored, judging by the cheerful, saucy letter he wrote to Kay. *"I am due to go on R&R to Penang next month for five days of eating, charvering, drinking, charvering, swimming, charvering, and if I get time, a bit more charvering! I believe that is the Old English expression, unless there's been a change since I left.*

"I must say I sure miss listening to jazz over here. Sometimes I want to blow so bad I think I'm going crazy. I guess once it's in you it stays in you. I'll bet old Newcastle is quite a swinging town these days. I can tell you, I could do with a night on the town. I haven't seen anything but mountains and jungle in seven months (I wish I could snap my fingers and get rid of the next five). How are the birds in Newcastle these days? All over the place I suppose, and every one in a miniskirt. It hardly bears thinking about, it's like another world. I'll probably drool and slobber when I get back, like a bloody animal. Sex is definitely a problem over here, there's not even any sheep! The worst time is when somebody gets the new 'Playboy'. Everyone goes apeshit for about 3 days. Regards to everyone, Kay, keep me posted."

By October 7, Tony was in Saigon enjoying himself, having learned that his next assignment was to be an Advisor to the Vietnamese Regional Forces. His friend Captain Jim Daily from the Eglin days at Ranger Camp, who had met up with Tony twice whilst in 'the boonies', remembers that an advisory role was not what most men wanted when they came out of the field, for very often the local forces were badly equipped, unmotivated and inept. "However, the regional forces had a high priority and taskings would come down for officers with several months in-country, Ranger qualification, good record and so on, which only some very good people could meet. They were after me when I was about to come out of company command. To get out of it I was sent up to interview to be the Corps Commander's junior aide and talked him in to letting me keep my company." But far from being disappointed, Tony took it in his stride and was even looking forward to it. *"We are waiting for our team equipment to get down from Cam Ranh Bay and are really doing the town. I have had a lot of fun since leaving the wild and woolly north. I will be stationed just outside Saigon with a company of Vietnamese Regional Forces, kind of like the 'Home Guard' to advise and help train them. It will be hard work and, poor living conditions but should be interesting and rewarding. And there is always a trip to Saigon to break the monotony."*

The US Army had initiated the Mobile Advisory Team (MAT) about six months previously. Once trained, the job of the members of the Vietnamese Regional Forces was to patrol their assigned areas to prevent VC activity, in particular the firing of rockets into Saigon and its Ton Son Nhut airport. As a unit leader, Tony accompanied his team on patrols, putting to good use the expertise he had acquired both in training and in the field.

"I still haven't had my R&R yet because of all this changing around, but I should get it fairly soon. By the time I get back from it, it will be almost time to come home! I am now a Co van me – which means American advisor. I am also referred to as a Trung uy (pronounced Choong wee) meaning 1st lieutenant and I wear the two pips of the Vietnamese Army on my uniform. It's a lot of fun to be around the Vietnamese after being isolated in the hills for seven months.

"I bought a brand new camera recently, a real professional job, and it's been stolen already. Sometimes I want to blow my

brains out for allowing things like that to happen." So, no photos of Penang which was evidently worth the wait, for upon his return he wrote home excitedly on November 3 with a list of all the made-to-measure clothes he had bought.

"I just got back from Penang. I had a great time and spent almost $600. I bought a total of 5 suits, a light grey Terylene and worsted, a medium grey, a brown Dacron and worsted, a charcoal all-wool and a dinner suit! I should be a regular James Bond when I get back. I also bought a Rolex diver's watch and a stereo tape machine for my car, not to mention six shirts, two pairs of slacks and two pairs of shoes. Some of this stuff will arrive by parcel in about two months. Let me know when it does, and please unpack it and have it all pressed for me.

"I am intending to take a special flight home that goes back the other way round, stopping at Karachi and Beirut and God know where else. It should be more fun than flying east across so much ocean.

"I have just heard that my next assignment request has been approved. I will be going to US Special Forces (the Green Berets) which means another school and possibly language training before reassignment. I have asked for Okinawa but anywhere will do. I will be a captain by then which will really be great. I will probably have my own 12-man special team, all experts in their fields. I just can't see getting out right now and becoming a penniless bookworm, this stuff is too much my cup of tea and the money's good.

"Before I left the 101st I got a Bronze Star for Valor, how about that? Another Audie Murphy! 'It was hell, folks'! I enclose a copy of my Bronze Star orders, a little far-fetched but basically accurate." This was the first we knew about 'the little action' on May 31 at the Battle of Memorial Day Hill. Not only was he now safely out of the field, he had been awarded a decoration for his attack on the NVA bunker complex with the addition of the device for valour. He had also been accepted into the Green Berets, a great honour and an

206

exciting next step. What was more, he would be home again in less than three months.

An extra piece of paper was enclosed in his letter, written in large letters:

3 NOV 68
86 DAYS
29 JAN 1969

His letter to Kay went into a little more salacious detail about his exploits whilst on R&R. *"I refused to buy a girl like the rest of the GIs, as I have never paid for it yet and don't want to start now. The going was rough but I finally managed to de-flower a young Chinese virgin on my last night! I am meeting the buddy with whom I spent those five days, in Saigon this week. I know what's going to happen. I'll get drunk with him and end up buying my first piece of ass in desperation! It is very, very hard to get a nice girl-friend here, even though the women are some of the most beautiful in the world. Their custom forbids them to associate with foreigners and even though many of them think Western men are very hand-some, they would be terribly ashamed to be seen with one. This makes matters extremely frustrating and causes 'horny' Americans (and Englishmen) to seek out female companionship in the many du-bious bars in Saigon. The young ladies who work in such places are extremely westernised both in their dress and in their morals. They are of course looked down upon by the Vietnamese people, but they sure make more money – 15 to 30 dollars a go!"*

Explaining about his new job, it became clear that he was finding it very fulfilling. *"It's a much more stable existence, less dangerous, and really quite interesting to work with the people in their own villages. In addition to military advising we are also active in the pacification effort and hold MEDCAPS (Medical Civic Action Programs) in all the local villages. This is when all the sick come to us for treatment. Our team medic does most of this but on occasions I display my vast medical knowledge on sores and the like!"*

Then he proudly broke the news of his medal to her too. *"By the way, I got a bloody medal while I had that Recon platoon in the 101st – a Bronze Star with V for Valor – how about that shit! If you haven't sold my fantastic story to the Journal yet, that ought to do it. Christ! I'll have to fight the dollies off when I get to Newcastle in February – that's a bloody laugh, 27 years old and I still don't have a girlfriend. Either I've got leprosy or the world's worst luck. Back in the States I seemed to either meet married women or nobody at all. Then I've always had bad luck with the birds, haven't I? If it hadn't been for that Ronnie I probably wouldn't even be in Vietnam now. That's a curious thought.*

"Well, I'll really have to start laying some ground work on leave, because after 30 days I'll probably be either back over here or in Thailand or some other oriental spot. Anyway, I hope there are plenty of gorgeous, sexy birds in Newcastle these days.

"This Christmas will be strange. It'll be my first in a hot country and, without any Christmas trees, it just won't be the same. Anyway, see you in or around the middle of February."

Tony's plans for his leave were taking shape and he wrote home to give us an idea of his plans. *"You remember Kay who used to sing with Don Smith? Well, she writes to me once in a while and wants me to go up to Newcastle for a booze up. Apparently she is singing in one of the many new clubs there. Same as last time, I will also go back and spend a few days in Florida with Jack and Betty and Johnny and Shirley. We have a big reunion dinner planned in a lovely restaurant called the 'Moonraker' which is like the inside of an old ship. Then of course I have to make sure my car is still okay and get the stereo tape machine put in before driving to Ft. Bragg, N. Carolina, to start Special Forces training.*

"For Christmas I have sent Mum and Gay two handbags from Malaysia, made from some material called 'Batik'. They had some lovely materials and dresses, which I would have loved to have bought for somebody – but who? Same old problem, very depressing sometimes. Almost 94 years old and still no girlfriends. What I

<u>would</u> like if possible is a bottle of pure Silvikrin and a bottle of Pantene with oil because my hair seems to be falling out a bit. Have they come up with any miracle cures yet?

"What I would like for Christmas, but I can choose when I get home, is some stainless steel cufflinks to go with my suits. Would you find out for me where there is a good tailor who will do some alterations? I didn't have time to have them done in Malaysia, but all my jackets need a bit taking out of the backs. Keep writing. I don't get much mail these days. Everyone else on the team gets one nearly every day, and I get about one a week if I'm lucky. Balls to the world. See you in Feb." Always the same old complaint – too little mail. We had so little to say; days came and went without anything newsworthy happening. It was always so easy to postpone writing him a letter until there was something interesting to report. And I was excitedly planning my first Christmas as a wife in our new little home. Tony was not in the forefront of my thoughts.

But someone had been thinking of him and had gone to a great deal of effort. Faithful Peggy in California had been busy gathering together some special goodies. She regularly sent packages to him when he was operating with the Hawks, just as she had sent them to us in Datchet in those dark post-war days when Tony and I were children. He wrote to thank her and told her of the plans he was making for his leave and for his next assignment. *"The other day I was sitting quietly in my outpost minding my own business when the team CO staggered in with two enormous packages addressed to me. My mail situation being at an all-time low of approximately one letter every two weeks, I was not expecting anything more than a 'Nothing for you' from Captain Scheerer. Consequently I was as surprised as if Santa Claus had himself delivered them. Of course I didn't even have to look at the return address to guess who had sent them. Thank you so much for thinking of me. I have already contributed the 'START' to the team larder, but am saving the delightfully wrapped little packages for Christmas Day.*

"Having more time to myself now in the latter stages of my Vietnam tour, I am managing to dig in to some good reading. In order to make sure my barrels are both fully loaded for the numerous discussions I will no doubt be drawn into on leave, I am bolstering my practical experiences with some good factual reading. I am half way through General Giap's book 'People's War, People's Army', rather a typical Communist mixture of truths, half-truths and bare-faced lies, and intend to continue with 'Street Without Joy', 'Why Vietnam' and others.

"What is even more spectacular, I have enrolled with USAFI and have a correspondence course in my possession! None other than 'The History of Western Civilization, Volume I' (my fa-vourite period in history, attempted before while I was in the 82nd but not completed). While at the education centre I noticed a poster ad-vertising a GED college equivalency examination in five subjects. Apparently a pass in all these tests credits the student with the equivalent in semester hours of one year's college (just the job for a man in my position). I took the English Composition test, my mind reeling as I came out of the classroom, and decided that I would at-tempt Humanities, Social Studies, Natural Science and Mathematics at a later date, feeling sure that I would fail miserably at all these subjects. If I pass any one of them I will get credit for it, so it's all free with nothing to lose.

"I read November's 'TIME' from cover to cover, trying to understand a little of the world's monetary problems, but found by far the most entertaining article was the film review of 'The Shoes of the Fisherman'. Anthony Quinn's performance as the Head of the Roman Catholic Church is referred to as 'Zorba the Pope'!

"Lots of love, Tony

"P.S. What on earth are 'Humanities'? I haven't the foggi-est idea."

As the day to Tony's home leave grew closer, our parents realised that they would have to tell him the sad news they had kept from him for six months. His beloved dog, Mikey, had died. They had not felt they could tell him whilst he was under such strain in the jungle, and somehow had not got round to doing it at all. But his impending return meant that the news of 'Smiler's' death had to be broken. I can just imagine Tony surreptitiously blinking away the tears as he remembered his dear old friend, knowing that he would not be there at the front door to greet his master on his return home. He replied, *"I'm glad I wasn't there, or I would have been as upset as you were. When I read Dad's letter I went out of the outpost to the café round the corner and had several beers. I couldn't help remembering how Mike and I had grown up together. He almost represents an 'era' in my life - there'll never be another 'Smiler', no other animal could grin that much. Now, anybody that didn't know him will never really believe it."*

Writing home on Boxing Day, Tony was still counting the days. *"28 days and a duffel bag drag! That's GI terminology for days left."* The New Year, 1969, arrived and so did his last letter dated January 11. *"10 days and a duffel bag drag! I hope the house is warm these days, my blood is as thin as water after a year in this climate.*

"I can't really estimate when I will be home exactly because of the haphazard flight back. My booked flight, on the 21ˢᵗ, takes me to Karachi and I have to start hitchhiking from there. I wish we could go someplace for a week's holiday, like Majorca or some other winter sunspot. Datchet is certainly going to be rather cold and bleak. I don't suppose there's anybody there at all I know now, what with Brian being in Malta. Why don't you check on the winter holiday areas, I should have about $500 with me when I get home and I definitely don't want to tour Devon in the snow again, not even if Aunty Nancy [Tony's Godmother, living near Exmouth] *is joining the Catholic Church. I've had enough of Catholicism over here to last me a lifetime. The RC priests are as bad as the Communists. They try to entice as many people away from Buddhism as they can, and laud it over the community as if they are the ruler, requiring that they are obeyed by the members of the church and ignoring the hamlet*

chief almost entirely. The Catholics all live together around the church and have nothing to do with the rest of the hamlet. You can imagine my problem trying to train the hamlet 'People's Self Defense Force' when there are actually two: one Catholic and one Buddhist, neither of which will co-operate with the other! Choc oi!

"It's the same all over the world, every religion thinks that it is the right one, and everyone else is wrong. It's almost farcical, as if we didn't have enough problems, the people who are supposed to be the 'goodest of the good' are far more nuisance than the others. If Communism doesn't succeed in dividing this country, Catholicism certainly will.

"See you soon, Tony"

Back in Datchet preparations were in hand for his home-coming. His made-to-measure clothes from Penang were, as he had requested, pressed and hanging in his wardrobe and up in Newcastle Kay was ignoring the Twelfth Night rule to take down her Christmas decorations. She was keeping her tree up as a surprise for Tony, even if it took him till late February to get there. In Saigon, too, a celebration was being planned and on January 19, Tony's team-mates, including Captain Scheerer the Senior Advisor, held a small going-away party for him at the MAT team house in Binh Trung just a few miles outside Saigon. Tony was in buoyant mood, his next coveted assignment was signed and sealed and his first tour of duty in Vietnam was almost over. After a few beers, he left the party, jumped into the team jeep and drove off into the city. He had not gone far before a motor scooter pulled out of a side road. In an attempt to avoid it the jeep went off the road, struck a telegraph pole and overturned. Tony was thrown out. His skull was fractured.

CHAPTER TEN

Captain Scheerer and the other partygoers, alerted by some local Vietnamese people to the accident, followed them to the scene. They found Tony lying in the road, deeply unconscious and called a Medevac helicopter, which airlifted him to the 24th Evacuation Hospital, Long Binh. There he remained in a coma whilst efforts were made to notify us.

I was preparing to go out to play cards with my parents-in-law, a regular Sunday evening fixture, when the phone went and Mum, with wavering voice, said that I was not to worry, but Tony had had an accident in a jeep and was in hospital quite seriously ill. I remember trying to make light of it and recalling the time when he had swerved to the wrong side of the road in France and ended up in hospital with a broken arm. "Trust him!" I said, with rather too much false jollity in my voice.

The news had been broken to my parents in person by a young Lieutenant stationed with the US Army at South Ruislip, just outside London. Lt. Jim Greenberg had found his way to our house in Datchet and knocked, apprehensively, at the door. The sight of a young, grave man in US Army uniform greeted Mum as she opened it with her usual wide smile. Jim quietly asked if he might come in as he had some serious news. He asked Mum and Dad, too stunned to ask more, to sit down while he read them a telex message:

"The Secretary of the Army has asked me to express his deepest regret that your son, 1ˢᵗ Lt. Anthony G Harbord was placed on the seriously ill list in Vietnam 19 January 1969 as a result of a

*compound depressed frontal skull fracture. He was the driver of a
military vehicle on an administrative mission. When trying to avoid
hitting a motor scooter the vehicle went off the road, struck a telephone pole and overturned. In the judgement of the attending
physician his condition is of such severity that there is cause for concern but no imminent danger to life. Please be assured that the best
medical facilities and doctors have been made available and that
every measure is being taken to aid him. You will be kept informed
of any significant changes in his condition. He is hospitalized in
Vietnam. Address mail to him at the hospital mail section, APO San
Francisco 96381.*

*Signed, Kenneth G. Wickham, Major General, US
Army, the Adjutant General"*

So he was well enough to receive mail? That was a good
sign, surely? We wrote immediately. On the envelopes, we asked
that someone read the contents to him if he was unable to do so himself. 'On an administrative mission' – so he had sustained his
injuries whilst carrying out his duties. That was all we ever knew
until I traced Alan Scheerer all these years later and I learned with
shock about the leaving party. My parents never knew the truth, that
Tony had probably had a couple of beers too many and was not paying full attention to his driving. But then again, I could be doing him
a grave injustice and no one will ever know the exact details.

Mum was distraught; she wanted to be with her son. She
had nursed him through all his childhood diseases, held him for hours
in her arms through the night while he sobbed with pain from a per-
forated ear-drum aged six, comforted him when he had opened up his
heart to her in despair at his luckless love affairs. But he was thousands of miles away and besides, he was in a war zone. It was out of
the question. Unable to sit and do nothing but wait for the next bulletin, she took the unusual step of calling long-distance to speak to
Peggy who might, just might, be able to do something. But all Peggy
could give was reassurance, followed swiftly by a letter of support.

214

Chapter Ten

*"My darling Vi – I heard your voice telling me this appall-
ing news just five minutes ago – and I am still numb with shock. But
somehow I must reach out to you and together we _must_ believe that
all the marvelous scientific knowledge that is now trained upon him
will pull him through. One _good_ thing is that no time was lost – Had
he been up in the jungle, perhaps not found for several hours, and
then transported to a Field Station for a bit and finally to a Base
Hospital, it might have been much worse. At least he was in Saigon,
where he was rushed to the main hospital immediately.*

*"And, too, he is so tough, so completely in the best physical
condition possible, that he will put up a tremendous fight. O Vi, your
calm voice reading out the message was so fine – so exactly how the
daughter of your Father would take this news – and I who am much
weaker stuff could only choke and sob.*

*"But my love and faith and hope are with Tony and with you
and Bill, my dearest.*

"Your devoted, Peg"

Six nerve-racking days went by. Dad felt powerless. He
contacted the American Embassy in London demanding that the Ambassador look into the case and find out more information for us.
The house was never left empty in case the phone rang or Jim Greenberg called. No news was good news. But then America was at war
and Tony was but one of thousands of casualties. But the first news
had arrived quickly, hadn't it? Backwards and forwards raced our
mental reasoning. Up and down and back up again went our hopes.
Our letters should have arrived, Tony would know we had had the
news and were rooting for him, he would be fighting back, just as
Peggy had said. Jim Greenberg visited Datchet again on January 25
with the next bulletin.

"Additional information received states that the condition of your son, First Lieutenant Anthony G. Harbord, is stable.
He is still on the very seriously ill list. Extent of brain damage,
if any, cannot be determined at this time, he is semi-conscious

but not talking at this time. The prognosis is guarded. Evacuation from Vietnam not contemplated at this time.

"You will be promptly advised as additional information is received."

"Semi-conscious but not talking." Well, that was an improvement, surely? Having heard the news about Tony, his friend Brian who was not in Malta after all as Tony had suspected, visited Mum and Dad on Sunday January 26. He comforted them with the fact that he himself had sustained a badly fractured skull some years previously, and had made a complete recovery. He made them laugh at the fact that he had been as crazy before the accident as after. At that moment there was a knock on the door and Jim Greenberg stood there, uneasily, the third bulletin in his hand. Brian stayed to hear its contents, suddenly appalled at what he saw as his untimely attempt at levity.

"Your son 1st Lt Anthony G Harbord has been removed from the serious injured list and placed on the very serious injured list. In the judgement of the attending physician his condition is of such severity that there is cause for concern. You will be promptly advised as additional information is received."

Jim was deeply troubled at the anguish his visit had caused, especially as he had, over the past week, been received by my parents with kindness, hospitality and understanding over the difficulty of his unenviable task. My parents were deeply shocked. Mum rang me in distress to tell me of this latest, terse communiqué and our frail hopes began to collapse. It had all gone so horribly wrong. Tony should have been home by now and was instead lying critically injured on the other side of the world.

The last bulletin arrived two days later, but was not delivered to my parents. On a dark and wild night of rain and high winds, I answered the knock at my door. An apprehensive Jim Greenberg stood there. I knew instantly what was coming and wanted to hear it. But Jim had clearly rehearsed over and over again just what he was going to say and how he was going to say it. He asked me to go through into the sitting room and to sit down. He took the bulletin from his pocket with shaking hands and, standing over me, at last delivered the expected, awful words. Tony had died the previous day from his injuries. His body would be shipped back to England, all admin would be taken care of by the Army who would supply a headstone, his effects would be returned to the family, etc; I wasn't listening. What was Jim doing here? Were Mum and Dad out? Then came Jim's request. He implored me to accompany him to Datchet, to tell my parents the dreadful news myself, as he just could not bring himself to do it.

In a state of complete shock, I pulled on my raincoat and my husband Mike and I got into the waiting car for the forty-minute journey to Datchet. How on earth could I tell my parents that their only son was dead? What can one say? The minutes counted down to my awful assignment and I still had no idea how I would break the news. The car pressed on through the foul night and all too soon pulled up outside their house. The curtains were drawn, the lights on. I got out and walked alone to the front door, unseen. My visit was unexpected and Mum opened the door with a smile of delight at see-ing me but the next instant she saw the look on my face. "He's dead", was all I could utter as I stumbled into the hall.

*

Removed to the US Army Mortuary in Saigon, Tony's body underwent a post-mortem. But first it was officially identified by comparing the fingerprints obtained from his lifeless body with those he had provided three-and-a-half years previously when, so full of life, he had cheerfully and expectantly signed on as a regular soldier back in Los Angeles. The post-mortem revealed that he had sus-tained a right frontal compound depressed skull fracture, and also fractures of the right maxilla and humerus. He had died from these injuries which had been exacerbated by bilateral pneumonia. A 71cm surgical incision confirmed this last complication. But the attention paid to his body did not end there.

On 2 February his remains arrived back at the Dover Air Force Base in Delaware, through which Tony had passed on his way to Vietnam just one year before, and his body was then embalmed. The report comments: "Aspirated remains, cosmetized face, sealed incisions, waxed lips, reshaped, sealed and waxed forehead. Bandaged head." He was ready for his last flight home, escorted by a US Army officer, to Mildenhall in Suffolk, where instead of reaching his destination tired but happy and ready to enjoy his thirty-day home leave, he would arrive in a coffin.

Back in Saigon Tony's American and Vietnamese colleagues in the Advisory Team held a memorial service on the roof of the building where so recently they had all celebrated the end of his tour. Captain Scheerer, who had visited him in hospital during the days he lay unconscious, gave the eulogy. It was to bring us some comfort, for he said:

"Tony welcomed his Advisor assignment. He enjoyed working with the Vietnamese people and was eager to help them help themselves. He was especially effective working with them on operations in the field. Tony liked the Vietnamese and they liked him, as was evidenced by the number of Vietnamese who inquired about him following the accident and the sorrow they expressed both orally and visually when told of his condition and then of his death. The rapport Tony established with the Vietnamese was of great assistance to this team in accomplishing its mission.

"Just a couple of weeks ago, two Vietnamese soldiers had a jeep accident at the edge of this hamlet. One of them was killed. Tony expressed to me that he had been driving for many years and had never seen a fatal accident until coming to Vietnam and had now seen three such accidents. It is indeed tragic that such a vehicle accident should befall Lt Harbord. Tony will be long remembered by all those who knew and worked with him here in Vietnam, both American and Vietnamese."

Peggy's volley of letters continued:

Chapter Ten

*"My precious Vi – all these days I have been close to you –
I wake, and you are my first thought – I go to sleep at night thinking
about you.*

*"But there are no words to say to you – only to love you and
ache for you and agonise.*

*"Slowly you will find a way to pick yourself up and go on,
knowing that Tony is going on, that he is as much your son as ever he
was, that nothing can take from you what has been, and nothing can
change the fact that his curious and painful experience of the past
three years was a wonderful and developing experience for him. The
boy who stopped here on his way overseas was a far more mature
and controlled person than before he entered the army. And the letters we got during the past year show a tremendous gain in insight
and maturity through the months in Vietnam. Terribly as I hate that
war and abhor the stupidity that got this country into a land war in
Asia, in this particular instance the effect on the boy we love was
good.*

*"Hang on to that, dearest Vi – the loss to you is frightful,
but it is just possible that Tony had learned through this experience
all that he needed to learn in this particular life. William Penn once
wrote:*

*"They that love beyond the world cannot be separated by it.
Death cannot kill what never dies.
Nor can spirits ever be divided that love and live in the
same principle; the root and record of their friendship.
If absence be not death, neither is theirs;
Death is but crossing the world, as friends do the seas; they
live in one another still.
For they must needs be present, who love and live in that
which is omnipresent."*

Tony's body reached the funeral directors in Slough, two
miles from Datchet, on 4 February and the funeral was to take place
two days later. During those two days Mum agonised over whether
or not she should go to see his body. Badly as she wanted to touch

him, kiss him and say a final goodbye to her beloved son, Dad and I
– perhaps fearful of being drawn in to accompany her – persuaded
her that his injuries may well have been so severe that she would gain
nothing from a last look and could indeed be left with a sight she
would never be able to erase from her mind. How I wish she had
overruled us and followed her heart. How I wish we had all gone, for
I found out thirty years too late from the funeral director who had
received Tony's body that the skill of the embalmers had rendered
his face seemingly untouched by trauma. We would have seen him
looking as he always had in sleep and we would have accepted his
passing. As it was, six years later when the US prisoners of war were
eventually released from their horrific captivity in North Vietnam, I
watched the news night after night, close up to the screen, watching
the families embracing their traumatised long lost sons and brothers.
I felt, quite irrationally, that somehow Tony's 'death' had all been a
dreadful mistake, that it had not been him inside his coffin and that
all the time he had been held prisoner and would step from one of the
troop carriers on to the tarmac tired, thin, but smiling and alive.

Knowing that Tony had been planning to visit Kay in Newcastle, I wrote to her within a couple of days of receiving that last
bulletin. My letter was forwarded from the Oxford Gallery to the
Newcastle club where she was then working, and was handed to her
and read by her while she was on stage, in a break between numbers:

"Dear Kay,

"I'm sorry I don't know your other name, but I felt I had to
write.

"Tony Harbord, my brother, was involved in a fatal acci-
dent on Sunday 19 January in Vietnam and he died on Monday 27
from head injuries. I remember him saying that you were good
enough to write to him occasionally and I understand he was plan-
ning a visit to Newcastle.

"It was so ironical that he was due to leave for home on the
24th but we have to console ourselves that something much worse
might have happened if he had gone into the Green Berets as

220

planned and returned to Vietnam. I'm so sorry to have to write this
letter to you, Kay.
"Yours, Gay"
Kay was devastated. The Christmas tree was still there in her home covered in lights and trimmings, waiting for him. She had also asked the drummer in her current band to allow Tony a number or two on 'the skins', a request that had been immediately granted.

The funeral was held in the village church where Tony had once served as an altar boy and where I, less than a year before, had been married on a day when Tony had been 'humping the boonies'. Relatives, friends and village people crowded into the church that cold, February day. The Stars and Stripes flag had been provided as a matter of course by the Army to drape the coffin, but Mum refused to allow it to be used, insisting that Tony had been an Englishman. Whilst not blaming America, she certainly needed no reminders at this final stage as to the root cause of his death. And so the bare wooden coffin, bearing a single wreath of spring irises, stood beside us as we struggled through the service. We sang, or tried to sing "He who would valiant be, 'gainst all disaster". Words of comfort came from all quarters but we were stunned. As the hearse pulled slowly away from the church on its journey to the crematorium, the local village policeman stopped the traffic and raised his arm in a pro-longed salute. His presence was quite unexpected and his silent tribute still touches me deeply after all these years.

As many as could cram into the little house in Lawn Close came back for refreshments and, as so often happens in particularly sad circumstances, there was a great degree of relief. The worst was over. Eighteen dreadful days had passed since we had first had news of Tony's accident and in a strange way the funeral had been a tri-umphant affair. People had sung, their voices filling the big stone church. The organist had chosen some appropriately stirring and encouraging music to send us out into the world and the ordeal of the day was behind us.

I got back home to find a letter from Kay asking for details of the funeral arrangements. I replied next day, telling her with regret that it was all over. *"Thank you for your letter. I was so sorry to have had to break the news to you. I rather gathered from your letter that you were a greater friend of Tony's than we had realised and it must have been a shock to you.*

"It was very thoughtful of you to ask about the funeral, but actually it was held yesterday – the day I received your letter. We had been dreading it so much, but quite honestly it was an incredibly wonderful day. The service was – although quite agonising – very beautiful, and so many relations and village people turned up that the church was quite full. I think what was most upsetting was that the long-awaited Tony was there right next to us in the aisle and we couldn't see or hear him. But of course his spirit – the real Tony – was not inside the coffin. All that was there was the part that looked like him.

"You are quite right in remembering him as he <u>was</u> – so many people become embittered and ask Why? But we – and, I believe, you – can understand that grief over him is the last thing he would have wanted. He was undoubtedly happy at the time he had his accident, because he was so looking forward to coming home and I'm sure he didn't know much more during the week of his illness. In the army he had at last found fulfilment and a purpose – for that we must be grateful.

"I cannot help thanking God that he <u>was</u> taken from us that way. Who knows what might have happened to him if he had gone into the Green Berets and returned to Vietnam? He might have been captured, tortured even. I also feel that his injury was so serious that had he recovered from the fractured skull, the extent of brain damage (which to this day is unknown) would, I am sure, have prevented him from ever leading a normal life and Tony – so proud of his fitness and strength – would never mentally have been normal again. That would have been a greater tragedy.

Chapter Ten

"We can all find comfort in the fact that while he was alive we all loved him so much and I can assure you that all the letters of sympathy and support from countless people like yourself have immeasurably lessened the great burden of grief and I thank you most sincerely for the part that you played in Tony's life."

Peggy, still struggling to help from so many thousand miles away, whilst nursing her dying husband Bill, wrote again to Mum. *"You are so constantly with me – as I sit by Bill's bed, as I drive over to the market – as I carry trays to the nurses – you are right there – and I wish there were some way that I could carry a little of the burden you are struggling with. I know there isn't, but the ache to help is almost physical.*

"Just yesterday I talked with a woman I know and learned that three years ago her son was in a frightful motor accident in Florida. He lived – but he doesn't know his father or his mother. He lies helpless – alive – but knowing nothing, fed by tube. He's in a nursing home down in Florida and they go every two months, and come back broken with grief and praying he can die.

"Never, never feel that everything wasn't done for Tony. Never feel that had you gone you might have saved him or he might have known you. The tragedy is that a wretched little motor scooter had to dart out ahead of him and that he couldn't stop on what was probably a rain-slick road.

"Some people have short and vivid lives, others take life at a slower pace and live longer. What we have to do is to accept.

"I think of my brother - dead at seventeen – and only now have I come to realize that his life was complete. Age didn't matter. And so we grieve for those of us left behind. We mustn't grieve for them."

Back in Vietnam, Harvey Watson had received word of Tony's death in a letter from Dixie. Not only did he feel grief for the loss of another good friend, but it also set him wondering about Tony's prophecy that night in the Blue Room in Destin, Florida. The thought had not escaped Dixie either, but she was the fortunate one who eventually welcomed her loved one home alive.

With the funeral over, the tide of nervous energy that carried my parents and me through that awful time began to dissipate and despair was never far away. Tony's ashes duly returned from the crematorium and, in a simple ceremony in the churchyard, Dad carried the remains of his son and placed them into the ground. A terrible moment for a man who, because of his own old-fashioned upbringing, had so often felt unable to display overt affection for his children. And now it was too late to make amends as far as his son was concerned.

Grief at the loss of a loved one is always painful, but in my parents' case it was prolonged almost beyond enduring because of the way reminders of the tragedy continued to disrupt the process of coming to terms with Tony's death. For in the months that followed, the procedures covering administrative minutiae seemed endlessly protracted. Paperwork concerning the US Army's provision of a bronze marker for his grave ran into many pages, as did correspondence with Jack Weygant, Tony's nominated Power of Attorney, who held many personal effects that Tony had left behind in Florida. In addition, there were the effects from Vietnam, which reached England at intervals over several weeks. They were perhaps the hardest to bear, for in one package were things such as his pipe and tobacco pouch, toothbrush, shaving kit, signet ring, Vietnamese phrase book and undeveloped films. And a lock of soft brown hair. We never sought to find out whose it was, it was too personal, too sad to think that the person from whom it had been taken had meant so much to him that he had kept it safe amongst his other belongings. There was the watch he had been so pleased with, the writing pad upon which he had written his last excited letter, every item caused pain. And then we received back the letters we had written him immediately after his accident, when we had hoped fervently that he might be conscious enough absorb their contents. Marked "Deceased. Return to Sender", we could never bring ourselves to open them and read what we had written in such hope and desperation.

Another package contained medals and citations, soon added to when the Department of the Army informed my parents that Tony's Bronze Star with V device was to be enhanced with the Oak Leaf Cluster. But it was the citations that meant most to us, for they captured Tony's humanity, a far more precious thing to us than a medal in a case. The Military Assistance Command citation accompanying the First Oak Leaf Cluster award commended his work with both the Hawk Recon platoon and his later MACV assignment:

"For distinguishing himself by exceptionally meritorious conduct in the performance of outstanding services from 1 February 1968 to 27 January 1969 while serving as a Reconnaissance Platoon Leader, 101st Airborne Division and later as Assistant Team Leader of Mobile Advisory Team III-81, Lieutenant Harbord continually demonstrated outstanding leadership ability while participating in combat operations with his platoon. His exceptional knowledge of tactical manoeuvres and sound judgement contributed significantly to the success of the reconnaissance missions and increased the morale of the entire unit. Later as an advisor, Lieutenant Harbord again displayed great perseverance, dedication to duty and broad military knowledge in his efforts to improve the training and operational effectiveness of the unit and its personnel. Participating in numerous combat operations, he was noted for the inspiration he provided the Vietnamese soldiers and was instrumental in assisting them in successfully accomplishing their assigned missions. His professionalism, sound judgement and personal courage enabled him to establish an outstanding working relationship with the Vietnamese and, as a result, his advice was often sought and readily accepted. Through his untiring efforts and unselfish giving of his time and energy, Lieutenant Harbord was instrumental in improving the morale and living conditions of the soldiers of the units he advised. First Lieutenant Harbord's professional competence and outstanding achievements were in keeping with the highest traditions of the

United States Army and reflected great credit upon himself and the military service."

Although Tony had never mentioned it in his letters, a month before his death he had been awarded the Vietnamese Medal of Honor, 1st Class, by the Vietnamese Government in recognition of his work with the Vietnamese. Again his relationship with them is specifically mentioned:

"During his tour of duty as an Advisor in Vietnam Lt. Harbord participated in many operations and contributed valuable ideas to Civic Action & Regional Defense activities in the territory of Gia Dinh sector. In addition, he actively took part in visits to families of war victims at out-of-the-way villages. Therefore, Lt. Harbord has won the hearts of the local people."

And so he had. For, as Alan Scheerer had remarked in his eulogy at Tony's memorial service at Binh Trung, many Vietnamese had enquired about Tony's condition after his accident and had expressed sorrow when learning of his death.

Tony could not have been in a more high-risk situation; more First Lieutenants were killed in Vietnam than any other officer grade and the years 1968 and 1969 saw the highest casualties of the war. California, where he had enlisted, was the State with the highest number of deaths at 5,572. A letter from the Governor of California, one Ronald Reagan, expressing his deepest sympathy, highlighted the ambiguous nature of Tony's nationality for he had, of course, been registered at Peggy's address in Beverly Hills and, for the purpose of administration, was considered a Californian despite never having taken out US citizenship. This lack of determining a serviceman's country of origin has made it impossible to ascertain how many other Britons might have died in the service of the US forces in Vietnam. Three men are listed in the records as coming from England, but in each case they were the sons of American servicemen stationed overseas at the time. Exhaustive research has led me to assume that Tony was the only British officer killed in the Vietnam

Chapter Ten

War whilst serving in the US Army. A tragic distinction, but one which has made his story all the more special.

*

At a quarter to midnight on 31 December1999 I quietly left a neighbour's Millennium Eve party. The champagne was coming out of the fridge, the fireworks were ready to be set off in the garden, but I slipped home. Before going out that evening I had arranged some candles and photographs on a table. There were Mum and Dad on their wedding day, Mum and her baby son looking up to see the RAF bombers on their way across the Channel, Dad reading *Babar The Elephant* to me, aged two, and Tony resplendent and beaming in his US Army uniform. I lit the candles and, oblivious to the noise of fireworks and people laughing and dancing in the street, I concentrated long and hard upon the three people who had shaped my life from the beginning and who had meant so much to me. I thanked them for their unconditional love, I asked them for help when the going got tough and I promised Tony that I would finish the book about him that I had only just sketchily started. Refreshed, sustained and ready for the new millennium, I blew out the candles and returned to the party.

Two months earlier a strange thing had happened. During a moment of idle reflection I had wondered what the time delay had been between Tony's death and funeral. I had not yet found Kay whose letters from me held the answer. Telephoning each of the funeral directors in Slough to ask them to check their records was the only way to answer this particular question which became something of an irrational obsession. I had not bargained for the time it seemed likely to take, for the age of the computer has yet to be embraced by English undertakers. I called the two whose names seemed the most familiar to me and, with reverential courtesy, they kept me appraised of their occasional visits to their archives until it became clear that neither of them had dealt with Tony's funeral. The third one was a direct hit and yielded far more than a date, it gave me the end of Tony's story.

227

On the other end of the phone was Mrs Newman, the lady who, as a new employee, had received and tended Tony's body thirty-one years previously. Not only had he been among the first of her charges, the case had of course been quite unusual and she remembered it in detail, down to the black cuffs on his uniform. It was she who told me how unmarked his face had been, thanks to the efforts of the embalmer. It was a difficult thing to hear, for I recollected Mum's agony of indecision about viewing Tony's body.

Having obtained the information about the funeral date, I prepared to hang up. "Before you go," added Mrs Newman, "the flag is still here". I had not known about the Stars and Stripes. She explained Mum's antipathy to the use of it at the funeral and asked me if I wanted it, as it had sat on a shelf in their offices since 1969. There was no question, of course I wanted it, and a few days later I drove to Slough to collect the flag, folded like a blanket and still inside its sealed wrapper. I did not quite know what to do with it, but knew from my American military friends that it should be specially folded into triangular form. I rang the US base at RAF Mildenhall, Suffolk, which Tony had used to get his free military air-hops home and back again, and where his body had been flown from Delaware. The Public Affairs Officer at the Headquarters 100th Air Refuelling Wing told me to send the flag to her department and informed me that in due course the Color Guard would fold it properly, whereupon it would be returned to me.

Late in the morning of 6 January 2000, I was still in my dressing gown, energetically vacuuming the downstairs carpets having taken down the Christmas decorations. Thousands of Christmas tree needles had sprayed themselves in all directions as I had struggled through doorways and down passages with the rapidly denuding tree, and, absorbed in my noisy task, I almost did not hear the phone ring. An American voice on the other end announced himself as Staff Sgt Dennis Brewer from the Public Affairs Office at Mildenhall and he was asking me a favour. "Ma'am, would you do us the honour of allowing us to fly your brother's flag this afternoon at the first

retreat of the millennium before formally folding it as you have requested?" I answered his question with one of my own, short and to
the point. "How long would it take me to get there?" There was just
enough time, for the winter days were at their shortest and retreat
would be sounded long before dusk fell at around 4.30 p.m.

I jumped into the shower, dressed faster than ever before,
stuffed Tony's medals and other insignia into a bag (because Sgt
Brewer had apologetically asked for verification), and ran to my car.
Mildenhall was over a hundred miles away and I would have to get
around London. There really was not a minute to lose. Making for
the nearest eastbound motorway, I eventually relaxed and began to
plan the rest of the journey to Suffolk. Two hours later I crossed into
the county. Inexplicably, and irrationally, I began to get excited.
Not at the thought of the ceremony awaiting me, but more a feeling
that Tony himself was going to be there. At the first signpost to Mildenhall my heart started to beat rapidly, and then I saw the airport's
perimeter fence and, crazily, a part of me believed I would shortly be
holding Tony in my arms. It felt so right, so possible.

I made it, with time enough before the retreat for Sgt
Brewer to escort me to the place where Tony's flag was flying gaily
in the stiff Suffolk breeze against a brilliant blue sky. I was filled
with pride, love and grief. Alongside the Stars and Stripes fluttered
the RAF flag, denoting the dual purpose and long allied history at the
base. Having respectfully checked my credentials, Sgt Brewer took
me to the place reserved for me for the short retreat ceremony. The
two national anthems were played, and as the many military personnel assembled there saluted, Tony's flag was slowly lowered, folded
with impressive precision and respect and finally presented to me
with the words "From a grateful nation". I could no longer hold back
the tears, but I felt I had honoured him in a way that would have
made him proud of his kid sister

POSTSCRIPT

———————————

Tragedy was soon to strike the families of three main characters during the writing of this memoir.

In March 2002, Rick Knight was found dead in his apartment in Bisbee. A cocktail of drugs and alcohol may have proved too strong for his heart.

Later that same year, in September, Ernie Flores finally succumbed to his aggressive brain tumour.

And in June 2003, Kay Rouselle suffered a fatally fractured skull in a terrible accident in her home.

I thank God that I managed to find them in time.

GH
2008

www.ingramcontent.com/pod-product-compliance
Lightning Source LLC
Chambersburg PA
CBHW031153270326
41931CB00006B/260